THE EASY EXPERT
IN
AMERICAN ANTIQUES

THE EASY EXPERT *in*

Fine comb-back Windsor armchair made in Pennsylvania, probably Philadelphia, about 1760. (Courtesy of Sotheby Parke Bernet, Inc., New York.)

Moreton Marsh

AMERICAN ANTIQUES

Knowing, Finding, Buying,
and Restoring
Early American Furniture

J. B. LIPPINCOTT COMPANY / PHILADELPHIA AND NEW YORK

Illustration Credits

All photographs furnished by owners, dealers, auctioneers, and publications are credited in the captions. Illustrations from Henry Hammond Taylor are marked (HHT), and drawings and photographs not otherwise credited are by the author. All objects photographed (with the exception of Figure 154) were privately owned and /or available for sale at the time the pictures were taken.

The first edition of this book
appeared under the title
*The Easy Expert in Collecting
   and Restoring American Antiques*

U.S. Library of Congress Cataloging in Publication Data

Marsh, Moreton.
   American antiques.

   First ed. (© 1959) published under title:
The easy expert in collecting and restoring
American antiques.
   Bibliography: p.
   Includes index.
   1. Furniture—United States—Collectors and
collecting. 2. Furniture, Colonial—United
States—Collectors and collecting. 3. Furniture
—Repairing. I. Title.
NK2406.M395   1978   749.2'14   78-9050
ISBN-0-397-01287-X
ISBN-0-397-01288-8 (pbk.)

This book is dedicated
to the curious,
the willing,
and the patient

CONTENTS

10. THE BASIC STEPS OF RESTORATION

11. MORE DETAIL ON RESTORATION

PREFACE

"You can learn anything from a book," my daughter told me when she was twelve, and it's true. If you want to learn something about American antiques, especially furniture, here is a book. Where do you find antiques and how do you recognize them? How can you tell what is genuine and really old? And what about fakes? How do you know a fake when you see one? All these questions we go into, in considerable detail.

Many antiques on the market are altered, damaged, or broken. Are they worth restoring? How should they be restored? The mysteries of authentication and conservation are many, but they are all explainable, and here we take pains to explain them.

How easy is the Easy Expert? That is a tough question. Easier, I would say, than conducting a symphony, flying a jet, or getting a Ph.D. in geophysics, and harder, of course, than riding a bicycle, cutting the lawn, or even unplugging the kitchen sink. Somewhere in between.

Expertise in antiques rests on the mastery of two elementary disciplines:

the appreciation of good design and the understanding of workmanship. The quality of design may be a matter of opinion. Most critics agree that the finest Chippendale furniture of all time was made in Newport and Philadelphia about 1760–80, but I know many sincere, intelligent people who don't like it. Accepting your interest in antiques, I think I can take your good taste for granted, but I would not want to mold it. You know what you like, and when I tell you what I like, feel free to snicker.

Workmanship is a different story. It is a technical consideration of methods and materials—the workman's skill. The quality of workmanship is usually quite obvious even if the details require more than a casual look. Without getting too technical, I have done my best to cover these details in full. You need not become a cabinetmaker yourself to learn about workmanship. You may have neither the time nor the inclination, but if you have a fine chair with a broken leg, you should know how the leg was made before you ask someone to repair it. More important, once you have learned the details of workmanship, you will be able to tell at a glance whether a chair came from eighteenth-century Newport or from twentieth-century Grand Rapids.

This book developed from a series of articles written by Henry Hammond Taylor for the magazine *Antiques,* beginning in 1926. He was a distinguished expert and amateur restorer in Connecticut, and in 1930 he published his *Knowing, Collecting and Restoring Early American Furniture.* For a very long time that was the best manual on the subject, and it became my guide when I started working with antiques in Boston in the forties.

Taylor's philosophy endures, but methods and materials of restoration develop and expand in time, and by the late fifties it came time to revise the technical part of his book. I took on the job, and it turned out to be difficult. Henry Taylor had died long ago, and I had questions. How does one divide responsibility with someone who cannot argue his side?

My editor was the late Tay Hohoff, whose perception was a legend in New York publishing circles in those days, and she thought that we should have a new book and that it should be called *The Easy Expert.* I rewrote the text to reflect my own experience but in a manner I thought would have satisfied Henry Taylor, and it was published in 1959. Not long afterward I received a letter from Henry Hammond Taylor II in Connecticut, saying that he was Henry Taylor's grandson, that the family had seen the book, and that I showed the same respect for the subject that his grandfather had. That pleased me no end.

Now almost two more decades have gone by, and technology waits for no one. It is time to do it over again. The ease of reproduction of photographs has much improved, and most of the photos in the present book are new. Materials have changed, especially glue and varnish, and the value of antiques has skyrocketed. No longer can one use old spinning wheels to make chair slats and old blanket chest boards to replace table tops. Antiques have become a form of investment, and there are problems with insuring them. The Easy Expert has to know about all these things, and they are fully covered in the present book. The knowledge and understanding of American antique furniture has greatly expanded, and I have tried to include as much of it as I think is useful. Any reader wishing to go further may consult the Bibliography at the end of the book.

Many people have helped me. The staff of Samuel T. Freeman & Co. guided my camera to many interesting details and bravely posed for it with selected objects. John Freeman was disappointed that my book was not to be about purebred fowl, but he opened his photo files to me just the same. Charles Santore advised me on Windsors, and Robert Stuart on hardware. My wife, Carol, served as arbiter in many questions of style and substance. Good people in the trade gave me the pictures I needed, and they are individually acknowledged. In the fourth estate, Lita Solis-Cohen and Sam Pennington kept me posted on the facts of life, including a few of those secrets. The manuscript was creatively edited by Thomas M. Voss.

Part One

1
ANTIQUES

Antiques are magic—bridges to the past, specimens of history, roots. In a fast-paced, transient world, they satisfy our desire for stability and our longing for continuity of purpose. "This table has been in the family for five generations," a man says with pride, and thus salutes his ancestors. No matter how little he may actually know about them, he is fortified by the thought that they lived and worked and faced up to their problems, and that he himself is a link in a chain anchored in the past and reaching into the future.

Perhaps it is not surprising that the finest collections of early American material were assembled by industrialists who spent their working hours banishing the old way of life, but whose free time (and money) was devoted to picking up the pieces of the era they helped destroy and fitting them together again in a nostalgic image of the "good old days." Henry F. du Pont (Winterthur), Henry Ford (Greenfield Village), John D. Rockefeller, Jr. (Williamsburg), and the Wells brothers (Old Sturbridge Village) spared no effort in assembling outstanding collections and housing

them in appropriate buildings—some original, some transplanted, and some totally reconstructed on the basis of slender evidence. Many other properties were painstakingly restored by the National Park Service, by private owners, or by local groups working with much more modest means but often achieving marvelous results. Some years ago, a group of enthusiasts organized themselves into the National Trust for Historic Preservation, which began in Washington, D.C., in a very humble way but rapidly grew into a major national undertaking. Obviously, the desire to preserve the American heritage is widely shared.

Besides the sentimental urge to recapture the past, another force is even stronger: the desire for good design. By a happy combination of social and economic factors, the time of the American Revolution coincides with a high point of grace and good taste in the design of American furniture. The basic elements of style obviously came from abroad, but American craftsmen simplified and abstracted the complex designs of Chippendale, Hepplewhite,

17

and Sheraton, producing a series of forms that are elegant and light, brilliantly proportioned, and, so far as I can foresee, eternal in their appeal to the eye searching for beauty.

WHAT IS ANTIQUE?

In the broadest meaning of the word, *antique* means simply *old.* That, at least, is the popular notion. Yet we certainly don't mean *old furniture* when we say *antique furniture.* As collectors we may not always find it easy to draw the line between what is antique and what is merely old.

Most serious writers on early American furniture agree that 1830, or even a little earlier, marks the end of the period when true antiques were made in America. That was the time when the steam engine became common and factory mass production began. In the urge to produce consumer goods for a burgeoning population, craftsmanship and design began to suffer. I agree with the view that in order to qualify as antique, an object must not only have been made prior to 1830 but must have some artistic merit or esthetic appeal.

And here, I think, we have the crux of what is or is not antique. A true antique must be the handmade product of an individual craftsman or group of craftsmen and must reflect, within the limits of the medium, the personality of the maker. It may be a rude bench made by a farmer on the spur of the moment or a block-front secretary on which two men worked for a year. The point is, an antique cannot be a piece that came out of a machine and would have come out the same no matter who pulled the levers.

Machines were not introduced everywhere at once. Small cabinetmakers in the country continued to produce ac-ceptable handmade furniture even long after 1830, while prominent firms like Duncan Phyfe in New York were beginning to use machinery even before 1820. For that reason it is difficult to fix a rigid date line between *antique* and just *old.* To draw the line, we must consider *how* a piece was made as well as *when.*

Hitchcock chairs, for example, were in production before 1830, yet all their parts were machine made, almost in assembly-line fashion. Consequently, they are not antiques in the sense that the word is used in this book. The pine furniture and slat-back chairs made by the Shakers, on the other hand, may date as late as 1860, but each piece was individually made and most certainly does reflect the sociological and religious beliefs of its makers. We need not hesitate to call this early Shaker furniture antique.

The Shaker chair-making establishment in Mount Lebanon, New York, became a mechanized factory in the early 1870s and greatly expanded production. The operation was successful for decades, and chairs were still being made there in the late 1920s, following the old patterns and preserving the original simplicity of design. The late Mount Lebanon chairs are common in the antiques trade and now in great vogue, but are they *antiques?*

THE LINGO OF THE EXPERTS

The world of antiques has its own language. The purpose is to make description easier, I suppose, but it does not always work out that way. Several writers have produced glossaries of the lingo, and a few have had a measure of success, but the problem of selecting a usage to follow is still with us.

Should we use the words that were

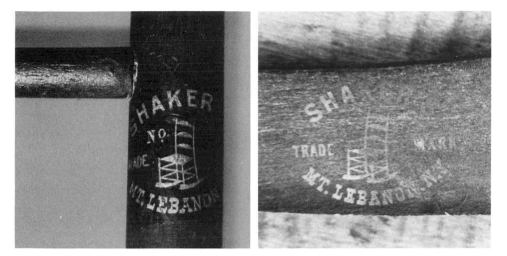

1. Trademarks on late Shaker chairs: left, *gold-lettered decal on the rear leg of a low-back side chair and,* right, *on the rocker of a "No. 3" slat-back chair, both after about 1875. Chair making at Mount Lebanon continued without much change in style or workmanship until the late 1920s.*

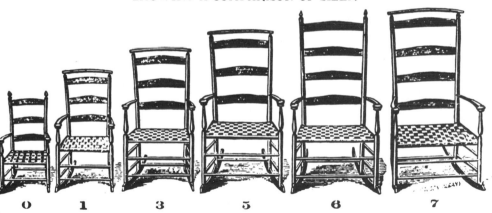

2. Shaker rocking chairs from the "Centennial Illustrated Catalogue and Price List of the Shakers' Chairs, Foot Benches, Floor Mats Etc., Manufactured and Sold by the Shakers at Mt. Lebanon, Columbia Co., N.Y." (Albany, 1876).

current in the trade when the furniture was being made? Should we follow the terminology used by present-day academics in their learned writings? Or should we adopt the jargon now current among antiques dealers and auctioneers? There is plenty wrong with each of these alternatives.

It may come as a surprise, but the exact meaning of most of the specialized vocabulary of the furniture trade before 1800 is now lost. We have many bills, wills, and inventories but only a few illustrations and not a single accurate glossary. The style books offer elegant drawings, but the accompanying text is brief and vague on details. Language always develops, and the same word may take on different meanings in time. Even if we could reconstruct the cabinetmakers' vocabulary for a given period, it would surely conflict with common usage at other times.

For example, the words *highboy* and *lowboy* were unknown in the eighteenth century. *Dressing table* described what we now call the lowboy, but there seems to have been no specific word for the highboy, and it was lumped with the other forms of high chests. What we now call a shield-back chair (fig. 37) was known as an urn-back chair when it was made because the design of the back often incorporated a neoclassic urn motif. What was sold in 1770 as a "scrutor" (a contemporary corruption of the old French *escritoire*) is now called a slant-top, fall-front, drop-lid, or Governor Winthrop desk, and the British call it a bureau (fig. 3). Where does that leave us?

Academic terminology has a valid purpose, of course. Every term is carefully defined to facilitate precise communication. Unfortunately, different authors often use different definitions,

3. *Late Colonial oxbow-front slant-top mahogany desk with good claw-and-ball feet, perhaps from Massachusetts. The shells on the lid seem too small and appear to be made from the wrong kind of mahogany. They may have been added long after the piece was made. (Courtesy of Samuel T. Freeman & Co., Philadelphia.)*

4. Simple birch slant-top desk, probably from New Hampshire, about 1780–1800. The Hepplewhite brasses are original, yet the desk itself is what most people would call Chippendale (43½" high, 21" deep, and 39½" wide, overall).

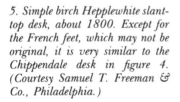

5. Simple birch Hepplewhite slant-top desk, about 1800. Except for the French feet, which may not be original, it is very similar to the Chippendale desk in figure 4. (Courtesy Samuel T. Freeman & Co., Philadelphia.)

6. Cherry secretary from Connecticut, about 1780–90.

7. *A good, simple, early Federal cherry secretary. The French feet, line inlay, cock-beaded drawers, and stamped oval brasses are concessions to the Hepplewhite style, but the basic lines are about the same as in the Chippendale secretary in figure 6. (Courtesy Samuel T. Freeman & Co., Philadelphia.)*

and their aims may be esoteric. When a famous professor in a big university describes a chair with a certain word, the students all follow because they know what is good for them. The resulting usage may spread beyond the local campus but usually doesn't. Academic terms have the advantage of being on record, but they tend to be stilted, and that limits their use by the public.

The lingo of the antiques trade is as changeable as the weather. It often varies from place to place. It is swept by fads from time to time. The trade has its favorite academics and may follow them up to a point, but it is a fickle friendship because the purpose of the trade language is to sell the stuff, not to explain it. Auction catalogs may try to be academic, but usually they come closer to reflecting the trade lingo of the time. The last thing I want to do here is to compile another glossary, but if we are to understand each other, perhaps we should go over some of the more important words and explain what they mean in this book—be that right or wrong.

PERIODS

A *period* is a certain length of time within well-defined limits. For the sake of convenience, I have arbitrarily followed the convention that separates early American furniture making into three periods:

> *Pilgrim* (1620 to 1720)
> *Colonial* (1720 to 1776)
> *Federal* (1776 to about 1830)

Yes, I know that the word Pilgrim can hardly be used to describe a whole century, and scholars rightly object to this usage. Few colonists thought of themselves as Pilgrims after about 1640 or 1650, and the "Plimoth Plantation," in spite of its great schoolroom popularity, was in fact a very small settlement and only one of many. Nevertheless, the term Pilgrim Century was popularized by Wallace Nutting, and, as far as the antiques trade is concerned, it stuck.

STYLES

A *style* is a subtle concept and cannot be defined so simply. We can say that a piece of furniture is of a certain style when most of the features of the piece reflect some model or some convention of design. For example, a piece with pad feet may be of "Queen Anne" style. The fact that Queen Anne was thirty years dead when the style now bearing her name flourished in the American Colonies has nothing to do with the matter.

Indeed, we must not confuse periods with styles. The English designers Chippendale, Hepplewhite, and Sheraton created styles that bear their names, but English styles have little time significance in America. The trouble is that some terms used to describe periods in Europe may describe styles in America. *Empire,* for example, is a definite period in the history of France (1804–15), but in America it is merely a style, with no precise implication of time.

Styles come and go, one blending into another, and it is unwise to be too rigid about style classification. The desk in figure 4, for example, is clearly Chippendale in style, is it not? Too bad some ignoramus stuck the oval Hepplewhite brasses on it! Let me tell you about that. I examined those brasses very closely, and they are original. No one would deny that they are Hepplewhite, yet Hepplewhite's *Cabinet-Maker and Upholsterer's Guide* does not show any such brass. On the other hand, if we look through Chippendale's *Gentleman and Cabinet-Maker's Director*, we shall not find anything that resembles this desk even remotely. A new search through Hepplewhite's book will not reveal any such desk either, but it will show some chests of drawers that are not too far removed in style. So is it a Chippendale or a Hepplewhite desk? Life is too short to brood over such things.

Style is our principal guide to dating early American furniture, but different styles were in fashion in different places at the same time, and the margin of error, in all dating by style alone, can be great. In the absence of recorded evidence, few pieces can be dated closer than about twenty years with any degree of confidence.

A *type* is a kind of construction or a utilitarian form or a conventional object. For example, Windsor construction is a type, the bookcase-top secretary is a type, and a burl bowl is a type. The secretary may be of the Colonial period and Chippendale in style, or it may have been made in Federal times and be Empire in style, but regardless of period or style, it is a type of furniture now known as a secretary—which, incidentally, is still another phonetic corruption of the word *escritoire*.

Then there is a welter of expressions like *Hadley* carving, *snake* foot, *ogee* line (from the French *ogival*, meaning the style of pointed arches—in other

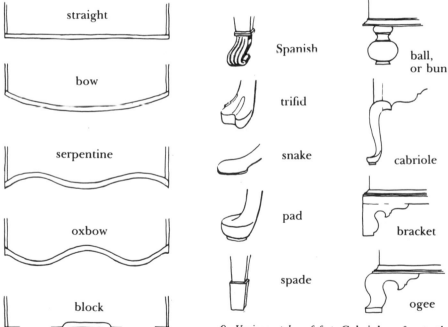

8. *Styles of drawer fronts, as seen from above. A well-shaped front greatly enhances the value of a case piece.*

9. *Various styles of feet. Cabriole refers to the whole leg. A cabriole leg may end in a Spanish, trifid, pad, or claw-and-ball foot. Feet similar to the pad foot but pointed are sometimes called slipper feet (see fig. 33).*

words, Gothic), *Chinese* Windsor, *Spanish* foot, *willow* brass, *shell* carving, and so on, most of which denote details of decoration or form. The number of these terms is very large, but I shall try to pick out the most important ones as we go along and make their meanings clear by small illustrations. The terms are listed in the Index.

Finally, some authors of profound prose and fancy auction catalogs delight in architectural terms like *plinth, spandrel, pilaster, pediment, medallion, cornice,* and so on. These are standard concepts of the classic tradition, well defined in any good dictionary of the English language.

QUALITY OF DESIGN AND WORKMANSHIP

The earliest (Pilgrim) furniture usually follows the English style of the times, and often one must look closely to decide whether a Pilgrim piece was made in America or brought here from England. The distinct American style first appeared early in the eighteenth century, found broad acceptance, and flourished in the Colonial period. The peak was reached about 1780, and in the Federal period the style diversified, matured as tastes became more sophisticated, declined perhaps, and finally capitulated before the onslaught of factory mass production.

10. *A spring-pole lathe. A narrow thong passes from a springy pole in a loop over the work and to a treadle on the floor. The workman made his cut on every downstroke and then let the spring pole turn the work backward and lift the treadle back up. Early Windsor chair legs were made this way, and lathes like this were still used in remote districts early in the twentieth century (see J. G. Jenkins, "A Chiltern Chair Bodger,"*Country Life *[London] 18 [1955]: 684–86). Original drawing by William P. Osborn.*

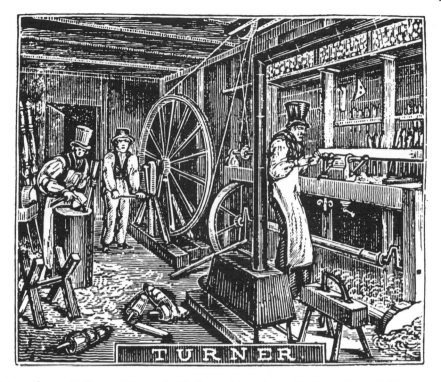

11. More advanced lathes could be cranked by foot or driven from a "bull wheel" cranked by a muscular apprentice. (From Edward Hazen's Panorama of Professions and Trades *[Philadelphia: 1839] in the University of Pennsylvania Library.)*

The superior level of technical skill of the seventeenth- and eighteenth-century European craftsman did not diminish when he moved to America. Even the work of minor cabinetmakers of Revolutionary times shows technical achievement well beyond the capabilities of most modern artisans. It would be difficult to find a man today who could turn Windsor chair legs by eye the way American wrights did 200 years ago, cranking their rickety lathes by foot (fig. 10). How many craftsmen do you know who are able to produce tight dovetails like those found on the common sea chests used by American sailors of 150 years ago? It is the ageless beauty of early American pieces, com-bined with their utility, quality, and consequent durability, that maintains the continued demand for them.

VALUE

The value of an antique piece of furniture, like the value of everything else, is what the buyer is willing to pay. Now a piece may be particularly valuable to us because it was willed to us by dear old Granpaw Stevens, whom we remember for the candy he brought us when we were three. This family piece is presumably not for sale, so we should not talk of how much it is worth, for senti-mental value cannot be expressed in dollars. Similarly, Benjamin Franklin's library chair, the one that converts to a stepladder, is not likely to come up for sale, and the impact of its authenticity certainly could not be replaced if (heaven forbid!) it should burn up. Therefore, we can hardly estimate its value.

Price is determined by the old law of supply and demand. The supply of antique furniture in circulation is gradually decreasing, as the better pieces find their way into museums or come into large collections that ultimately become museums. The demand, on the other end, fluctuates irregularly but shows a pronounced and steady long-term increase. As a result, the value of good antique furniture climbs higher and higher.

That does not mean that the value of one particular piece will continue to increase along with the average. Fashions and fads affect the demand. When some popular and influential collector decides to go after such-and-such, others are likely to follow, and the supply of such-and-suches being essentially limited, their value may take a spurt beyond all expectations. Similarly, the interest in a type or style may wane gradually, and the prices may hit the doldrums. It is not exactly like the stock market, but the situation is not too different. We shall say more about that in chapter 4, Antiques as an Investment.

Even so, one can still furnish a home with original antiques at roughly the cost of "store-boughten" furniture. It takes a little doing, to be sure, but therein lies the sport. As a rule, the cheapest new chest in a furniture store will cost more than an equivalent semi-antique piece in an auction, and good new "contemporary" or "period" furniture will cost about as much as original antiques displayed by the better antiques shops. It is a curious paradox

that a really good antique reproduction is almost always priced higher than a good original. The original, of course, is not listed in a catalog and cannot be ordered by size. It is there, just the same, and with a little knowledge and much patience we shall find it. And if we now carefully restore it to its former state of beauty and utility, we shall have the satisfaction of accomplishment that could not have been ours had we merely ordered the piece from a department store.

That is the basic difference between new and antique furniture. Modern furniture, including reproductions of antiques, no matter how good in style and workmanship, loses more than half its value as soon as it leaves the store. Who wants secondhand furniture? If you don't believe me, just try selling something you recently bought! On the other hand, if some antique piece looked great (to you, on the auction floor) but now does not (to your spouse, in the house), just take it back to the auction and have it sold again. Chances are that it will bring what you paid for it. If you are lucky, it may even bring more.

Good antiques are much more plentiful in the northeastern United States than anywhere else in the country. In New England, eastern New York and Pennsylvania, New Jersey, Delaware, and Maryland the supply is greatest and the prices lowest. New York City is traditionally the marketplace for the best antique furniture, with Philadelphia not far behind.

The buyers, on the other hand, show no such lopsided geographic distribution. As a result, American antiques tend to travel south and west, and the farther they go the more expensive they get. It is not just the cost of transport that causes prices to increase but

12. A country auction in eastern Pennsylvania.

also the inevitable profit that dealers must make every time a piece changes hands. A simple chair picked up for $50 in a small shop in Intercourse, Pennsylvania, may later appear in a fine location in Los Angeles marked $250—and the price could be "right" in both places.

Naturally, all collectors want to buy as well as they can. Somehow, the talk among collectors always turns to money, not as a boast of power but as a measure of collecting skill. If a collector has bought wisely, he or she will be only too happy to tell you the exact price. Anybody can buy almost any-thing with money, but skillful collectors find real sport in seeing what others did not notice, going where others have not been, picking up a bargain just by being clever. Naturally, you must know what things are worth. If you have followed the auctions and perhaps kept notes on cards or in a little book, you will soon get a very good idea of what to expect—in other words, you will gradually learn the art of appraising. A little error every now and then should not dismay the fledgling appraiser. I know a local auctioneer with whom I play games on appraising. We both look at a piece of furniture and write

13. There is a dirty, worn, but sound hutch table in original condition amidst all that stuff not worth mentioning, but don't think that it has not been noticed just because everyone's back seems to be turned! The auctioneer knows it is there, and he will put it up when he thinks the time is ripe.

down on slips of paper the price we think it will bring at auction. As a rule, our estimates agree within 10 or 20 percent, and once in a while we both get fooled by a factor of two or more. Once I saw a piece sell for thirty times the preauction estimate.

Some of the major auction houses issue profusely illustrated catalogs and make price lists available after each sale. Bear in mind that the ultimate bidders may have known something not mentioned in the official descriptions in the catalog, and remember that any photograph shows only what it wants to show. Armed with those precautions, you may peruse priced catalogs and get a fair idea of prices. The trouble is that the best catalogs cover mostly fancy stuff. Ordinary, everyday pieces do appear occasionally in these auctions, but the prices they bring there are often erratic. The diversity in manners of

running an auction is another important reason why auction prices are not always a reliable guide to values. A widely advertised and skillfully staged auction in a classy atmosphere will bring much higher prices than a seedy sale in some old warehouse on the wrong side of the tracks, even if some of the merchandise is exactly the same.

Those are some of the reasons why it is quite impossible to compile a useful price catalog for antique furniture. We have detailed catalogs for coins and postage stamps, and annual lists of the auction prices of rare books, but available guides to furniture prices are of little use. The variables are far too important to be simply listed. A piece of furniture cannot be described in a standard way, and even if it could be, the comparison from place to place and from time to time would be misleading.

2
WHERE AND
HOW
TO BUY

One of the main reasons why searching for antiques is so much fun is that it takes you into such a great variety of places. Auction galleries offering regular sales are established in many cities. Free-lance auctioneers hold sales "on the premises," as they say, or on the lawn in front. Antiques shops and flea markets abound. Regular newspapers and specialized publications catering to dealers and collectors carry classified advertising of antiques for sale by private persons. In any case, you can expect to do much looking before you find a good authentic piece in any of these places, but if the stuff were stacked in every corner, what would be the fun in collecting?

AUCTIONS AND AUCTIONEERS

Most of the surviving early American furniture was made in East Coast states, much of it is still there, and it regularly turns up in auctions. That is scant solace to you, I know, if you happen to be living in Dallas or San Francisco, or for that matter anywhere far from New England or Pennsylvania.

Then you may find that local auctions go on but hardly ever have an antique piece consigned to them, and you may have long ago given up trying to follow them. Once in a rare while someone may advertise an "antique auction," but even then you are likely to find great latitude in the interpretation of the word antique. I remember auctions in Denver where rusty bicycle parts and battered gas-station utensils were boldly hawked as "antiques." Collectors in the midwestern, southwestern, and western states are probably best advised to cultivate the local dealers. I have met some very good ones, from Arkansas to Oregon.

There are big auctions and little ones, elegant and sloppy ones, folksy and formal ones, honest and crooked ones, but they all have these things in common: the goods are as you find them, the prices are unpredictable, and all sales are absolutely final. In an auction you are on your own. If you find a piece that interests you, you must examine it with great care before the actual sale, decide how much you are willing to pay for it, and let it go with a

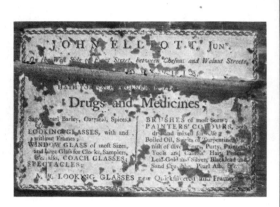

14. *"Now this fine Chippendale mirror, ladies and gentlemen—it's all original and a labeled piece! Circa 1790! What am I bid? . . ."*

smile if someone else wants to pay more.

Collectors must absolutely never fail to make a careful inspection of anything they might possibly want to buy in an auction. The novices in the auction crowd buy things they have barely seen, and from twenty feet away at that. They soon reach the conclusion that the world is full of surprises. However, if you look around during the exhibition before the sale, you will observe the experts poking at the furniture, turning it over, pulling out drawers, and looking at the backs. They may look at many more pieces than they intend to bid on, but when a lot they are interested in finally appears during the sale, they know what it is.

Auction attendants have the knack of showing a piece in a way that makes serious flaws inconspicuous to the casual observer. Once I saw a small drop-leaf table handled and shown so skillfully on the open stage of an auction hall that most of the audience, including the unhappy buyer, never noticed that one of the drop leaves was torn off and missing.

In most auction houses you can leave your bid with the auctioneer or an assistant if you have no time to attend the sale. As a rule, the bid will be used competitively and honestly, but there are a few auctioneers who only use such bids to jack up the price, and such auctions you had best attend yourself. If you are all out to buy a certain piece, you will do well to look at many others in great detail—to camouflage your interest.

15. The auctioneer, his clerk, and his spotters.

Many a bid has been pulled out of the air by fast-talking but observant auctioneers, with the overanxious collector feverishly bidding against a nonexistent opponent or even against himself. I have seen auctions where the moose head on the wall was the most active bidder in the room.

Most auctioneers will gladly estimate the price that a given piece is likely to bring, but you should not take the figure for more than what it is—an educated guess. If the auction is honest, no one can tell what a piece will bring until the last bid is in and the hammer has fallen.

FANCY AUCTIONS

Some years ago I went to a very fancy auction staged in a tent on the lawn of a small castle near Tarrytown, New York. I could not make it for the inspection but came to watch the sale just for my own education. The crowd was very elegant, but the furniture I saw being brought out certainly wasn't. The chairs were skinned, the case goods looked altered, and some of the "primitives" they were touting were primitive only in terms of the talents of the fakers who had made them up. Just the same,

it was a grand social occasion, and the prices went higher than you would have seen in the finest shops at the time. The auctioneer was brisk to the point of rudeness most of the time, except when a famous lady managed to bid in a piece. Then the tempo of his chant would noticeably slacken and he would puff himself up, announce the knockdown price, and finally recite, so no one could miss a syllable, "Sold"—pause—"to Missuhs"—pause—"John D. (ahem) Rockyfellah"—pause—"the Thuhd!" He would then sit in a roseate glow for a while before he picked up the next item.

Celebrities in the audience have a way of raising not only the auctioneer's blood pressure but the prices as well. Bidding high in such auctions is a very expensive way of making an impression.

HOW TO BID

On the average, the top price you should pay in auction is about two thirds of what the same piece would bring in a shop. Against this apparent price advantage you must balance the time, bother, and inconvenience of it all, as well as the considerable risk that the piece you have just bought at auction may have a serious flaw you did not notice before. Personally, I like to buy in auctions, but some collectors prefer not to take the risk and buy only from reputable dealers.

Auctioneers are usually likable people, and most of them are friends with everybody. Some are great wits, and a few are regular clowns. They think fast, and many of them have phenomenal memories. They will know you by name after your first purchase and will greet you by name years later. I know one chap who can tell me, several weeks after an auction, the exact price any piece brought and who bought it. If you ask him the value of a mahogany Chippendale chest of drawers, he can recite the approximate prices of all the chests of that description that have passed through his auction in the last five years, and he can do the same thing for cars or pianos or diamond rings.

Some auctioneers find it convenient to adopt an attitude of haughty condescension toward their public. The attendants in these auctions often follow the example of the master, with his nose held high like the bowsprit of a Bath schooner. It is one of the curious aspects of the auction business that this ill-mannered attitude toward the public, surprising and reprehensible as it may seem to the uninitiated, actually promotes the commercial success of the house. The crowd gets sore at the auctioneer's jibing, and the vindictive customers bid higher "just to show him." I have often had reason to believe that the haughtiest auctioneers get the best prices, and the most deliberately disrespectful attendants get the best tips.

To a good auctioneer, money is the basic element. Literally, he is the fellow who knows the price of everything. So when we need something appraised, a reputable auctioneer will be the man to ask, for he is eminently qualified to estimate what a piece would bring at auction, and he has no commercial interest that might cloud his judgment.

COMMISSIONS AND RESERVES

Auction houses collect a commission on the sale of the goods consigned to them, and it may vary with the value of the articles consigned. A house may list a fixed commission of 20 or 25 percent on ordinary material, but if asked to sell a single Philadelphia highboy, they might be willing to do it for much less. When you have something to sell, you may have difficulty deciding whether to offer it to a dealer or consign it to an auction house. In my experience, dealers will offer less for a piece brought into their shop than they are willing to pay for the same item in an auction thirty miles down a country road. However, nobody can predict the exact price a single piece might bring at auction. Two identical chairs may bring widely different prices in the same house on two successive sale days. The consignor takes the risk of having to accept a low price, or possibly buying the piece back himself and paying the regular commission for the privilege. Owners are allowed to bid, and often do, in all sales that are not advertised as *unrestricted*.

Lately it has become a custom among the better auction houses to indicate *after* the sale which pieces were "bought in" because they did not bring the "reserve," meaning the minimum price the consignor was willing to accept. While a piece is still on the block, however, the bidders in the room never know whether they face a real opponent or are bidding "against the book."

Some auction houses advertise that their reserve is never higher than the lower limit of the official preauction estimate—a valuable clue for the wise bidder.

AUCTION CATALOGS

The catalogs issued by auction houses are often finely printed and illustrated with superb photographs. Some of the better catalogs have become collector's items in themselves and are eagerly sought on the rare book market. The famous Reifsnyder sale catalog, for example, originally issued by the American Art Association in New York for $2, now brings as much as a good Windsor.

Whatever form the catalog may take, from a roughly duplicated sheet to a slick volume rich with color, its purpose is to show each item to best advantage. Many catalogs try to generate an atmosphere of elegant scholarship and may flower with language all their own. Windsor chairs, good or bad, are always "rare." Anything big is "important" (to whom?), and "exceptional proportions" means simply *odd*. "Chippendale style," "Hepplewhite style," any other "style," or the word custom all mean *reproduction;* and "attributed to" means nothing at all. If something is seriously wrong, the catalog mentions the trouble in passing. Obviously, the detail is so trifling, a person of breeding would never give it a thought.

I have never seen a catalog that actually tried to deceive, but ordinary errors are common. We could hardly expect auction catalogers to be experts on everything, and even if they were, they could not possibly take the time to research every item. Furthermore, all catalogs I have ever seen contained some introductory paragraphs to the

16. Here is a good, early Colonial New England slat-back chair with crudely added rockers and a defective rush seat. Restoring it will cost more than it brought at auction, but it's worth it.

effect that the house is in no way responsible for the correctness or accuracy of any statement, etc., etc. As I have said before, in the auction hall buyers are on their own, and that is why I like auctions.

THE KNOCKOUT RING

There was a time, during the good days of Victoria and Albert, when British auctions were attended almost exclusively by dealers. Gentleman collectors bought through their agents, and the big dealers soon found it profitable to form a combine to eliminate competition among themselves and to discourage outsiders. The cartel became known as the Knockout Ring. (See, for instance, James Henry Duveen's *Art Treasures and Intrigue.*)

The system was really quite simple. The combine was formed at the beginning of an auction, and a bidder or several bidders were appointed with instructions on what pieces they were to buy. No one else in the combine would bid, but if some outsider had the nerve to bid up, the Ring would run him up to such a high price that he would soon learn to buy from the combine. In this way the Knockout Ring came to rule the important auctions, and only the crumbs went to nonmembers. At the end of each sale, the Ring members would get together and hold a second "knockout" auction among themselves to divide the loot. The total sum realized in this wildcat auction was often much higher than the sum of the Ring's purchases, and the net profit was divided among the members. In that way, a member of the Ring could realize a tidy sum at an auction without saying a word or raising a finger.

With the advent of income taxes, the princely warehouse collector became a thing of the past, and the initiative shifted, if not entirely to the little fellow, at least to the individual amateur with comfortable means. Most amateurs like to bid for themselves, and so it happened that more and more private people went to auctions until the Ring lost control and was reduced to competing with them.

In America the Ring was never as strong as in Britain, but it managed to survive, and we may still see it operating in the important auctions. In Philadelphia, the Ring is directed by a very good dealer who conducts the knockout auction by sealed bids and distributes the profit on the basis of a complicated formula based on how high the underbidders went in the secondary auction. It's fairer than the simple English system and keeps the members on their toes.

Dissension within the Ring is common. The dealers, of course, must buy at wholesale prices, but the private collector can pay a little more. As a result, it is an uphill fight for the Ring. Nevertheless, when you see a group of professionals all in a knot and tensely gesticulating after the auction, you are witnessing the last vestige of a once fiercely powerful monopoly.

SHOPS AND DEALERS

Antiques shops range from magnificent establishments with elegant addresses to abject holes-in-the-wall in the rundown part of the city. The dealers who operate these shops range from consummate experts to something very much less than that, and some of them make a good living while others don't even eke out the rent. However, I am reasonably certain that few if any of them get rich. Let me outline the basic mechanics of the trade.

In order to stay in business, dealers must sell for more than they paid. The markup may range from very little to several hundred percent of the purchase price, depending on how well the dealer bought, but it will average about

100 percent of the original purchase price. Against this seemingly large portion of the price, the dealer must charge the transport of the piece, minor repair and restoration, a share of the rent and normal business expenses such as heat, light, advertising, clerical help, salespeople's salaries, insurance, taxes, and all the thousands of minor expenses. Honest dealers offer fairly extensive guarantees as to authenticity, and any guarantee involves some risk and occasional expense. Furthermore, each piece represents a certain investment, and the dealer must write off the interest on this sum. If a piece should stand in the shop for a number of years, the interest might easily wipe out any remaining profit when the piece is finally sold.

The expert collector is well advised to be on friendly terms with the best local dealers. Many good pieces turn up through their grapevine, and few collectors have the time or the inclination to go to all the sales everywhere. When we buy a piece from a dealer, we may want to haggle over the price, remembering that many come down but some will not. We should consider all sales final, and once we have bought something, we should never complain about it.

At first, we may find it a little difficult to appraise the dealers we meet, for there are no obvious outward signs of knowledge and understanding. Having looked at a few good collections, and having spent some time with a few good books, we shall soon learn what matters and what does not. Then we can evaluate our dealers by the answers they give to a few technical questions.

In that way we discover that antiques dealers may be classified into three broad categories, which I call Kind Souls, Conspirators, and Antiquarians. The division between these three species is not sharp, of course, but the types are sufficiently distinct to be described one by one.

The Kind Souls are sincere and friendly. They will chat with a customer for hours, freely dispensing inaccurate information. They are full of good advice and are an inexhaustible source of stories. They try to be helpful, but their shops rarely contain anything that could properly be called antique. Once in a while they find a good piece, so that we cannot safely overlook them, but neither must we expect miracles. Most of them are in business for lack of anything else to do, which gives them a wonderful outlook on life. This is certainly the largest of the three categories. I would estimate that over two thirds of America's antiques dealers qualify as Kind Souls.

The Conspirators are a small minority. Their stock is often good, and their shops may be quite large. If you walk in on them clad in your most comfortable painting shirt and work trousers and ask them the time of day, they will tell you that the clock just stopped. If, two days later, you appear dressed for a White House reception, they will greet you unctuously, and when you ask the time they will answer in a way that implies that the highest honor of the land is about to be bestowed upon you. Everything they do is flavored with mystery. Their merchandise is not marked, and the prices they quote will quickly erode once the customer has indicated even passing familiarity with standard bazaar tactics. They talk of other shops with a curled lip, and when they go to auctions they scratch their rumps and make sneering remarks in the back of the hall. If you meet them there and ask about any piece up for sale, they will run it down with some enigmatic remark like, "What is wrong with that desk? Why, everything!" But should they succeed in buying the desk, they will immediately tell you that not only is it the finest desk ever to come through this or any other auction, they also happen to have proof that George Washington personally designed those little drawers to store his teeth in.

Conspirators are easy to outbid in auctions, but some of them like to bid against a well-known collector simply because they think the collector might have seen something they missed. On the other hand, it is a sport among mischievous experts to feign interest in a worthless piece and see to it that one of the Conspirators ends up high bidder. Many among the Conspirators are educated and would be worth knowing if it were not for the fact that they always try to put something over. The few serious fakes I have seen for sale were all in the shops of Conspirators.

The Antiquarians are in business to stay, often for several generations. Some of them go out for publicity; others let the world come to them. Their shops may be large or small, and their stock may be good or only fair, but the people in charge know their stuff, and some of them are real scholars. They are eager to discuss technical details if the customer shows appreciation. They are likely to have a good reference library. Usually they go out of their way to further the beginning collector's education. They may be young or old, male or female, affable or reserved, but they are the people we should seek out and get to know.

As a rule, Antiquarians do not seem anxious to sell. They will call attention to the desirable features of every piece but would not think of trying to conceal serious faults. They show their wares, and if the customer makes it eminently clear that it would be impossible to live another minute without this or that piece, they will indicate the grief of parting before they let it go. Some of them have a very fine stock, and the reason for that is, of course, that they are willing to pay the price. Israel Sack, one of the greatest American dealers, was known as "crazy Sack" around Boston auctions for the "outrageous" prices he would pay for good furniture, but the firm he founded has prospered and still bids like a fiend on very fine pieces.

JUNK SHOPS

Every now and then we hear of a collector who was prowling through a filthy junk shop and under a pile of moth-eaten debris found a Colonial tavern table that he bought for a song. Far be it from me to assert that the story is untrue. I can only say that I have been to hundreds of junk shops, and in the very few instances when I saw a piece worth having, the price was usually high. Junk-shop owners share the desire to hang on to their wares. From my own experience I conclude that hounding junk shops in search of treasure is largely a waste of time.

FLEA MARKETS

Flea markets are something else again. They are held in the country, as a rule, in or near shopping centers, in abandoned large stores, by the side of the road, or almost anywhere there is some flat ground to set up the tables with room for parking. I know one flea market in a drive-in movie and another in the basement of an active church. Flea markets have been around for years,

17. *Nothing in this flea-market display is antique! The white jug was made about 1890, the black one perhaps in 1910, and the pierced-tin "Paul Revere" lantern is new and not even as old as the used Dietz lamp behind it.*

but in the late sixties the custom caught on like never before, and now you can find them anywhere you go. On Saturdays and Sundays many people seem to enjoy sitting behind folding tables in the sunshine, and even more people want to come and see what is on those tables. Mostly it is not much, and some of the stuff may look as if it came straight from some trash can, but a few of these part-time dealers are skillful pickers, and once in a very great while I see some very nice things on their tables. Glass, pottery, ancient tools, small utensils, and, in the way of furniture, mostly chairs and small chests can be found in flea markets, usually but not necessarily at reasonable prices. When I consider the things I have bought in flea markets and balance them against the time and the gasoline it took to get them—well, profit isn't everything in life, is it? A flea market in good weather is lots of fun, and cover-

ing a big one is every bit as much exercise as a good round of golf.

PICKING

Such great early collectors as Irving W. Lyon, Henry Erving, Wallace Nutting, Luke Vincent Lockwood, and Walter Hosmer liked to acquire their pieces by a process known as picking. They would drive out into the country, manage to meet an old widow in an ancient farmhouse, convince her of their honorable intentions, and thus gain access to her attic. In the end they would buy what they wanted from the attic, or even from the parlor, at a mutually agreeable price—usually quite low.

This technique worked wonders when roads were still bad and cars few, but as more and more pickers roamed the landscape, the old farmers became cagier and cagier, until now it is hardly worthwhile to try the game. Only once did I gain access to a well-stocked attic, and then only through family connections, and I had to bring in an independent appraiser before my offer was accepted. Nevertheless, we may be tempted to try our hand at picking in the backwoods. As Henry Hammond Taylor has said, "Collecting from old country homes is most interesting, but it requires infinite patience, tact, and the ability to absorb vast quantities of sometimes not very interesting conversation."

If that seems like a challenge, then pack your wagon and head into one of the eastern states. Get away from the cities and off the main roads, stop at the gas station, and ask around. If you fail in your effort to buy directly from the source, you might be able at least to find one of the small "wholesale" or "shipping" dealers who collect antiques in the country and sell them in batches to large city dealers. These professional pickers may have a surprisingly good stock on hand, and their retail prices are sometimes lower than those in the city.

Following the classified advertisements in the Sunday newspapers is a modified form of picking. We shall find some of the strangest things advertised as "antique," and some of the prices demanded may give us pause. Apparently the world is full of people who think they can make their friends happy by telling them their antiques are worth thousands of dollars. Somebody makes an offhand remark, it's confirmed by a rumor, verified by a guess, and there you have it: the piece is most valuable indeed. It is no good to argue—the best you can do is to humor them.

In most cases we can tell by a phone call whether we should go out to look at the material offered. A few well-chosen questions will give us a rough idea of what there is, even if the advertiser seems quite unable to describe the piece. How tall? How wide? How many drawers? What kind of handles? Knobs? Brasses? What kind of feet? What kind of wood? Where did it come from?—those are the questions we might profitably ask. Even so, most of our visits will be in vain. However, every now and then someone has a first-rate piece and genuinely wants to sell at a reasonable price. Although I personally find it more fruitful to follow the auctions, I have bought a few pieces through the ads, and one certainly meets a lot of people that way.

Some years ago I was in Dallas on Sunday and saw an ad in the paper offering a Windsor chair. The owner made good sense on the phone, and I drove out to see it. From the outside the house looked like a thousand other North Dallas "Colonials" except that I noticed the shutters were real. But once in the door, I could hardly believe my eyes. Here was as neat a late-Colonial interior as I had ever seen anywhere, Williamsburg included! Every piece was right, and everything worked together, even the drapes, the Turkish rugs, and the handmade candles in the sconces. The Windsor was for sale because the owners had found another that fitted their set a little better.

In a corner I saw a shelf of reference books, *The Easy Expert* among them. The lady of the house noticed my attention and asked why I was interested. "Well, I am Moreton Marsh," I allowed, and she burst out laughing.

"I am Thomas Ormsbee!" she said, and nothing I could do the rest of the time I was there would convince her that I had really written this book.

3
HOW
TO
SELECT

First, let us examine the general rules and then see how they apply to the wide selection of antique furniture you will find on the market. When I consider buying a piece, I examine it from three separate points of view:

1. Are the lines good?
2. Is it genuine?
3. Is it in good enough shape to be useful?

The quality of the lines, of course, is obvious at a glance. You either like something or you don't, and there is no sense in trying to explain the reason why. Taste is a strictly personal matter, almost like getting married. If you expect to live with a piece of furniture, then it must please you, or you should not buy it.

Tastes change with the years, but a good piece remains good regardless of the fashions. When my wife and I were first setting up housekeeping, we went overboard for primitives. Everything had to be pine or we did not give it houseroom. Once we had a chance to get a carved Chippendale chair from a relative, but we picked a black Windsor instead. The Chippendale seemed much too fancy and did not interest us then, even though I now know that it was worth twice the sum total of all our possessions at the time. If I had the chance, I would swap all our Windsors for it today. Our tastes became more sophisticated as we grew older, and we happily accept fancy carving now, as long as it adorns a piece that is good in itself. It is only a matter of taste.

A good way to exercise one's taste is to study the style books (see the Bibliography at the end of the book). The three great classics, arranged in the order of decreasing usefulness, in my experience, are *Furniture Treasury* by Wallace Nutting, *American Antique Furniture* by Edgar G. Miller, and *Colonial Furniture in America* by Luke Vincent Lockwood. The texts may be a trifle out of date and some of the photographs muddy, but no other books offer so many pictures, systematically arranged.

More accurate descriptions and better (but fewer) photographs appear in the two volumes titled *American Furni-*

41

ture, one by Joseph Downs and one by Charles F. Montgomery; in *Eighteenth-Century American Arts* by Edwin J. Hipkiss; and in *American Furniture . . . Boston* by Richard H. Randall. Albert Sack's *Fine Points of Furniture* is a good brief guide to styles and values, and the deluxe *American Antiques* series gives excellent if random exposure to the very best from his shop. *American Painted Furniture 1660–1880* by Dean A. Fales, Jr., gives a systematic overview of styles and decorations. I have also found it useful to go through the ads placed by dealers in the magazine *Antiques* and in more ephemeral periodicals like the *Maine Antique Digest.* Old illustrated auction catalogs are also a good source.

By looking through these books, I can decide what I like, but genuineness is something else again. Whether or not a piece is "right," as they say in the trade, has to be decided on coldly impersonal grounds. No matter how much I may like a piece, if close examination reveals that it is all jazzed up— forget it!

FAKING, FAKES, AND FAKERS

Most of us are fascinated with the idea of counterfeiting. It has overtones of Sherlock Holmes, the implication of danger, if only the danger of getting burned, and all the other melodramatic aspects that are required as background for a good story. The literature on fake antiques is voluminous, and many people are so scared by the many tales of woe they read and hear that they come to think that museums are the only places where genuine antique pieces can be found—everything else being guaranteed fake.

Yet it is my experience that genuine antiques are common, but convincing fakes are a rarity. Furthermore, all the really good fakes I know are now in museums. The usual fake is so crude that anyone can learn to spot it at a glance. The collector of early American furniture may have problems, but recognizing fakes is not likely to be a major one among them.

First of all, there is hardly any such

18. *Antique looking, isn't it? A believer might even call it folk art and describe it as a "Pennsylvania salver with remnants of polychrome decoration," but it is just an old beer tray I decorated for a friend more than thirty years ago. It acquired its convincing patina by getting blown off the porch in a high wind and being lost in the shrubbery for a couple of years.*

19. Exceptional Hepplewhite gentleman's secretary-bookcase, probably Boston, about 1910. Yes, 1910! It has superlative lines, convincing patina, and genuine signs of wear, but it is an early reproduction —not a fake. It was made in the old way but with modern nails, screws, and other hardware, and interior surfaces show the marks of a mechanical thickness planer. (Courtesy Samuel T. Freeman & Co., Philadelphia.)

thing as a fake built from the ground up. It is quite impossible to whip up a highboy from some old barn lumber and make it look convincingly antique. Few men are alive today who can cut an accurate dovetail, much less carve a reeded quarter column or a reasonable facsimile of a shell. The price of good lumber and the wages demanded by the few remaining skilled workers are so high that it would cost more to have a piece copied than the original is worth. That is why good "handmade" reproductions usually cost more than original antiques even though these reproductions are made by factory methods in large numbers. The honest reproducer does not attempt to conceal the marks of rotary saws, automatic thickness planers, modern screws and nails, and the color of freshly cut wood. The faker has to worry about all these details and many more. I know one could have a simple piece faked so well that it would fool the Easy Expert, but such a joke would be costly.

The fakers, however, have one avenue open to them: they can improve on genuine antiques. The products of this endeavor are known as monkeys in the trade, and we shall discuss them as we come to the respective types. Some of these alterations would be obvious no matter what the faker could do. A wedded chest on chest, for example, or a fake scroll on a once-plain cupboard are easily detected by the techniques I shall discuss quite thoroughly. Fake inlays, fluting, carving, turnery, and similar embellishments are usually recognized by their crudity. The woodworking talents of most fakers seem to be pitifully inadequate to the lofty tasks they set for themselves. Only rarely do we run into a bit of fakery that shows great skill.

In Baltimore they are rightly proud of the finely inlaid Hepplewhite furniture made there in the early Federal period, and in 1947 they had a magnificent exhibition of the stuff with an elegantly illustrated catalog. The star of the show was number 16, a beautifully proportioned card table with a large, crisp griffin inlaid on the skirt. The table was widely known. It had come from the Reifsnyder sale (no. 505) and appears in Miller (vol. 2, no. 1516) and Nutting (no. 1030), among others. It is now in the Garvan Collection at Yale University.

The typical Baltimore inlay consists of neatly graduated flowers on the legs and delicate ovals on the panels, but this griffin was such a rare bird that he was oohed and aahed over at length. Many years later some smartie at Yale became curious about this unusual inlay. The table was taken apart and was found to have been assembled from English and American parts with new inlay added (Kirk, fig. 178)! It had been done well enough to fool everybody for decades, but let me assure you that such instances are very rare. Almost without exception, the faker relies not on skill but on the ignorance of the customer.

"UNIQUE" PIECES

If you ever find a print or a book of which no other copy is known, you will have made a worthwhile discovery. No matter how insignificant the picture or the text, uniqueness alone will generate interest in any printed work. But when you see a piece of antique furniture advertised as "unique," chances are very good that you have merely discovered another monkey.

It could be that some eccentric ancestor wanted a strange piece and

20. *An elegant folding card table, about 1790, with detail of oval-and-cornhusk inlay—a style of decoration often attributed to Baltimore. (Courtesy David Stockwell, Inc., Wilmington.)*

found a cabinetmaker to make it. Or some craftsman may have been a bit odd himself, and his product shows it. Perhaps so, but I can only say from my own experience that almost all the "unique" pieces I have seen in the trade were badly jazzed up or foolishly faked. Colonial and Federal cabinet- makers hewed close to fashion, as a rule. The orthodoxy of their designs came from knowing what they could sell, and when they went out of the regular way to create pieces like the ladder-back Windsor in figure 21, for example, they still remained within the framework of current fashion. Nobody

21. Unusual (but not unique) Windsor bow-back armchair in a strange mixture of styles. The thin seat and bamboo-turned legs show that it could not have been made before about 1810, but the ladder motif in the back is Chippendale (see fig. 34) and had been fashionable a generation earlier.

made oddities for the fun of it. They sold even less then than they do now.

THE MATTER OF CONDITION

When we have decided that a piece is in good style, and when it has passed all the tests of authenticity, then we are faced with the all-important question of condition. It is my experience as a restorer that most people tend to minimize, rationalize, or altogether overlook the condition of pieces they like. Some time ago I saw a simple Sheraton chest of drawers in an auction, and it would have been fine had it not fallen off a truck and in the process lost all four legs and much of the top. The chest was clearly not worth restoring,

22. From above, top, *this rush seat may seem only slightly damaged but,* bottom, *a look underneath reveals the seriousness of the problem. The seat must be entirely replaced if the chair is to be used.*

but I thought I might buy it for the lumber. Ten dollars would have seemed too much, but one unwary buyer went right on up, and I can just imagine the length of his face when his cabinetmaker told him how much it would cost to fix the chest. A reliable dealer would never dream of trying to sell a wreck to a customer, yet in auctions one often sees total derelicts

23. Late Sheraton mahogany-veneered chest of drawers with its original mirror, about 1820–40. (Courtesy of Samuel T. Freeman & Co., Philadelphia.)

bringing prices that compare with the price of a good piece in a shop. Most of us are optimistic, and it is a common tendency to underestimate the extent (and the cost) of necessary repairs.

Sheraton chests of drawers (like the one in fig. 23) are not cheap, but they are relatively common. I have seen more than a dozen of them sold at auction during the past year, so I know that I can afford to be choosy. If this one does not come up to standards, the next one may, or the one after that. A rare piece, on the other hand, like a Bible box with Hadley carving (fig. 30), could be a total wreck and I would still consider it. In all my life I have seen only six Hadley pieces offered for sale, and I would be quite willing to overlook a lot of damage on so rare an item. In between these two extremes one has to use judgment. In cases of doubt I lean away from damaged pieces. I pass by wrecked Windsors and slat-back chairs simply because it is difficult to repair them. However, I might take a beat-up framed chair if it were complete and original, for I know that I can repair it without too much trouble. We discuss this aspect of the various types of furniture both in this chapter and in chapter 11 on details of restoration, but let me conclude by emphasizing that it rarely pays to buy wrecks.

4
ANTIQUES
AS AN
INVESTMENT

This is not a book on finance, but antiques have been bought as a form of investment for a long time, and their investment potential cannot be ignored. It all started in Europe, when wartime runaway inflation, from the Napoleonic Wars to World War II, repeatedly destroyed the value of money and savings. In Europe, real estate ownership is restricted, so people turned to chattels, trying to preserve their capital. They bought fine furniture, Oriental carpets, glass, china, rare books, musical instruments—"objects of virtu." The antiques trade developed and prices of good things rose higher and higher, not only because of continuing inflation. The population was growing, the standard of living was rising, and the demand for valuable objects continued to increase in the face of an essentially unchanging supply.

In America we have never had a runaway inflation, but the steady creeping kind has made itself felt from time to time. The population and the standard of living have grown faster here than in Europe, and the supply of antiques has always been much smaller simply because there wasn't much property hereabouts until after the beginning of the Industrial Revolution. It is hardly surprising, then, that American antiques are so popular as a secondary investment medium. Not for a moment, however, would I suggest that chairs, desks, and highboys should replace stocks, bonds, and savings accounts; nobody should invest all his money in antiques. But if you have funds you don't need, if you know something about good things, and if you enjoy chasing after them—why not combine pleasure with a little business?

We are concerned here with long-term investment, say ten years or so. Short-term trading can be profitable, as shown by the relatively small proportion of antiques dealers who consistently make money, but it is a specialized business apart from just straight investment. Even so, private antiques buyers with investment in mind must learn a thing or two about business. Specifically, they must find ways of minimizing the difference between retail (when they buy) and wholesale (when they sell). In practice that usually means they do most of their buying and selling in auctions. Whenever they can arrange it, they buy in plain auctions and sell in fancy ones.

PRICES GO UP, BUT NOT ALWAYS

Over the years I have accumulated a large pile of sale catalogs from the leading auction houses. Some of them go back to the turn of the century, and many are priced, so that one can get a fair idea of how the prices have moved. It's rather a rough picture, nothing like the precise tabulations one can get for such things as the Dow-Jones Industrials, but clear enough. To paraphrase John Jacob Astor, the antiques market fluctuates. Let's start with the bad news.

In the late twenties the prices of antiques (and many other things) were bid up to dizzy heights, not to be equaled for several decades. "The stuff was turning into gold, right in my showroom," a New York dealer told me years ago. Things changed abruptly on those last few days of October, 1929. Many great dealers and collectors found themselves in a financial squeeze, and some fine collections had to be liquidated at once. Before long the market was flooded with good stuff, and prices tumbled wildly. The slide went on, and the same pieces were sold and resold at prodigious losses. One of my catalogs is dated January, 1930, and a dozen pieces from that sale reappear in another catalog dated January, 1932. In the intervening time, some of the furniture had been capably restored—all to no avail. When those same things were sold again, in the very same auction hall, prices dropped an average of 71 percent! As far as I know, the greatest loss was incurred on a sunflower chest, one of the earliest fine pieces made in the Colonies. It dropped from $4,200 to $325, a loss of more than 92 percent in only two years.

Prices continued to skid until about 1935 and then began to recover—very, very slowly. The war came, of course, and people thought about other things, but even by 1950 prices had risen no higher than 20 percent over the Depression lows. New interest appeared in the fifties, and by 1960 the antiques boom was in full swing. The highs of 1928 and 1929 were surpassed in the sixties, and prices continued to soar in the seventies. That is the good news—maybe.

Partly from those priced catalogs and partly from my own experience, let me document that fabulous boom in the antiques market. Look at the jug in figure 51. I bought it in a large, untidy antiques shop in Binghamton, New York, in 1945 for 50 cents. In 1976 I bought a slightly larger but otherwise very similar jug in a flea market in New Jersey for $30, and I think I got a good buy both times.

Now consider the fan-back Windsor in figure 42. A friend bought three of them in a weekly auction in Washington, D.C. for $60 in 1956. Two were in fair-to-good shape, one lacked a post, and all three were heavily painted white. They looked as if they had been in storage for fifty years, and I got stuck with restoring them. About a year later, in the same auction house, I spotted a fellow carrying a Windsor chair he had just bought for $2—slightly cut down but obviously a mate to the other three, with the same paint and the same dust on it. He was glad to sell it for $6. So here we had a set of four fan-back Windsors for $66 plus the cost of restoration. A single chair of that kind, in the "original" black paint but with turnings not quite as good as on those four, fetched $700 in Pennsylvania in 1976, and others have gone higher since.

In the late forties and early fifties I bought quite a few plank-bottom chairs like those in figure 96, and I paid an average price of less than $5 each. Some cost me only a dollar! Once, in Boston, I paid $8 each for two nice thumb-backs with original decorations on yellow ground, and my old notes show that I was very annoyed to have gone so high. Have you seen a chair like that on the market lately? Have you noticed the price? Plank-bottom chairs have certainly appreciated!

The particular comb-back Windsor armchair in the frontispiece is highly desirable but as a type is fairly common. They come up occasionally in the auctions I go to and are well represented in that pile of catalogs. Some of the chairs are better than others, but some auction crowds are more eager than others, so the effects even out. Here are some sales of such chairs for which I have records:

New York, 1928	$275
New York, 1931	225
another	325
New York, 1944	180

another	310
Philadelphia, 1951	210
New York, 1959	450
Philadelphia, 1966	3,300
Philadelphia, 1975	2,800
another, ordinary	1,250
Pennsylvania, 1976 (restored)	3,300
New York, 1977 (top grade)	10,000

That last chair appears in the frontispiece.

Next, let's look at decorated "Pennsylvania Dutch" dower chests. They are a marvelous product of American folk art, and one rarely sees two that are similar, but here I list only the best:

New York, 1928	$200
New York, 1944	240
two more, each	250
another, very fine	410
New York, 1958	675
New York, 1959	1,300
Philadelphia, 1966	6,500
Pennsylvania, 1973	10,500
another	4,300
Philadelphia, 1975	6,250
Hyannis, Mass., 1976	4,400
Pennsylvania, 1976	22,000
Toronto, 1978	10,000

24. Fine Pennsylvania dower chest · with incised decoration filled with sulfur, dated inside 1783. The base seems too large, and the feet are replacements. (Courtesy of Paul R. Flack.)

The chest sold in Philadelphia in 1975 for $6,250 and again in Pennsylvania in 1976 for $22,000 happens to be one and the same piece! It is illustrated in figure 24, and I shall get back to it presently.

Finally, let's look at the price performance of some unusually fine pieces, the sort of things a good museum would be proud of—shell-carved kneehole block-front desks, for example. Such pieces, in the finest Newport workmanship, appear in auctions from time to time. One sold in New York in 1932 for $6,300, a bargain; another, in 1948, for $7,000; and a third, in 1950, brought $16,000—still cheap, considering. A very similar desk came up in Philadelphia in 1971, without any great fanfare or advance publicity, and fetched $104,000 (fig. 25)! As an investment it would have amounted to about 7.2 percent compounded annually, if you bought in 1932, and 8.8 per-

cent had you waited for the third one, in 1950 (allowing 10 percent for the auctioneer's commission). That is a lot more than savings banks would have paid over the same period, and the 1971 price was not a fluke. Another such desk appeared in New York in October, 1972, and brought $120,000.

Fine Philadelphia highboys come up for sale surprisingly often. Here is a list of prices of Philadelphia highboys with good carving, partly gleaned from my catalogs and including some sales I watched myself:

New York, 1928	$1,800*
New York, 1929 (very fine)	44,000
New York, 1932	5,500
Philadelphia, 1937	1,650
New York, 1944	2,080
New York, 1959	9,000
New York, 1966 (very fine)	22,000

25. Shell-carved block-front kneehole desk of the Townsend-Goddard school, Newport, R.I., about 1765–75. This one brought $104,000 in 1971, which at that time was a record for an American case piece. (Courtesy of Samuel T. Freeman & Co., Philadelphia.)

New York, 1967	11,000
Philadelphia, 1973	51,000
Pennsylvania, 1977	15,000*
New York, 1977	
(damaged)	40,000
Washington, D.C., 1977	21,000*

As it happens, the three sales marked (*) are all of the same highboy. It is not a bad highboy and not a good one—just average. If you had bought it in 1928 and sold it forty-nine years later, even at the higher 1977 price, your money would have earned less than 5 percent, the way we have been calculating it. Had you bought the one in 1929 (a very superior specimen), held it for forty-nine years, and then sold it for $130,000, which would have been a record for a Philadelphia highboy, you would have earned less than 2 percent. You would be justified in reaching the conclusion that there must be better investments.

HOW AND WHAT TO BUY

How, then, does one buy antiques for investment? Exactly the way one would buy them for sitting on, eating off, or keeping one's socks in. Whether he knows it or not, the Easy Expert is already an investor. The techniques and tactics of buying discussed in this book are essentially the same for a young couple furnishing a house as they are for the seasoned investor protecting capital. The only difference is that the young couple would pay attention to the things they need for their house, but the investor would be considering what is likely to appreciate the most.

There are fads and preferences in the antiques business just as there are favorites and "tiers" in the stock market, and long-term investors do not try to follow short-term fashions. Investors have to buy well and can't afford to chase their rivals in the auction room. They must diversify their buying to minimize the risk of mistakes. They have to know the fair value of the things they are trying to buy, and if they can pick up a sleeper every now and then, that's frosting on the cake. In the average purchase they must know the right price and be willing to pay it.

The next question is *what* to buy, and that is not so easily answered. It is like any other financial advisory: if the guy with all that advice really knew how to make money, he would be doing it instead of telling you about it. The skilled investor develops a nose for investment and just *knows* what to buy. He or she may make a mistake once in a while, but that is only human. Everybody gets stuck from time to time; the trick is to learn from one's mistakes.

With the explicit understanding that the Easy Expert will take my advice just like any other advice—namely, with a grain of salt—here are my views on what may be good buys for investment:

1. Small, everyday stuff—the genuine-but-undistinguished antiques that frequently come on the market. Chairs, tables, simple case goods—even some of the popular semiantiques like dry sinks, commodes, and cupboards—are regularly seen in weekly auctions in the city, in genuine country auctions, and in antiques shops and secondhand furniture shops. Over the two decades from 1955 to 1975, these ordinary things showed the largest percentage increase in dollar value. Because of their wide utility, they have a ready market. The only problem is that they take up a lot of space per dollar invested.

2. Well-designed intermediate pieces with artistic merit. Here I would include the better desks with nicely shaped interiors and good figure in the

wood of the drawer fronts; Queen
Anne and Chippendale chairs of elegant proportions; good Windsors of all
kinds; small but neat chests of drawers,
preferably with original brasses; tip-top
tables with well-turned columns and elegant legs and feet; small Hepplewhite
and Sheraton tables and sewing stands;
neat lowboys and small highboys.
These pieces can be found in the major
auctions and in better shops, but don't
expect to get them cheaply—the average price will be in the thousands of
dollars. These things have utility, of
course, but their main value is decorative, and the quality of design makes a
lot of difference in the price. The market for the elegant stuff is limited compared with that for everyday things, but
there has been no shortage of buyers in
my memory. (We shall say more about
selling in due course.)

3. Big-time showpieces. governor's-
mansion furniture, historical pieces,
Philadelphia highboys, block-front furniture, bombé carcase goods, big fancy
secretaries, large sets of elaborate
chairs, very early American pieces, the
flag made by Betsy Ross, and all of
George Washington's furniture several
times over—these things come on the
market more often than most people
think. The prices begin at $10,000 or
so, and the sky is the limit. Most of us
simply don't have the money, but the
statistics gleaned from my catalogs also
show that these showpieces do not appreciate as fast as smaller things. More
important, they are difficult to sell.
That fact alone should be enough to
scare an investor.

The high-style pieces are often held
by people of high income. Instead of
taking their chances in selling (and
being taxed on the proceeds), large
taxpayers may find it more advantageous to have a piece generously ap-

praised, give it to an appropriate public
institution, and apply the full appraised
value as a deduction on taxable income. As a result, big-time furniture is
steadily shifting from private to public
ownership and out of the market.

SELLING

The price of a share of stock at any
given time will be very nearly the same
no matter how or where you sell it, but
with antiques it is a different story. The
price of a given piece could be much
higher or much lower, depending on
how and where it is sold.

Selling to dealers is rarely easy.
Their business is predicated on buying
cheaply, and their first offer is almost
always too low. Pushing them up to a
reasonable figure could be a drawn-out
process that some of us may not enjoy.
Good dealers know what they can sell,
and if the piece being offered does not
happen to fit their pattern, they will buy
it only if they can get it for very little.
Unless the dealer can be made to feel
some competition, he is unlikely to pay
the price to a private seller.

Competition is the heartbeat of the
auction trade, and auctioneers have an
obvious interest in obtaining the best
possible prices for their consignors.
Most auctions have reserves, which as
we have seen means that they will not
sell a piece unless it brings some prear-
ranged figure, and reputable houses
make sure that the reserves are reasonable. The honest auction is an open
marketplace and probably the best
means we have for establishing fair
market value.

We have already mentioned that
there are auctions and *auctions.* Now let
me illustrate the point with a documented example—the dower chest in
figure 24. The chest was sold in the fall

of 1975 in the ancient and respectable auction house of Samuel T. Freeman in Philadelphia for $6,250. It was an elegant sale with many good things, and the room was full of clever people. The Philadelphia auction crowd has many knowledgeable amateurs, and the dealers were there too, of course, sharp-eyed as ever. The chest was knocked down properly and in the open—no one present was willing to pay more, and many thought that the price was rather high. After all, the feet of the chest are not original.

The following spring the very same chest became the focal point of an elegant country auction in Pennsylvania. The catalog of that sale cost $6, and the chest was on the cover in full color. The sale was vigorously advertised well in advance. The three hundred reserved seats in the auction hall sold for $10 each, and about a hundred people were turned away when the tickets sold out. Prices of everything went very high, and when the chest came up, several people quickly ran it up to $16,000. From there, a contest developed between two bidders who simply wouldn't yield until the price reached $22,000! So here we have a chest that almost quadrupled in value in half a year by moving out into the country with skillful publicity and sharp merchandising.

Swings like that are exceptional, but I know several auctioneers who often manage to push prices above retail. There is an element of luck, of course, and that frightens many potential consignors in spite of the protection offered by the auctioneer's reserve.

FUTURE TRENDS

The next question is obvious: Will the prices continue to go up, or are we heading for another collapse like that of 1929? Of course I don't know the answer, but it seems to me that both alternatives may be valid. In the very long run, inflation of all currencies is likely to continue, living standards are likely to increase, and prices of good things can't help but keep going up and up and up. In the short run, a few years to a decade, perhaps, dips in the market are likely. As I said before, it fluctuates. Next time you have the chance to buttonhole an economist, inquire about the Kondratieff cycle. It is a projection made by a Russian economist in the early twenties, and it implies large-scale worldwide depressions every fifty or sixty years. Should we gird up for the early eighties? Many say it's nonsense, of course.

APPRAISALS

The price of anything is what the customer is willing to pay, but there are many occasions when one needs to have an appraisal of something one has no intention of actually selling. A hypothetical price must be estimated. If the appraisal is to have any weight, it should come from someone experienced in selling things and unlikely to be prejudiced by conflicts of interest. My first choice for such a person would be a reputable auctioneer. Most of them have lots of experience and a very good memory. Knowing the probable price of things is the heart of their business. Only if I really had to avoid the auctioneer would I ask a dealer for an appraisal.

Not that dealers do not know the price of things; of course they do. The trouble is that dealers always want to buy and never take no for an answer. An insurance appraisal, for example, should reflect the actual replacement cost at retail, but dealers always think in terms of wholesale. Once they have told you the retail price, they know you would not sell at wholesale. It is an obvious conflict of interest.

A good appraiser will charge a fee, normally based on the time he spends on the job, with some sort of minimum for spot appraisals. Some appraisers charge a fee in terms of a fixed percentage of the appraised value, but I have always thought that such a practice cannot serve the interest of unbiased accuracy.

A museum is the last place to go for an appraisal, but the public thinks just the opposite. Museums are beleaguered with people bringing in things and asking what they are worth. That is why museum curators go into hiding when they see someone coming with baggage. A museum has nothing to gain and much to lose from making appraisals.

Good curators can be most helpful in matters technical or historical. They are likely to know a great deal about stylistic details and their regional association. They will be at home in the library and know where to go to learn more about things. In other words, they are likely to be scholars. At the same time they are seldom buyers and hardly ever sellers. Forgive me, friends, but in my experience museum people are out of their element when it comes to buying and selling. It is not their line of duty. No one should ask them to make appraisals.

Some museums organize public appraising sessions as fund-raising affairs. You bring your piece(s), make a fixed contribution to the good cause, and visiting experts from some well-known auction house tell you what they think your thing is and how much it might bring in auction. Conservative board members may shudder at the thought of such gross display of collective materialism, but I have been to some of these affairs, and I think they are good clean fun and benefit all parties.

Part Two

5
WHAT
WE CAN HOPE
TO FIND

Having reviewed the elementary considerations in selecting antique furniture, we are ready to take a closer look at the wide spectrum of the market. We shall begin with the earliest American types and follow the development of styles as we go on.

PILGRIM FURNITURE

It will be a red-letter day when we find an authentic Pilgrim piece for sale in a shop, and when we see one in an auction we might as well hoist all the flags and fire a twenty-two-gun salute. I hesitate to go into a discussion of Pilgrim furniture, for it is unlikely that many of us will have the chance (or the money) to buy a piece of it. Many illustrations of Pilgrim stuff will be found in books by Nutting, Kettell, Miller, Cescinsky and Hunter, and others listed in the Bibliography. Splendid collections of Pilgrim furniture can be seen in the Boston Museum of Fine Arts, the Metropolitan Museum of Art in New York, and the Wadsworth Atheneum in Hartford, Connecticut. Examples of two Pilgrim chests, a highboy, and an armchair are shown in figures 26, 27, 28, and 29. A daybed appears in figure 50.

It is my opinion that even if Pilgrim furniture were not so extremely rare, it would be little suited for modern living. Pilgrim homes were singularly uncomfortable, and even the esthetic quality of some of the furnishings may be open to debate. Just the same, there is no denying the inspiration and the feeling of contact with an early Ameri-

26. Pilgrim molded chest, about 1680–1700 (HHT).

59

27. Late Pilgrim ball-foot chest, about 1710–30 (HHT).

28. Late Pilgrim six-legged highboy with trumpet turnings, about 1700–1720.

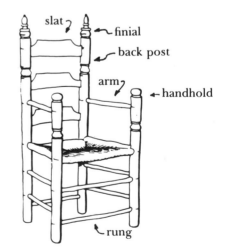

can past that comes from simple Pilgrim pieces like the Bible box shown in figure 30.

COLONIAL AND FEDERAL FURNITURE

Colonial furniture, particularly of the early styles dating from the first half of the eighteenth century, is very rare, and late Colonial and early Federal pieces are still none too common. We might say, in a crude statistic, that for each five hundred semiantique pieces

29. Fine Pilgrim slat-back armchair, about 1660–1700.

30. Late Pilgrim Bible box of oak with pine top and bottom and the characteristic Hadley carving on the front. Family tradition relates that the pigtailed initials refer to Abigail Ball, who was married in Durham, Conn., January 30, 1710. The box is 24½" wide, 18" deep, and 9" high and rabbeted and nailed from the front and back. The lid is attached with staple hinges.

on the market we can expect fifty late Federal, ten early Federal, five late Colonial, and only one early Colonial. The reason is, of course, that the population of the Colonies increased very rapidly in the eighteenth century, and the amount of furniture owned by the average person increased even faster as conditions became more and more comfortable. With the advent of wood-

31. *Two simple early Colonial chairs.* **Left,** *the banister-back is refinished after several coats of paint were removed;* **right,** *the primitive splat-back (Queen Anne) is in its original black. Both have newly woven splint seats; both are dreadfully uncomfortable, but their unquestioned age gladdens the collector.*

working machinery in the second quarter of the nineteenth century, good furniture became reasonably common—but somehow the style lost its purity as prices went down.

CHAIRS

Large numbers of chairs of all types were made in the eighteenth century, and many have been preserved. The most common type is the *slat-back* (or "ladder-back") chair with a woven seat (either rush or splint), a type still being made in many parts of the world (figs. 16 and 29). The quality of the slat-back lies in its proportions, in the fineness of the finials, and in the arms, if it has any. Pilgrim slat-backs are extremely rare, needless to say, and even early Colonial ones are fairly rare, particularly good armchairs.

Banister-back, splat-back (fig. 31), and *Flemish* chairs (fig. 32) come up from time to time, but the better grades, with good turnings or fine carving, are rare. However, these chairs are not particularly comfortable, and any vogue for them is likely to be brief. As a result, they do not bring high prices.

The seats of all these types present a problem. Originally they were mostly woven in rush, but a rush seat does not last very long, and we can expect to see various replacements. If we do find an original rush seat, it is very likely to be damaged or to become damaged the first time anyone tries to sit on it.

Cabriole-leg *Queen Anne* chairs (fig. 33) and the later Colonial *Chippendale* chairs (figs. 34 and 35) are avidly sought, and even primitive specimens bring high prices. The finer examples (fig. 36) usually have upholstered seats and elegant carving. These fine chairs are not particularly rare, by which I

32. A Flemish side chair of about 1720. The seat and back were originally caned and should be restored that way (HHT).

33. A Queen Anne splat-back (fiddle-back) chair with cabriole legs and slipper feet, about 1750.

34. Chippendale ladder-back chair, about 1760–80.

35. Very fine ribbon-back Philadelphia Chippendale chair with claw-and-ball feet, about 1770.

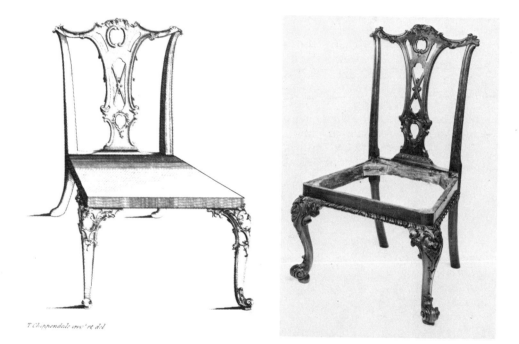

T. Chippendale inv' et del

36. **Right:** *Is this an American chair?* **Left:** *The design is straight out of Chippendale's* **Director,** *first published in London in 1754 but best known from the third edition of 1762. The chair was made in Philadelphia, probably not long after the book arrived, by a very capable craftsman who did not hesitate to improve on Chippendale's proportions and strengthen his design by well-placed additions. A pair of these chairs sold for $27,000 in 1977. (Courtesy of Sotheby Parke Bernet, Inc., New York.)*

mean that I could buy two dozen of them this afternoon, but only at the price of a good producing farm, with cows and all the rest. Single Chippendale chairs often bring more in auction than late-model luxury cars.

The early Federal *shield-back* (fig. 37) and other *Hepplewhite* chairs, and the later, severely straight-lined *Sheraton* styles (fig. 38) are also very popular, but their supply is more plentiful and the price rarely reaches the stratosphere. Still, we can hardly expect to pick up a good set of them for peanuts. Even just an isolated chair of that type is likely to attract lots of bidders. All these chairs were made for the rich people of the time—a group that was becoming very style conscious in Federal times.

But while the styles changed rapidly in the parlors of the new American aristocracy, the ordinary citizens furnished their houses with *Windsor* chairs—as practical a style as you could hope to find. Windsors were the chairs in public places, both sacred and profane, and even the Continental Congress, when it was not on its feet, sat in Windsors much like the ones in figure 39. (Only the President had a Chippendale chair.)

Windsors were made in profusion during the latter half of the eighteenth century. There were *bow-backs* (figs. 40 and 41) and *fan-backs* (figs. 42 and 43), with or without arms, as well as such armchairs as *low-backs* (fig. 44), *comb-backs* (frontispiece and fig. 45), *sack-backs* (fig. 39), and *arch-backs* (fig. 46). Bow-back, fan-back, and arch-back (continuous-arm) Windsors sometimes had back braces, as in figure 40. The *writing-arm* Windsor (fig. 45) was a practical chair-desk combination. Early low-backs are rare and should not be confused with the similar but much later semiantique "fire-house" or "captain's" chairs. The quality of Windsor leg turnings may be good, bad, or indifferent (fig. 48), and the fineness of the proportions of the whole chair will vary, but a good early American Windsor is unsurpassed in lightness and grace—a splendid example of the oft-repeated principle that good functional design produces articles of permanent beauty.

American Windsors are very different from their British counterparts.

37. *Hepplewhite shield-back chair, about 1780–1800.*

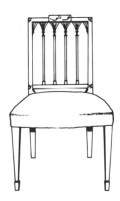

38. *Square-back (Sheraton) chair from Boston, about 1800.*

39. *Two sack-back Windsor armchairs (also known as hoop- or bow-backs). Both are from New England, 1780–1800, and superficially they look alike. The one at the left is ordinary, however, with simplified turnings, plain arms, and a poorly shaped seat; the one at the right has elegant turnings, well-proportioned knuckle-carved arms, and a well-shaped, rakish seat. On the underside of its seat, the latter chair is branded three times L. E. TERRY. (Courtesy of Richard A. Bourne Co., Hyannis Port.)*

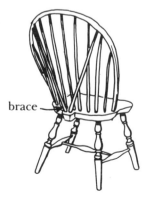

brace

40. *Braced bow-back Windsor of about 1780–1800.*

bow

41. *Ordinary bow-back Windsor, about 1800–1810, distinguished only by its nine spindles, instead of the usual seven.*

42. *A good fan-back Windsor and a late Colonial cherry tilt-top table with snake feet. The table is from Connecticut and carries a shiny Victorian varnish. The chair is a New England type, now finished in wax with the left post restored. The instrument on the table is a contemporary surveyor's compass.*

43. *A good chair can be unorthodox! This fan-back Windsor has good turnings, eight spindles instead of the usual seven, and leather upholstery, apparently original. (Courtesy of Pam Boynton, Groton, Mass.)*

44. *Early Pennsylvania low-back Windsor, about 1760. (Courtesy of Charles Santore.)*

45. *A graceful Connecticut comb-back writing-arm Windsor of about 1770. (Courtesy of Charles Santore.)*

46. *Arch-back (continuous-arm) Windsor of about 1780.*

47. *"Chinese" Windsor, about 1800.*

Among other things, British Windsors have a much greater variety of leg turning patterns, or even cabriole legs in front, and they often have a splat in the middle of their backs (fig. 49).

While Windsors are the most common among good early chairs, they are also the most devilish to fix. They are difficult to take apart, and damage that appears to be relatively minor, like a crack in the top of the bow, may mean that the whole bow has to be replaced —an operation that can bring forth strong language from the most patient of men. So it is doubly important to think twice before buying a wrecked Windsor. A missing spindle or a split seat is not a serious matter, but if the long bent members are in poor condition, then we shall be well advised to let someone else be the buyer. The suggestion has been made that pieces of a good but smashed Windsor could be hung on the wall to be enjoyed as sculpture. It is a novel idea, and I am sure there is no law against it.

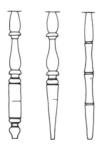

48. *Principal leg-turning styles of American Windsor chairs.* **Left,** *early Pennsylvania, about 1750–65;* **center,** *late Pennsylvania, about 1760–80, and New England, about 1770–1800;* **right,** *bamboo-turned, about 1790–1840.*

49. *Typical English Windsor armchair.*

SETTEES AND DAYBEDS

Relatively few eighteenth-century *settees* were made, so they are now very rare, and we shall hardly ever see one. After the Revolution, settees became more common. The late Windsor-type settees with the characteristic bamboo-turned legs were widely used in meeting places, and they are now often for sale. If you ever have to spend an evening sitting in one of them, you may agree that they are no substitute for the usual living-room couch. Just the same, they can be handsome, and a thin foam-rubber cushion can make them bearable.

Daybeds of any period are rare, and early ones are extremely rare (fig. 50). In general they follow the style of contemporary chairs from late Pilgrim to early Federal time, but they went out of fashion toward the end of the eighteenth century, presumably replaced by the newly popular sofa. The daybed has six to eight legs supporting a narrow frame covered with rush, stretched linen canvas, or a network of ropes with a mattress on it, like that of eighteenth-century beds. At one end is a backrest, often adjustable, which usually reflects the design of chair backs of the period. The daybed is a large and relatively fragile piece of furniture, so it is not surprising that so few have survived. For that reason, perhaps, they are much sought after by sophisticated collectors.

CHESTS, HIGHBOYS, AND LOWBOYS

Six-board chests in pine are probably the most common true antiques extant (fig. 51). When I began collecting, the plain nailed chests of rabbeted construction were valuable only as a source of wide old pine boards for restoring the tops of simple tables, but that seems like an awfully long time ago. Demand has caught up with supply, and any old crate will fetch a good price today if it is early enough. Even more desirable are the better-made dovetailed chests with good molding around the base and some kind of feet. Usually they have a *till* inside and perhaps a secret drawer underneath it (fig. 52). Some

50. Pilgrim daybed from Pennsylvania, about 1700–1720.

51. *The six-board chest, lowest-ranking type of true antique, is the joy of the homemaker, who always finds something to store inside. This particular one is of pine, 36″ long, 18″ high, and 16″ deep, with a till and a small drawer inside. Note the superb dovetailing and the odd cross-grain patch applied by some previous owner. Judging by the hardware and the workmanship (cast-iron hinges, marks of the gash saw), one can estimate the age as late Federal. The escutcheon is new.*

have a drawer or two in the base (fig. 53), and a few are elegantly decorated (fig. 54). These better chests usually had locks, but sooner or later somebody always tried to get in without a key. As a result, most of the chests show a jagged hole where the lock once was. Chests with locks intact are rare.

The more elaborate *blanket chests* may have the front divided into false drawer fronts with a real drawer or two below. They are still fairly common. The gen-

52. *Till and secret drawer often found inside six-board chests and blanket chests. Note how the corner of the till lid has made a mark on the underside of the chest lid.*

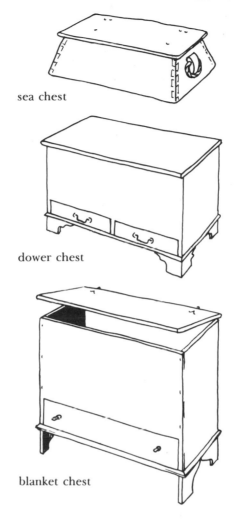

sea chest

53. *Common chest types.*

dower chest

blanket chest

eral design of the blanket chests persisted from late Pilgrim times right up to the Victorian era, but we shall be able to date any particular one by the details of style and workmanship. The early pieces are, of course, rarer and much more desirable, even though usually not much more expensive. In auctions, a skinned and brightly shellacked Empire blanket chest will often bring a higher price than a good early piece, caked with dirt.

Very early Colonial *chests of drawers* with their typical cotterpin brasses (or at least bona fide scars where the cotter pins once were) are not easy to find (fig. 157). The better ones are made of maple or some other hardwood, and the simpler ones are of pine. These pieces are rather fragile, and those that one sees are usually wrecked. The weak brasses are almost always gone, the drawers banged up, and the carcase often rickety. The underbody of the

54. Late Federal pine blanket chest from New England, sponge-decorated and pin-striped to imitate mahogany veneer and line inlay. Painted country furniture in such condition is very desirable and brings high prices. (Courtesy of the Maine Antique Digest.*)*

early *highboys* is often missing. Nevertheless, such late Pilgrim (fig. 28) and very early Colonial pieces warrant considerable restoration simply because they are so rare. If you insist on finding them in perfect condition, you may have to look a long, long time.

Later (but still early) Colonial chests and highboys in the Queen Anne style are more plentiful but still by no means

55. Early Colonial Queen Anne highboy, about 1730–50 (HHT).

common (fig. 55). This period probably marks the high point in the design
of highboys. In my opinion, at least,
few styles can match the lightness and
grace of a simple Colonial highboy with
a bonnet top and slender cabriole legs
(fig. 56). These pieces are sufficiently
distinctive so that they are likely to have
been properly cared for. When we do
find one, it will probably be in good
condition. The wood is usually maple,
often finely figured, for most of these
highboys come from New England.
They were made from about 1740 to
1790. The remarkable Philadelphia
highboys, richly carved in mahogany,
have outdone these simpler types and
generally date from about 1760 to
1790. Perhaps I should not even talk
about Philadelphia highboys (fig. 57).
Occasionally they do come up for sale,
but a good one will cost as much as a
two-bedroom house.

56. *New England bonnet-top highboy, about
1750–70 (HHT).*

Here we should say something about
"divorced" highboys. Later in this
chapter we talk about wedded pieces—
secretaries, chests on chests, and such
—which are produced by marrying two
carcases that were not meant for each
other. With highboys it is the other way
around: they are frequently divorced.
Beware of a tall chest that is not quite
tall enough, has a cornice that seems
just a little too strong, and shows the
type of drawer treatment normally
found on highboys. Examine the feet
with care, and you may find that they do
not belong. Perhaps you have before
you the divorced top of a highboy.
Similarly, be careful about *lowboys* that
seem just a little too high. The usual
height of a lowboy is 31 inches, give or
take about an inch (fig. 58), but the
lower part of a highboy, in all other
respects identical with a lowboy without a top, is usually somewhat larger
and about two inches higher. This is

57. *Philadelphia highboy, about 1760–80
(HHT).*

58. Queen Anne fan-carved lowboy, about 1750–70.

not an iron-bound rule, and many matching lowboy-highboy sets do not show this difference, in which case a fraudulent lowboy could be recognized only by its spurious top board. A complete highboy is naturally worth much more than its component parts, but it may not be easy to sell. An ignorant dealer may decide he could do better splitting it up, or some contentious heirs, squabbling over the estate, may decide to be "completely fair," giving the top to Minnie and the base to Mack. Don't laugh—I have witnessed some wild goings-on among heirs to good collections. A Philadelphia dealer I know once bought the base of a highboy from one branch of a feuding family and waited eight years before they tipped him off that "the other side" was now sending the top to the auction. "That is the way to buy them," he says, "if you can arrange it."

Simple chests of late Colonial or early Federal age (fig. 59), with four or five drawers and made of almost any native wood, or of mahogany, are not exactly common, yet they certainly are not rare. Even *tall chests,* with seven or more drawers, are often seen on the market. They are handsome and useful, so that we must expect to spend some

money if we need one. A little damage should not surprise us. The original brasses are usually gone, some drawer lips may be chipped, and the feet may be damaged or missing. The carcase and the top should be in good condition; otherwise the piece may not be worth fooling with. I remember walking into a large antiques shop, many years ago, somewhere in Massachusetts. There in the semidarkness I saw row upon row of early chests, desks, and highboys, stacked one on top of the other—a superb assortment, except that every single one of them was bashed up beyond any hope of restoration. This fellow apparently collected derelict carcase goods. I can hardly think of a more futile pastime.

The quality of all chests makes itself evident in the proportion of drawers and molding. The drawers should be graduated in height, increasing downward about one inch per drawer. On the better chests, the tops of the drawer sides are molded in a double arch, and simple quarter-columns add a touch of style to the corners of the carcase. Moldings should be well selected, the one around the top usually stronger than the bottom one, but both in harmony with each other and with the chest as a whole. Proportions and good lines are doubly important on the simpler pieces.

A *chest on chest* has two separate carcases placed one on top of the other, the top one usually slightly smaller (fig. 60). They are not too rare, but we must examine them with special care to make sure that the two halves were actually meant for each other. If the piece is wholly authentic, all drawers will show identical detail of workmanship, and the rough boards that cover the back will match.

On all these chests we shall pay close

59. Top, *elegant Chippendale chest of drawers, probably Philadelphia, about the time of the Revolution;* bottom, *underside view of the leg.*

attention to the drawers themselves. It is difficult to make a drawer from scratch, so fakers often adapt odd drawers to fit a particular carcase by gluing matching boards over the planed-down fronts of old drawers. Whether the applied board is the front of an original drawer from the carcase, or whether it is just a piece of old wood that matches the carcase, the surgery is not too difficult to detect, even if it was skillfully perpetrated. The glue line will

60. *Fine chest on chest, about 1770–90 (HHT).*

show on the sides and top of the drawer front, and when it is concealed (as it can be on lipped drawers), the wood inside the drawer front will be obviously different from the wood outside. Old holes drilled for previous brasses will not go through, and the board will often appear to be abnormally thick. This sort of assembly is clearly outside the limits of legitimate restoration.

Chests of solid figured wood ("crotch" mahogany, "burl" walnut, and curly or bird's-eye maple) and chests with shaped fronts—*bow-front, serpentine, oxbow*—as well as all but the simplest highboys and lowboys are fairly rare, especially if they are Colonial (see fig. 8). *Block-front* (fig. 61) and *kettle-base,* or *bombé* (fig. 62), chests are very beautiful, extremely rare, and among the highest-priced pieces of furniture I know. One can buy a pretty fair

61. *Block-front chest of drawers with shell carving, Newport, about 1770.*

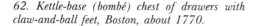
62. Kettle-base (bombé) chest of drawers with claw-and-ball feet, Boston, about 1770.

yacht for the price of a good block-front chest made by one of the Newport masters.

DESKS

What I have said about chests applies generally to desks as well. The early *writing boxes* (also called *Bible boxes,* fig. 30) are rare, but if we should ever find a Pilgrim piece, it may well be one of these boxes, for they are small and durable.

The early Colonial *desks on frames* (fig. 63) are also very rare; the later desks with cabriole legs and pad feet are more often seen but just as eagerly sought, for they can be handsome and useful. As a result, both early and late desks on frames command a good price.

The late Colonial and early Federal *slant-top desks* (figs. 3, 4, and 5) are relatively common, but, being one of the most practical inventions of all time, they bring a high price even when quite plain. The quality of such a desk is often determined by the grade and figure of the wood used and by the fineness of the compartments and drawers

63. Early Colonial desk on frame, about 1720–30 (HHT).

64. *An early Federal tiger-maple slant-top desk of simple lines with an elaborate secret compartment. Pull out the upper one of the two drawers behind the little door, reach in to push aside a simple wooden latch, and the whole middle section comes out, revealing two upright compartments and five little drawers. There is even some contemporary scribbling on the back of the drawers. This kind of detail adds interest (and value) to any piece.*

65. *Hepplewhite tambour desk, about 1800–1820.*

under the lid (fig. 64). If the desk has a bookcase on top it is now called a *secretary,* and its price may well reach the stratosphere if, in addition, the front is shaped (figs. 6, 7, and 8).

Tambour desks are one of the most elegant types of the Federal era (fig. 65). They have a writing leaf that folds out, and their pigeonholes and drawers are concealed behind a rollaway curtain of wood slats. They were never too common and are now quite rare. In the Harding-Coolidge-Hoover era, Seymour-style furniture returned to the spotlight, and some very fine reproductions of his tambour desks were made by hand in the old manner but without any intention to deceive. With a little dust on them they now look exactly like the originals—from a distance.

Other late types are the *falling-leaf (butler's) desk* (fig. 67), either Hepplewhite, Sheraton, or Empire in style, and the simple boxlike *schoolmaster's desk* (fig. 68). They are common, but their cost may be high even so.

The damage to desks is usually much the same as to chests, with the additional problem of the lid, which is very

often split and sometimes gone altogether. This is a fairly difficult thing to repair, for any new wood will have to be matched with greatest care to avoid a spliced-up look on the one board that first strikes the eye.

Beware of the secretary with a top that almost but not quite matches the base, and carefully scrutinize the doors if they are glass. The tops of secretaries are ideal victims for the "improvers" of antique furniture. Some years ago, the public demanded glass doors, but Colonial secretaries almost always had paneled wooden doors. Only the late Federal and Empire pieces often had glass doors. It was a favorite trick of the sharp peddlers to wed a nondescript desk to some sort of crate with old sash in front and to call this unholy union a "Colonial secretary." Some of these creations are ridiculously crude, but others may be quite subtle. We must carefully examine the top board of the desk. If it was meant to carry a bookcase on top, the board will have been made of some common wood, planed but certainly not finished. If this board is finished and matches the sides, we

66. Elegant Hepplewhite cylinder-top lady's secretary, probably Massachusetts, about 1800–1810. The finials are missing and the brasses are wrong, but that did not stop it from bringing $14,000 in 1975. (Courtesy of Samuel T. Freeman & Co., Philadelphia.)

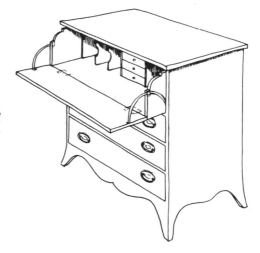

67. Hepplewhite butler's desk, opened to show interior. This style was popular in Federal times and is occasionally referred to as a fall-front or falling-leaf desk.

can be fairly sure that it was meant to show and that the bookcase is a later addition—even if no fraud was intended on the part of the old-timer who simply wanted a place to keep his books. But regardless of when the top was made, the wedded secretary is much less valuable than the same piece made all at the same time.

The door hinges on the secretary top also deserve close scrutiny to see if they are fastened where they always were. If the door or the frame shows hinge scars, or patches intended to cover up hinge scars not reflected in the corresponding place on the opposite member, chances are the doors and the frame were not meant for each other. In auction, the altered secretary with fake glass doors may bring a better price than a good piece in original condition.

CUPBOARDS

Early cupboards are rare, and very early ones are almost nonexistent, in spite of the fact that they were fairly

68. Schoolmaster's desk, Federal and later.

69. *Pennsylvania open cupboard of about 1750–1800.*

commonplace in Colonial times. Kitchen furniture, as a rule, is not preserved. Many of the cupboards we shall see offered for sale will have come from Pennsylvania and will be Federal or later. They will have been made to stand alone (fig. 69) or to fit into a corner. Often they are in two parts, with top and bottom framed independently. They are usually made of pine, tulip poplar, or walnut, and the doors are (or at least were originally) solid wood panels.

Again, the public likes glass doors of the kind one finds on the rare early Federal corner cupboards. Everyone knows how profitable it can be to give the public what it wants—hence all the improbable and ill-fitting glass doors one sees on so many cupboards. If the fraud is not obvious at a glance, the expert will look to make sure the hinges are where they belong, as we have already done on the secretary discussed earlier.

If the faker can't find suitable glass doors, he may simply remove the wooden doors and artfully scroll the inner edges of the door-frame opening. The result may be pleasing if the man with the jigsaw happened to have a flair for design, but the antique value of the piece is quite destroyed by such embellishment. These cupboards were almost always painted, and skinning them down to bare wood is a mistake; but even when the outer surfaces have been stripped, the inside edges of genuine scrolls will show traces of old paint. The fresh wood exposed by the faker's saber saw will be bare or uniformly stained to mask the newness of the cut. Genuine scrolls were usually finished with a chisel and are not likely to show any saw marks at all.

WARDROBES

In the Hudson valley it is a *kas* (a Dutch word), in Pennsylvania it is a *Schrank*

70. Large cherry wardrobe (or press), about 1760–80. The fluted quarter columns and the brasses make it Chippendale, but the basic design is European and harks back to the Renaissance. (Courtesy of Samuel T. Freeman & Co., Philadelphia.)

(German), in New Orleans it is an *armoire* (French), and the British call it a *press,* but all this bewildering variety of terms describes essentially the same thing: a large cupboard behind paneled doors with a few drawers underneath (fig. 70). To be internationally impartial, I call it a wardrobe. It is a large piece of furniture for storing clothes.

Wardrobes are usually demountable. The doors and the top come off and the sides come apart for moving. The basic design is ancient and goes through the sequence of styles with very little structural change. The style is all on the outside, and good wardrobes are rare.

71. Elegant, small, Hepplewhite sideboard in a bright, new finish with crotch mahogany panels bordered by rich checker inlay. The cornhusk decoration on the legs suggests Baltimore, 1780–1800. (Courtesy of Samuel T. Freeman & Co., Philadelphia.)

SIDEBOARDS

Sideboards are a product of the Hepplewhite style, and as such they first appeared in early Federal times. Chippendale side tables are known, but they rarely have the drawers one associates with sideboards and never the compartments below. These precursors of the sideboard are very rare in any form. Proper sideboards were made in relatively large numbers and are therefore fairly common today. The smaller examples (fig. 71) are particularly useful for modern living and thus are likely to bring a better price than their larger cousins (fig. 72), but not always. Just recently I saw a huge monster of a Sheraton sideboard go for an enormous price, or so it seemed to me. With the Hepplewhite pieces, the quality of inlays, the choice of veneers, and the overall proportions determine the value. The quality of the reeding and grace of the legs are also important on Sheraton sideboards, which are, furthermore, less common (fig. 73).

TABLES

Good tables, even Colonial ones, are not too rare, but the demand for them is great and the price consequently high. Style more than age determines the rarity of a table. Early Colonial *butterfly tables* (fig. 187) are about as rare as antique furniture can be, good *gateleg tables* are still very rare, *chair tables* (fig. 74) and *tavern tables* (fig. 75) are merely

72. *A large and ordinary-looking Hepplewhite sideboard, about 1800. The top is warped, the sides are cracked, bits of veneer are missing, and the brasses are absurd replacements. Is it worth a second look? The expert will notice that under the darkened varnish the crotch mahogany veneers of the main panels are well matched and the line inlay is precise. (Courtesy Samuel T. Freeman & Co., Philadelphia.)*

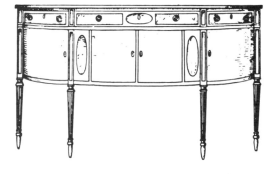

73. *Sheraton sideboard with reeded legs, about 1800–1820 (HHT).*

rare, and *tilt-top tables* are seen quite often (fig. 42). But if the tilt-top has an elegantly carved, scrolled border, then it is a true aristocrat among tables and very valuable (fig. 76). For that reason, the expert will make quite sure that the carved border is original before writing a check. Tops of this kind are almost always carved from a single board up to three feet wide. A faker will be hard put to find such a board nowadays, and if he tries to make it up from narrower boards, the glue lines will give him away. Another way to fake it is to carve

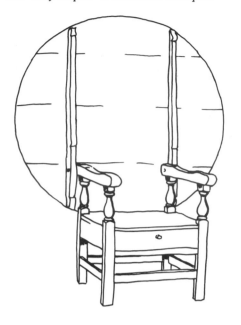

74. Early Colonial chair table, all pine.

the border from another board and glue it onto an old plain table top. The grain of the carved molding is then not likely to match the grain of the old top, and there will be a glue line in between, of course. The bases of some English tilt-top tables are similar to their American counterparts, and one also has to look out for that.

Drop-leaf tables are fairly common, and the late varieties with rectangular tops and turned legs, two of which swing out on wooden hinges to support the leaves, are very common, though

75. New England tavern table in pine and maple, about 1750–80. The top may be a bit warped and the feet a bit bashed, but it is all original, and that means a lot. (Courtesy of the Maine Antique Digest.)

76. Bottom, *scalloped ("pie-crust") tip-and-turn table with claw-and-ball feet, about 1760–80;* top, *the top is usually carved from a single piece of wood, as shown in cross section. Tables of this quality are expensive but not very rare.*

hardly ever cheap (fig. 77). *Card tables* with a double top that folds out are not too rare, but fine examples are not easy to find (fig. 20).

Many tables on the market are altered—particularly the rarer and earlier varieties. We have to crawl underneath with a flashlight to appraise a table properly, and we may be fooled even so. A museum curator once told me that the only way to evaluate an antique table is to take it apart, but some shop owners are likely to take a dim view of that.

The expert will pay much attention to the condition of tables. A slightly wobbly frame can be glued up, and a missing stretcher is no catastrophe, but a warped or seriously cracked top is often very hard to repair, and broken

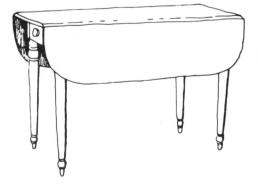

77. *Late Sheraton drop-leaf table with turned legs, about 1820–40.*

78. *Simple Colonial candle stand and corner chair. The chair is refinished and has a new rush seat.*

legs can be most difficult—particularly if any wood is missing. Unless the table is of a very rare breed, it is no bargain if it is wrecked.

STANDS

Among the small tables, or stands as some prefer to call them, we may see an early Colonial one every now and then —usually on four legs (figs. 78 and 79). Later Colonial and early Federal stands follow the pattern of *tripod tables* (fig. 80). During the late Federal era, small four-legged *sewing stands* (fig. 81) became fashionable. Usually they have a drawer or two in front, and occasionally small drop-leaves on the sides. Some of them originally had a cloth bag underneath, hung on a frame that slides out like a drawer. These stands are very useful in the modern home. The simple ones are quite common, especially in the later styles, so the price is usually reasonable. Fine specimens, however, are expensive.

BEDS AND CRADLES

Antique *high beds* are not too rare, but good ones—made of figured wood or handsomely carved—are not easy to find. Originally these beds consisted of four high posts joined to a stout frame with a network of ropes running either through holes in the frame or over a series of pegs in the rails, and with a light framework on top to hold the canopy, often called the tester. A well-turned late-Colonial curly-maple bed with gracefully curved sweeps for the canopy may be a thing of beauty, but if we intend to use it we shall be well advised to equip it with a modern mattress. George Washington may have managed with just a straw mattress on the ropes, but generals were tough in those days.

Antique beds are small by modern standards, and we can hardly hope to find one that fits a modern mattress. More likely, we shall have to have a mattress made to order, and that will cost something, but the regal feeling of snoozing under an elegant tester may justify the trouble and the expense. Many old bed frames are extended to fit modern dimensions, but I would not encourage such surgery. If you need a long bed, get a reproduction.

Antique beds are high to begin with, and when you add a modern spring and mattress, together about 12 to 14 inches thick, it may be quite a climb to get up there. My own solution to the problem is to fit a sheet of half-inch plywood inside the bed rails, flush with the top edge, and lay an extra thick (5- or 6-inch) foam mattress on top, covering the plywood and rails to their outside edges. The mattress will have to have the corners cut out to fit the bed posts, but that is not too difficult with foam. If you now put a pea, or even a pecan, in the middle of that plywood under the mattress, I'll bet there isn't a princess around who could feel it.

I doubt that any modern mother would be willing to keep her baby in one of the low, hooded boxes in which our ancestors spent their first months. Thus deprived of its fundamental utility, where does a cradle go? You may keep it in the guest room, where it is not in the way, or in the living room, where it is. I have seen cradles used by the fireplace, to hold wood, but they

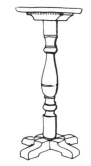

79. Early Colonial candle stand, about 1700–1740.

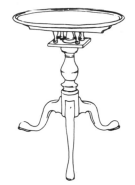

80. Late Colonial tip-and-turn tripod stand with snake feet and revolving birdcage top, about 1760–80.

81. Sheraton sewing stand, 1800–1820 (HHT).

are not strong enough for that, and the logs will wreck them in no time. So what do you do with an antique cradle? Exactly. The demand being so restricted, cradles rarely bring much of a price. Unless they are of a distinct style, cradles are not easy to date, except that the common spool-turned varieties are very late, perhaps not even antique.

DOUGH TROUGHS

When you make bread you require a largish vessel, somewhere in a warm place, where the dough may rise in good order. Large rectangular troughs were often used for that purpose, and in Pennsylvania the dough trough became a fairly elaborate piece of furniture, often with handsomely turned and stretchered legs, as in figure 82. These troughs are quite decorative, so one often sees them in the living room these days. Their value is largely determined by the quality of the turnings. Good dough troughs are rare, for only a small fraction have survived the rigors of farm-kitchen utility.

MIRRORS

Many styles of antique mirrors are seen on the market, but most of them are Federal or later. American Queen Anne mirrors are extremely rare (fig. 83). Good Chippendale ones are offered from time to time, but some of the fragile fretwork is almost always broken. All-original, undamaged Chippendale mirrors are rare (fig. 14).

Federal mirrors are usually plaster over a wood base, with gold leaf applied to the surface—a dreadfully fragile combination (fig. 84). Damaged places on these mirrors can be repaired, of course, but it is not a simple matter, as we shall see in Part III of this book. These mirrors often contain one or more decorative panes of glass with pictures painted on the back (*églomisé* is the fancy word for that), and if these pictures are good, they notably increase the value of the mirror. If you see two ships blasting away at each other, then you can bet it is the *Constitution* vs. the *Guerrière,* the *Constellation* vs. *l'Insurgente,* or the *Enterprise* vs. the *Boxer,* and the mirror will go very high (see, e.g., the painting on the clock in fig. 88). Before you pay the price, make sure of the age of both glass and painting. It is not too difficult to change a trivial decoration into a plausible battle scene on the back of the old glass.

Empire and later mirrors are usually undistinguished and, of course, very common. Many have been removed from chests of drawers and were not

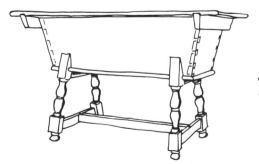

82. *Pennsylvania dough trough of about 1760–1800.*

83. Queen Anne mirror, 1720–50, about 46"
high. The glass is in two parts, usually beveled,
and the upper part may be engraved. The frame is
usually veneered. The glass was certainly imported,
and even the frame is not likely to be American.
(Courtesy of Herbert Schiffer, Exton, Pa.)

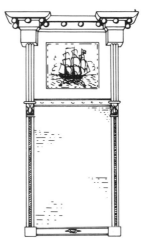

84. Federal mirror, gilt over pine, about 1800–
1820, about 42" high.

originally intended to hang on the wall.

All the original mirrors will be of wavy glass, often stained and dulled by the years. If the original glass was replaced by the flawless modern product, the value of the mirror is greatly impaired. Occasionally, the old glass may have been resilvered; this is much less objectionable. We can easily check if the glass has been disturbed by inspecting the nails that hold the wooden back to the frame of the mirror: each nail should be in its proper hole; there should be no modern nails and no extra holes. I have seen few mirrors in altogether untouched condition.

Some old-timers may remember the ancient ditty:

Little Willie at the mirror
Licked the mercury all off,
Thinking in his childish error
It would cure the whooping cough. . . .

At the funeral, Willie's mother
Sadly said to Mrs. Brown:
" 'Twas a chilly day for Willie
When the mercury went down."

The old mirrors were, in fact, "silvered" not with silver but with tin amalgam in a fairly thick layer. Modern mirrors are coated with aluminum or other metals, but the coating is extremely thin. When the metal is backed with a coat of paint, as it usually is, then it may be difficult to gauge the thickness of the metallic coating. If it is important to verify the authenticity of the coating, we can resort to a chemical test. Mercury is easy to detect chemically, and good chemists, unlike good gilders and woodcarvers, are fairly easy to find.

CLOCKS

Several good books have been written about antique clocks by people who know much more about the subject than I do (see Bibliography). Unlike furniture, clocks are not too difficult to trace to their original maker, for most of them have a name or a label inside. Colonial clocks are extremely rare, and later ones are rare to common, roughly in inverse ratio to their age. Imported works, as a rule, are much less desirable than American ones, even though the equivalent domestic product is usually cruder. With tall clocks, at any rate, the case determines the value, unless the works are by a particularly celebrated maker.

SOUTHERN FURNITURE

Colonial and Federal furniture made south and west of Baltimore is now very rare, and one could advance many reasons why that should be. Hurricanes, fires (New Orleans had big ones in 1788 and 1794), and the Civil War all took their toll, and there always was a regional preference in the South for imported furniture in the latest style. Saving "old stuff" was not a prevailing custom. All these factors have been argued at length, but it all adds up to the same thing: genuine southern pieces

85. *Tall (100″) walnut clock with wooden works by Daniel Oyster of Reading, Pa. By style alone, I would date the case about 1780, but depending on whom you believe, Daniel was either fourteen or sixteen at that time. He lived to a ripe old age, and it seems likely that he installed the works long after the case had been made. (Photo courtesy of Samuel T. Freeman & Co., Philadelphia.)*

86. *Patriotic brass finial intended for an American clock, overall height 6". (From the anonymous catalog of an English brass stamper, about 1780–90, in the Victoria and Albert Museum.)*

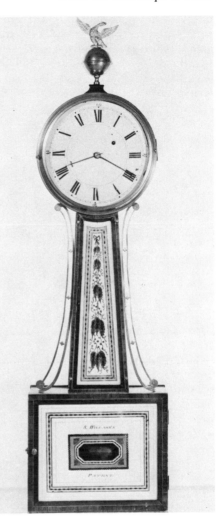

87. *Very fine banjo clock by Simon Willard, about 1810. It sold for $3,250 in 1976. Compare the eagle finial with figure 86. (Courtesy of Richard A. Bourne Co., Hyannis Port.)*

are almost impossible to find on the market.

Besides mahogany, southern cabinetmakers used native woods because they were both plentiful and good, so that wood is now our best guide in recognizing genuine southern workmanship. Bald cypress (*Taxodium distichum,* not a true cypress) is fairly obvious; yellow pine and slash pine *(Pinus palustris, P. taeda,* and *P. caribea)* are a little more difficult, but easily distinguished from the northern white pine *(P. strobus).* However, the difference between southern walnut *(Juglans nigra)* and English walnut *(J. regia)* may be subtle, even under the microscope. Just like their northern brethren, southern

88. Pillar-and-scroll clock by Eli Terry of Plymouth, Conn., easily dated about 1815 by the stylized painting of a naval engagement of the War of 1812. (Courtesy of Samuel T. Freeman & Co., Philadelphia.)

cabinetmakers rarely used oak as a secondary wood because pine was plentiful and much easier to work.

Southern styles cover a very wide range, from the conspicuous French provincial lines of early Louisiana furniture (fig. 89) to the clear-cut Baltimore style of Federal furniture made in Virginia and Georgia. When people moved from Pennsylvania to Kentucky, for example, they brought their style with them, and the diversity of the new population accounts for the great diversity in southern styles. References to documented southern pieces are listed in the Bibliography (Burroughs, Gusler, Poesch, and Speed Art Museum). Hunting southern antiques is a great sport because it is so difficult.

LATE FEDERAL FURNITURE

Although the Sheraton influence was quite pronounced, the principal style of the late Federal period was Empire. It was an American adaptation of the new style that developed in France during the short but dazzling period that followed Napoleon's coronation as Emperor in 1804. The British adaptation of this style goes by the name Regency, referring to the regency of George IV. Introduction of the style in America coincides roughly with the ap-

89. Louisiana armoire of about 1760–1800. The massive demountable hinges are typical of French provincial furniture of the eighteenth century, the feet and skirt are pure French, the exterior wood is walnut, which could be French, but the inside is of cypress and thus leaves no doubt that the piece was made in America.

pearance of steam-driven woodworking machinery, which permitted great expansion of productivity but brought about a cheapening of quality and a decline in the purity of design.

More furniture was made in America during the twenty or thirty years of the late Federal period than in the two hundred years that preceded it. So it is that, among true antiques, Empire furniture is by far the most common and, on the average, the least well made. Fine lumber and rich veneers were available to the Federal cabinetmaker, and he often used them with abandon. Concurrently, slipshod methods appeared when it became clear that thin veneer could cover a multitude of sins.

The expert can well afford to pick and choose here. We should pay attention to internal construction details and quality of the wood. Many cabinetmakers continued to use old quality methods, and some designers did not let the new freedom from mechanical restriction corrupt their lines. Conse-

quently, we often find first-rate Empire pieces, particularly chests of drawers with the characteristically large top drawer (fig. 90); falling-leaf (butler's) desks, looking much like the chests but

90. Empire chest, 1810–30 (HHT).

91. Left, *late Federal (Sheraton) sewing stand of rich tiger maple with fine bird's-eye veneer on the drawer fronts. The interior is pine, one drawer knob is restored, and the piece is refinished.* Right, *the Empire chair, of the same period, has been cleaned of its dingy varnish and will now receive a cane seat. Late Federal furniture is common, but the fine wood and sound craftsmanship of these two pieces raise them above the ordinary.*

with a writing compartment inside the top drawer; sewing stands with one or two drawers (fig. 91); drop-leaf tables with straight, turned, or reeded Sheraton legs; and expanding *pedestal tables,* often with many extra leaves. Chairs of this period usually have cane seats and are designed to please the taste of those who think Windsors are stark (fig. 91). Imperceptibly they grade into purely machine-made products, and we are in for some lively hair-splitting when we try to decide which of them still qualify as true antiques.

SEMIANTIQUES

With the flowering and decline of the Empire style we come to the end of what can properly be called antique furniture. Nevertheless, even long after 1830 much furniture continued to be made that should be mentioned here. I am thinking particularly of chests, *wash stands* (fig. 92), *commodes* (fig. 93), cupboards, and *dry sinks* (fig. 94) made of pine or tulip poplar and originally painted. Only a few were made by hand. Most were factory made by the thousands, but some of them managed to retain vestiges of the simplicity of the earlier country furniture. In the trade these late pieces are often called semiantiques, which seems to describe them quite well.

This is the furniture for the beginning collector. It is easy to find, and if we just don't happen to have the price

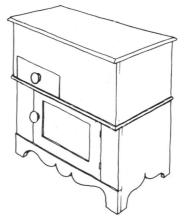

92. Semiantique wash stand, mid–nineteenth century. These stands were almost always painted and striped.

93. The lowly commode, a popular semiantique of about 1830–80.

of a first-class highboy, a cheap pine bureau will fill the space until circumstances improve. A pine commode will do very nicely to conceal a collection of bottled refreshments or a modern tape deck in an otherwise early American interior. And if we have never refinished a piece before, a semiantique will offer good practice. Semiantiques are often found in the rough, and that is the best way to buy them.

Some of the semiantique furniture was originally decorated with painted and stenciled fruit and floral designs and striping in contrasting colors (fig. 95). Occasionally we may find a piece with the decorations preserved, and it would be wrong to strip such pieces down to the bare wood. The decorations may seem silly to present-day champions of the "pine look," but the day is not far off when semiantiques

94. A dry sink of about 1830–80.

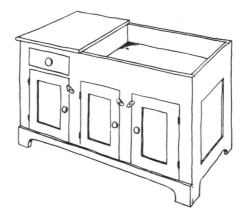

95. The back of a late Pennsylvania half-spindle chair, about 1840, with bright hand-painted decorations on a yellow ground. Paint in such condition is rare and makes an otherwise ordinary chair much more desirable. The missing spindle is a minor restoration problem.

with original decoration will achieve a degree of rarity.

LATE WINDSORS

The quality of Windsor design also gradually declined in the nineteenth century. The gracefully turned Pennsylvania and New England leg patterns (fig. 48) gave way to the trivial "bamboo" turning, which ultimately lost all proportion. The H stretchers were gradually superseded by box stretchers. The back became simpler, spindles became fewer, and seats were less well shaped. The graceful fan-back evolved into the *step-down comb,* the *thumb-back* (fig. 96), and the *half-spindle back* (fig. 95). Again, it is hard to tell where to draw the line between antique and semiantique.

Most of these late types are common. We shall find them caked with many layers of paint, and they bring little in the rough, for it is a tedious job to refinish them properly. Occasionally

we may see one in the original green, black, or yellow-ochre paint with stencil-and-stripe decorations still intact (fig. 97). Once I restored a whole set of them. In this condition they are fairly rare, and I make every effort to preserve the decorations.

HITCHCOCK CHAIRS

Lambert Hitchcock (1795–1852) established his wood-turning shop in Connecticut in 1818 and at first produced only chair legs and spindles. Gradually he took to making complete chairs and rockers in the Empire style, and by the time he left the firm, in 1843, his factory had over a hundred employees and was making more than a thousand chairs a month. His machine-made chairs were cheap and sturdy, and they carried his name far and wide. They are characteristic of the Yankee peddler of the mid–nineteenth century, and they are still good chairs, but insofar as the exclusive clan of true antiques can be

*96. Left, a "step-down" Windsor and, **right**, the very common "thumb-back," both refinished, both showing the degraded bamboo-turned legs and poorly shaped pine seats characteristic of the beginnings of mass production. These late, ordinary Windsors are often called plank-bottoms.*

97. Worn remnants of original stencil-and-brushstroke decoration on an arrowback chair of about 1830. It may not look as rich as it once was, but any effort to clean the design is very likely to damage it. One might protect it with a very thin coat of good varnish and no more.

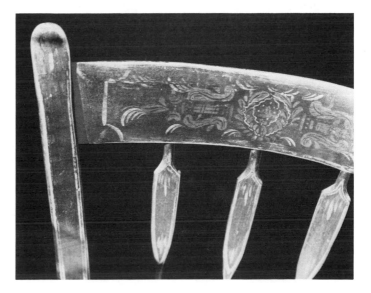

98. Fancy chair, probably Connecticut, 1820–30, in the original black paint, grained over red ground to imitate mahogany, pin striped, and highlighted with gold. Many people would not hesitate to call it a "Hitchcock chair," but, in the absence of a mark, it would be difficult to be certain. (Courtesy of Samuel T. Freeman & Co., Philadelphia.)

quently seen. Original decorations are rarely preserved.

Many factories produced "fancy chairs" in late Federal times, but Hitchcock's are without doubt the best known. The discriminating collector usually demands that they have their original black paint over a red undercoat, and that the stenciled decorations be intact.

Some Hitchcock chairs are signed in stencil on the back edge of the seat. L. HITCHCOCK.HITCHCOCKS-VILLE.CONN. WARRANTED, with the N's in CONN. correctly oriented, is said to have been the earliest signature, used between 1825 and 1832. After that, when Hitchcock's foreman and brother-in-law became a partner in the firm, the label became HITCHCOCK.ALFORD.&CO HITCHCOCKS-VILLE.CONN / WARRANTED with the N's usually but not always reversed. The partnership was dissolved in 1840 and Hitchcock moved to Unionville, where he made more chairs until he died in 1852. These signatures are found only rarely and greatly increase the value of any chair. They need to be checked out with due care.

If the chair has been repainted, we may be able to strip the paint just down to the original coat and reveal the decorations well enough so they can be seen. Failing that, we might repaint the chair and restencil it with bronze powders, following the designs and instructions given in the excellent books by Brazer and by Lipman (see Bibliography).

The Hitchcock factory in what is now Riverton, Connecticut, was reopened in 1948 and again produces chairs in the old style, signature and all. We should have no trouble recognizing these reproductions (but *are* they reproductions?) by their modern appearance, but the task may become more

established, Hitchcock chairs do not quite make the grade. Why? Simply because they very definitely were made on a repetitive, assembly-line basis. Nevertheless, the Hitchcock chair has many devotees, and some of them may go after me with a hatchet for what I have just written.

A well-decorated Hitchcock chair can be pretty, and most of them are reasonably comfortable. Those with solid-wood seats are usually best preserved, but the earlier rush-bottoms and the later caned varieties are more fre-

difficult fifty years from now, when the paint has had a chance to check and to crawl a little. Perhaps we need not worry over that. If you want to know everything there is to know about the Hitchcock operation, look up J. T. Kenney's *The Hitchcock Chair.*

DUNCAN PHYFE'S EMPIRE

The American Empire style is often loosely connected with the name of Duncan Phyfe (1768?–1854), who came from Scotland and eventually set up a small shop in New York City in about 1792. His designs were sound, his business acumen even sounder, and his shop soon developed into a mechanized factory. Phyfe was a true eclectic, and the main source of his success

was a keen perception of the tastes of his customers. His early pieces are Hepplewhite, Sheraton, and Adam, but he went into Empire in a big way and followed with the multitude of derivative styles we loosely call Victorian. Europe was boiling with new styles in the first half of the nineteenth century, and Phyfe tried them all. His range was so wide, it may be hard to believe that all the authenticated Phyfe pieces could have come from the same shop. Phyfe labels are rare and command a high price.

BELTER FURNITURE

One more name deserves mention here: John Henry Belter (1804–63). He arrived in New York from Germany in

99. *Expanding pedestal table in the Empire style now associated with the name of Duncan Phyfe, probably New York, about 1830. This specimen is dingy and a little bashed (note the chipped foot), but the lines are right, the contrasting mahogany and satinwood veneers are elegant, the metal ornament is neatly worked, and the carving is crisp. Obviously the piece is worth spending some time on. (Courtesy of Samuel T. Freeman & Co., Philadelphia.)*

100. *Empire dining table in mahogany, probably New York, about 1840. The center section expands accordion-fashion to make room for additional leaves, and an elaborate system of hinges and sector gears keep the legs of the midsection evenly spaced, regardless of how many leaves are used. This sort of unabashed gadgetry is characteristic of New York furniture of the mid–nineteenth century.*

101. A carved, laminated rosewood sofa in the exuberant Victorian rococo style made famous by John Henry Belter in New York, about 1850–65. It may not be antique, but it has its devotees and will bring a price. (Courtesy of Samuel T. Freeman & Co., Philadelphia.)

1844 and developed a process of bending rosewood and laminating it on steel forms to achieve a remarkable freedom of shape. His curvaceous tables, chairs, and sofas in the "new rococo" style were elaborately carved and handsomely proportioned (fig. 101). The new manufacturing technique also made them very strong.

Belter was a huge success after about 1850, but his factory was a one-man show and failed four years after he died. It had attracted a host of imitators who made similar furniture more cheaply and less well. Authentic Belter pieces are rare and highly desirable. Even the better imitations bring a good price.

ACCESSORIES

This is a book about furniture, but I want to say a few words about accessories that complement antique American furniture. People collect a wide variety of accessories—quilts, coverlets, hooked rugs, butter prints, stoneware, slipware, silver, pewter, tools, lighting devices, and much more—so that the following is necessarily a small sampling of some of the more popular things.

QUILTS AND COVERLETS

Pattern-woven coverlets in three contrasting colors became popular in the second quarter of the nineteenth century, following the introduction of the Jacquard system of weaving. Most of them are signed and dated in the weave and come from Pennsylvania, New York, and Ohio. They are not rare but bring good prices. Quilts come in an infinite variety of styles and colors and were made at home since Colonial times, but early specimens are now extremely rare. Most quilts on the market were made in the second half of the nineteenth century. Many books on quilts and coverlets have appeared in the wake of the recent interest in them. My favorite is *Quilts in America* by Patsy and Myron Orlofsky.

WOODENWARE

Many wooden articles were made for the early American homemaker. These things were called *treen* in their day and are now widely used as decorative accessories. Large and small bowls, mortars, butter prints and molds, spoons, and ladles are the most common. You will find them well described in Mary Gould's book, *Early American Wooden Ware.*

These small items are not usually preserved, so that very early treen is now rare. The mortars, butter molds, and spoons we find in the shops are usually very late, most of them made in the second half of the nineteenth century. Similar articles are still being made and used in the conservative rural districts of Switzerland and the Black Forest. Gingerbread molds with figures of ships, windmills, horsemen, and baroque cavaliers and their ladies, often beautifully carved, are imported from Holland, almost without exception. Carved American gingerbread molds are known, but I have never seen one for sale.

102. Left, *slip-decorated, salt-glazed stoneware crock marked* F. B. NORTON & CO / WORCESTER, MASS. *That dates it about 1865–80.* Right, *the bottom shows the characteristic swirl made by the potter's twisted wire as he cut the finished crock off the wheel. The swirl guarantees that the piece was hand thrown, but many potters used smooth wire, which left only indistinct marks, and some deliberately wiped off the marks.*

STONEWARE

Salt-glazed jugs and crocks, like the one in figure 102, have been "thrown" (as the potters say) on the wheel by hand since Colonial times. Technically known as stoneware, they are made from a special high-fire clay mined mostly in New Jersey. Inside they are lined with a film of low-melting clay dug near Albany, New York (Albany slip), and outside they are glazed with salt that was thrown into the blazing kiln at white heat. At high temperature the salt vaporizes and combines with the clay of the pot to form a thin layer of glass (sodium silicate) on the surface. The process, incidentally, releases chlorine gas, which tends to kill all the trees in the vicinity. That is one reason why salt-glaze potters were not always welcome as neighbors.

Salt-glazed stoneware is dense, impervious to liquids, and durable. Colonial and Federal stoneware is rare, mostly because the population was so small then. That changed very quickly in the mid–nineteenth century, and from about 1840 to 1910 stoneware was the favorite container for everything from pickles to whiskey. Ranging in size from a quart to about five gallons, stoneware crocks and jugs are often marked with the name of the maker or the distributor (fig. 103). Salt-glazed stoneware may be decorated with cobalt-colored slip or with incised patterns. Some of the decorations are pleasant, even bold and lively. These nicely decorated pieces are in great demand and bring big prices, even though they are relatively common and usually rather late. Most of the pieces are difficult to date by style alone, and one resorts to checking the period when a certain mark was in use. Donald Blake Webster's *Decorated Stoneware Pot-*

103. *A crock stamped with the name of the maker —FULPER BROS. / FLEMINGTON, N.J.—and inscribed with the name of a customer. The Fulper pottery was started in 1805, but this crock is much later, perhaps 1880.*

104. *Early jugs are pear-shaped, but not all pear-shaped jugs are early. This one is marked E. L. FARRAR / BURLINGTON, VT., and that makes it fairly late. Ebenezer Farrar was active about 1850–70.*

105. Shoulder jugs are very late, about 1900 or later, usually glazed brown and white (not salt glazed), and made in molds (not thrown). In the sixties I saw them still being made industrially in Ohio, with "pulled" handles attached by hand.

106. One of a pair of good Federal andirons, about 1800–1820. (Courtesy of Samuel T. Freeman & Co., Philadelphia.)

tery of North America is particularly useful for this purpose.

FIREPLACE UTENSILS

Forged iron hooks, jacks, trivets, tongs, spits, trammels, toasters, andirons, and waffle irons can be found in the antiques trade in endless variety. Since the supply is so very large, one may suspect that imports play a part in maintaining it. Few of the objects can be dated, and even fewer identified with a region.

Handsome andirons of polished brass or bronze are not too rare (fig. 106). Almost all are Federal or later, and the quality of their turning determines their value. Their iron parts, on which the burning log rests, are often scaled off and thin, or even replaced by a new piece welded on. These old blacksmith welds produce a step where the new iron is lapped onto the old. Underneath, the old andirons are almost always riveted where the brass joins the iron (fig. 107). Modern andi-

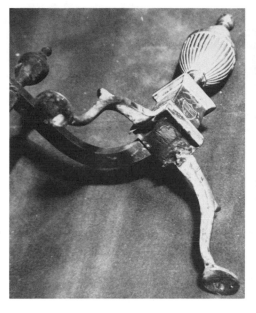

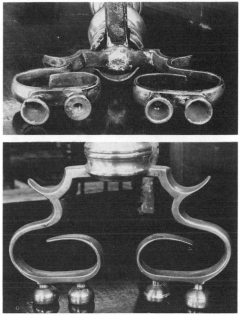

107. *Underside of a good, early Federal andiron. Note the riveted construction.*

108. *One of the four feet of this late Federal andiron (about 1820–50) is a modern replacement.*

rons are bolted together, usually with square nuts.

FIRE MARKS, FIRE BUCKETS, AND SUCH

Like so many other things, fire insurance began in Philadelphia, at the urging of Benjamin Franklin. The Philadelphia Contributionship for the Insurance of Houses from Loss by Fire was organized in 1752. The symbol of the new organization was four clasped hands, and subscribers indicated their membership by displaying on their houses a lead casting of the symbol, mounted on a wooden shield marked with the policy number (fig. 110). That was the first American fire mark.

In time, other insurance companies were organized. The Mutual Assurance Company for Insuring Houses from

109. *Household furnishings including an andiron very similar to the preceding. (From the* Specimen of Printing Types and Ornaments Cast by L. Johnson *[Philadelphia: 1844] in the Library of Temple University.)*

110. *An exceedingly rare mark: the four clasped hands of the Philadelphia Contributionship, always cast in lead. This particular mark was issued in 1775. (Courtesy of the Philadelphia Contributionship for the Insurance of Houses from Loss by Fire.)*

Loss by Fire issued its first fire mark in 1785, a tree cast in lead and mounted on a wooden shield. It is one of those remarkable coincidences that this very mark, the No. 1, is still preserved and now hangs in the main offices of the company (fig. 111). In New York, another mutual assurance company issued copper and cast-iron marks with an eagle, and beginning in 1794 the Baltimore Equitable Society used two clasped hands cast in iron and mounted on a board.

All these marks are very rare. It has been years since I have seen a genuine one in the trade. The first reasonably common marks are the hydrant-and-hose cast-iron ovals of the Fire Association of Philadelphia issued from 1817 for more than fifty years with only minor changes in design (fig. 113). These marks, usually in the later variants, are occasionally seen in the antiques trade.

Genuine marks almost always had

111. *First of the "green tree" marks, issued by the Mutual Assurance Company in Philadelphia, 1785, heavily refinished. The tree is cast lead. (Courtesy of The Mutual Assurance Company, Philadelphia.)*

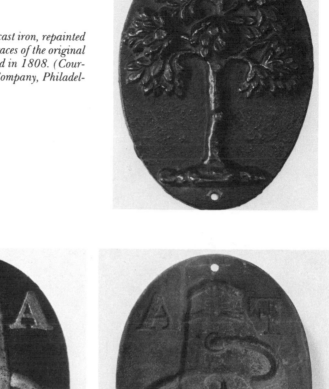

112. A later green tree mark in cast iron, repainted several times but still showing traces of the original policy number, No. 2234, issued in 1808. (Courtesy of The Mutual Assurance Company, Philadelphia.)

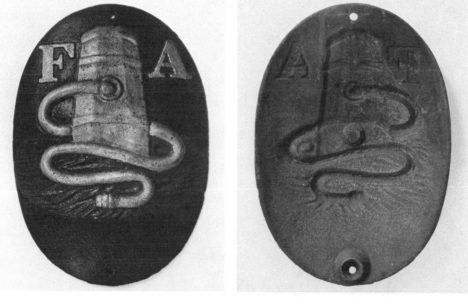

113. Most commonly found are the late issues of the Fire Association of Philadelphia. This is the front and back of their last mark actually used, issued about 1875–76, distinguished by its highly convex form and the drainage knob at the bottom nail hole, designed to make the mark stand off the wall. The paint is not original.

the policy number painted below the company's symbol. The additional thickness of paint protected the wood or metal underneath, so that traces of the number are usually still discernible in slight relief, no matter how badly the mark may be weathered. Fire marks look nice on old houses, and they have been made since the 1920s purely as a decoration with no intent to deceive anyone. Some of these new marks were issued by the old companies and their successors for advertising purposes and usually bear the year of the company's founding in the place where old marks would have the policy number. Many of these modern marks have been mounted on houses and exposed to the weather for half a century, and it may be difficult to tell now what is genuine and what is not.

The Contributionship marks, originally always of lead, are often imitated in cast iron. The "green tree" marks

114. Somewhat less common and very desirable, no doubt because of the elegant engines, are the late marks of the United Firemen's Insurance Company of Philadelphia, first issued in 1860. This particular mark dates from 1876. Note the severe corrosion along the lower rim on the back.

115. Fire buckets come in pairs and are usually marked with the owner's name to facilitate return after use. They are made of leather and hold about two gallons each. (Courtesy of Mary Page, Warner, N.H.)

116. Carding, spinning, and weaving wool. (From Edward Hazen's Panorama of Professions and Trades *[Philadelphia: 1839] in the University of Pennsylvania Library.)*

were also lead until about 1805 and cast iron after that. Among the cast-iron marks, the experts tell new from old by exact measurement and sometimes also by weight, allowing for obvious corrosion. The best comprehensive catalog of fire marks is Alwin E. Bulau's *Footprints of Assurance.*

Fire buckets were made of leather, sometimes elegantly painted (fig. 115). They vary considerably in size but average about two gallons. They often bear the name of the owner and a date, which may be either the year of the owner's joining the fire company or the year that the particular company was founded. All that, presumably, was an aid in sorting out the buckets after a fire in which more than one company was involved. The buckets almost always come in pairs. They are not exactly common, but one sees them in the trade from time to time. The earliest I have ever seen was dated 1797.

Fire hats, fire belts, fire axes, salvage bags, firemen's tunics, megaphones, and a host of other fire memorabilia appear in the antiques trade, almost all dating from the second half of the nineteenth century. I think I have told you just about everything I know about them.

SPINNING WHEELS, KETTLES, AND CANDLE MOLDS

Spinning wheels (the large ones made for spinning wool and the little ones for flax), brass kettles, and candle molds are staples of the antiques trade, and they are often thought of as very old. Yet the wheels and kettles are machine-made products, and almost every one of those we shall see offered for sale was made after 1850. Candle molds are difficult to date, and they are still being made by hand, in the old way.

6
EVIDENCE OF
AGE AND
AUTHENTICITY

The expert walks up to a piece that is offered for sale and just looks at it awhile, eyes roving over it; or steps back, head cocked a little; or runs a hand over the top and the sides in a seemingly absentminded way. But by this time the expert already knows whether the piece is interesting, even though only ten seconds may have elapsed since it was first spotted.

If things do not seem right, the expert moves on. "The first impression must be good," a well-known dealer once told me. Detailed examination of the interior is worthwhile only if the outside appearance is pleasing.

If the expert likes the piece, a careful examination of the pertinent details comes next. Pull the piece away from the wall and look at the back, then pull out a drawer, look inside, and run a hand over the underside. If it is a chair, pick it up and look underneath. If it is a table, take out a flashlight and peer under the top. Pay particular attention to the feet of the piece, because they are often altered. The whole routine may take only a minute, like a doctor examining a newborn baby. A few looks

and a touch here and there—the secret lies in knowing where to look and what to look for.

At this point—with few exceptions—the expert is moderately certain whether the piece is genuine, how much it has been restored, roughly when it was made, and what general region it came from. Beginners are often amazed by such seemingly incredible ability, and they are likely to ask, "How do you *know?*" The answer is that the expert knows from experience. Good dealers have handled thousands of choice pieces, and experienced collectors have seen many things and are used to looking long and hard before they shoot. They are experts mostly because they have learned to remember and associate significant details. Stylistic details change from period to period and from region to region, and the expert can date a piece by its style and may be able to associate a given piece with a certain region, and perhaps with a maker or a group of makers, even if the identity of the craftsman may be long lost.

I would not want to pretend that you

113

will learn the fine points of expertise from this chapter. All I can hope to do here is outline the most important concepts—where to look and what to expect. The rest will come from studying a few good books and from examining furniture in museums, shops, auctions, and private collections—in brief, from looking at all the antiques you can possibly gain access to.

WHAT IS "RIGHT"?

Very few pieces are signed, even fewer are dated, and still fewer are reliably authenticated by records of ownership. A few rough contemporary illustrations appear in old newspapers, in trade catalogs, and on labels. Many inventories, wills, and similar documents offer fragmentary descriptions of furniture. From all this evidence we have learned rather well how things were done at various times in many places. There are gaps in the record, of course, but the information collected is surprisingly extensive. You will find it summarized in the good books (see Bibliography), in serious magazine articles, and in museums that like to show technical detail.

The vast majority of the furniture we see bears no helpful marks and lacks authentication of any sort. So we compare the remembered features of authenticated pieces with the features of the item before us. We form a mental picture of what to expect for this period, type, and style and then compare this picture with the naked reality, point by point. The style books will be helpful to refresh our memory, but much will depend on our personal outlook. Cheerful extroverts will be fooled because they took things for granted, and crabby skeptics will miss good items because they expected too much. The world being full of people who love fooling others, all I can say is, Let us use the old bean—the results may surprise us.

"I never judge on a single detail," Joe Kindig told me when we were chatting one day in his shop in York, Pennsylvania. "I pay attention to all of them. There may be a dozen points to consider, but when five go right, five wrong, and two are uncertain, then there is not a man alive who could tell if the piece is right. I never take the chance. I let someone else buy it. Oh, I've been stuck a few times, and always just because I did not look as carefully as I should have."

With a little exercise, our eye will soon become educated to the point where it can tell at a glance what is "right." If the subsequent examination forces a reversal of the first opinion, nothing is lost—as long as we keep our findings to ourselves. We shall soon find that our mistakes become fewer and fewer as we gain experience. When I think back on the bloopers I pulled when I was a beginner, it makes me cringe.

Some time ago I chanced by a shop with a handsome tall secretary in the window. From across the street it looked terrific. I entered the shop and asked the price. A stupendous figure was casually dropped. These things used to upset me, but I said nothing and went about the routine of giving the secretary that close-up, roving look. Well, the brasses were fancy Chippendale willow and too large; the scars of Hepplewhite brasses showed underneath. The feet were ogee and too small; marks of the band saw were clearly felt on the under part of their scrolls. The piece was walnut, but the front of the top bookcase section was just a shade darker than the bottom section. The lid was nicely inlaid with a star and two initials, and the bottom section had quarter-columns in front. The top section was plain, and what is more, it was 1½ inches deeper than the width of the board that formed the top of the desk carcase, so that the bookcase section protruded in back like a balcony. Furthermore, the bookcase section was too narrow and showed just enough of the top board of the desk carcase to let me see that this board was walnut, finished, and the same color as the front. Need I say more? This "secretary" was a jazzy product of a hasty wedding.

Let me now describe the procedure I used to appraise that secretary and the technique I always follow in examining pieces that are new to me.

THE COLOR OF OLD WOOD

"On the inside I go almost entirely by color," Albert Sack once told me. Bare wood matures with time, and only time will produce the various shades of brown characteristic of antique furniture, depending on how much the wood was exposed to air and light. If the internal structure of a slant-top desk is of pine, for instance, the back will be very dark, almost black, where it stood against the wall (fig. 117). The outside backs of the drawers will be considerably lighter, and the sides lighter still. The little drawers in the writing compartment under the lid are protected and will be very light, perhaps just slightly yellowed, and may, in fact, seem surprisingly new. It is this gradation in color of the unfinished wood that testifies to the genuineness of all the parts. Surfaces equally exposed are equally darkened. Short of elaborate and repeated staining, I know of no artificial process that could simulate this color gradation.

Various woods darken to different shades of brown, and tulip poplar turns grayish. In every case we have a discoloration that is uniform, depending only on exposure. There is no easier way to detect a new drawer, a new table top, or those elementary fakes, the wedded secretary and the falsely united chest on chest.

The notion is widespread that anyone could easily falsify antique furniture by making it of old wood that already has the right color. The faker's life would be easy indeed if that were true. First of all, a whole barn full of old wood may not contain two boards of matching color, and we could hardly expect them to be of the right width, length, and thickness for the purpose

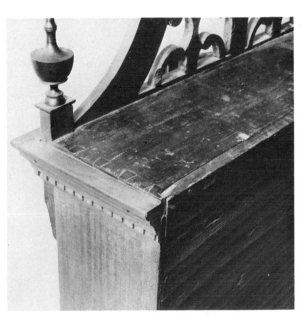

117. *Back view of the secretary shown in figure 6. The dovetails of the carcase are clearly visible, and the rough planing of the backboards is evident. These surfaces are bare wood, now almost black with age.*

we may have in mind. Any piece of wood has to be cut somewhere, and the color of the cut will tell the tale.

THE KINDS OF WOOD

The kinds of wood a piece is made of, especially the secondary (inside) wood, can be helpful in deciding provenance and thus, indirectly, genuineness. Most woods can be positively identified under the microscope from thin slices taken lengthwise and across the grain. The technique is available in specialized laboratories, but in a dark antiques shop or the crowded exhibition before an auction we have to rely on more casual inspection. White pine *(Pinus strobus)* and yellow birch *(Betula lutea)* are usually associated with northern New England, tulip poplar and cherry with southern New England, tulip and walnut with Pennsylvania, and cypress, of course, with the Deep South. It is not an ironclad rule, just a general guide. The lumber trade became very active in late Federal times, and desirable woods, like large logs of white pine, were shipped all along the East Coast. Nevertheless, if someone shows you a Queen Anne Boston highboy made of maple, for example, and the secondary wood turns out to be tulip poplar instead of pine, treat that as a warning signal—like a red light on the dash.

WEAR FROM USE

When a chair stands against a wall, it rubs against it once in a while, and sooner or later a flat place appears at the point of contact. Such wear is seen on the back of the bows of Windsors, on the back of combs, and on the backs of finials of slat-back chairs (fig. 118). Rungs and stretchers will be worn by contact with countless feet (fig. 119),

and the wear will be greater where it is easier to put one's feet. Chairs with two rungs in front will show greater wear on the bottom rung, except in the case of children's high chairs, where the top rung will be more severely worn.

Table tops will have all edges worn smooth and corners rounded. Marks of countless matches struck and the stain of many greasy hands will show on the underside of table tops, outside the skirt. Drawer runs will be worn to a curve and hollowed to a point where

118. The worn finial of a maple slat-back chair. Finials are usually most worn at the back, where they come in contact with the wall (HHT).

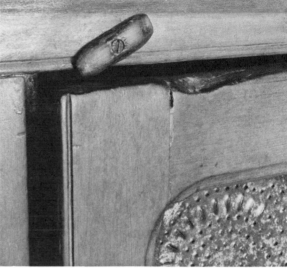

120. *Genuine wear does not always indicate great age. The door of this Maryland pierced-tin pie safe has a turn-button lock but no handle, so a deep groove has been worn into the soft tulip poplar by the fingernails of many homemakers right where they grasped the door after pushing the turn button aside with their thumbs. Yet the cupboard has all the earmarks of a machine-made product and could not possibly be older than about 1840.*

119. *Colonial slat-back, mushroom-post child's high chair. Note how the top front rung is almost worn through from contact with all those vigorous, tiny feet. If we seem vague about the age of this chair, it is because this type was made from late Pilgrim times on through the Revolution, with minor variations in style.*

they may have to be repaired, and marks of fingernails will be evident near the pulls of pine drawers. Cupboard doors will be worn where fingernails grasped them for opening and closing (fig. 120). The inside surface of desk lids will be scratched and spotted with ink—evidence that our forebears worked there, wrote letters, and made out their accounts.

Although we always expect to find wear on a genuinely old piece, even deep wear alone is not necessarily proof of great age. Late semiantique plank-bottom chairs may be just as well worn as early Windsors, and Victorian tulip-poplar cupboards, commodes, and chests may show greater wear than one would expect on a Pilgrim piece. It is all a question of how much use that particular piece has had and how resistant the wood of which it is made. Wear alone is no test of antiquity. The genuine wear that my children inflicted on our dining-room chairs is enough to make them look antique even if they were not.

121. *The expert peers into a Hep-plewhite sideboard . . . and finds a label! That more than makes up for all the faults. (Also shown in fig. 72.)*

NAMES, DATES, AND LABELS

Early American cabinetmakers rarely left their marks on their product. We may examine hundreds of fine and genuine pieces without finding any indication of who made them. When, at last, we discover a scrawled inscription, it is likely to have been left by a previous owner, long after the piece was made.

Isolated dates cannot be trusted for the same reason, and it is, in fact, a favorite indoor sport in faking circles (particularly in Europe) to carve plausible-looking dates on genuine antiques.

So it will be a memorable day when we find an authentic signature on the outside of some drawer, a stamp branded into the pine bottom of a chair, or a time-darkened label pasted

122. *Rubbings of brands found on the underside of Windsor chair seats (about one half actual size).*

in some obscure place (fig. 121). Many marks are illustrated in some of the books listed in the Bibliography. The rarity of such marks naturally increases the value of the pieces that bear them, but it is not easy to estimate how much. An ordinary chair bearing the name of an unknown maker is still just an ordinary chair (fig. 122), but a simple table

with the rude label "Made by John Townsend, Newport" would be very valuable indeed.

It would be difficult (but not impossible) to counterfeit well-known printed labels. Advertisements clipped from old newspapers may look a little like labels, but most of them have printing on the back, and that gives them away. Inscriptions are easy to cook up. John Townsend's bold signature could be copied; in fact, a skillful penman with a sharp goose quill, a bottle of brown ink, and a little practice could produce a diversity of authentic-looking inscriptions, replete with long *s*'s and suitably misspelled words. Outrageous, preposterous, incredible fakes have appeared in the autograph market, and some have gone undetected for years, so why

123. *Maple Philadelphia chair with a rush seat, probably from the shop of William Savery, about 1750. The Savery name is magic, and if this chair had his label the price would more than double. (Courtesy of Samuel T. Freeman & Co., Philadelphia.)*

124. *Signature incised on the underside of the desk in figure 3. Why is the J in Joseph Davis's name reversed? It might indicate that he had done some work for a printer. It is not a practiced signature, and one may surmise that it was made by an early owner.*

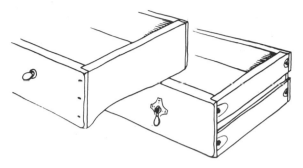

125. *Pilgrim drawer construction, rabbeted and nailed.*

not on furniture? I think that this kind of fakery is rare, but it happens. I know one inscription, on a very important piece once owned by Luke V. Lockwood, but a trustworthy witness told me some years ago that he had handled that very same piece many years before,

and at that time there was no inscription on it at all.

STYLES OF DRAWER CONSTRUCTION

The method of constructing drawers varied characteristically as time went by, so that drawers are a big help in dating a piece. Pilgrim drawers, made after the English fashion of the day, were rabbeted and nailed (fig. 125). They usually move on runs that fit into a groove in the sides of the drawer, about halfway up. A broad dovetail

126. *Single broad dovetail from an oak-front tavern table drawer of about 1700, held in place with hand-forged nails (HHT).*

127. *Fairly wide dovetailing on the drawer of a ball-foot chest of about 1725. Cotter-pin brasses (HHT).*

sometimes appears at the front (fig. 126). Pilgrim drawers are never lipped.

Colonial drawers have three or four stubby dovetails on each corner (fig. 127), and the bottom is no longer just nailed but fits into a groove that runs around the front and sides of the drawer (fig. 128). One or two nails in the back keep the bottom from rattling around. The bottom may be quite thick, in which case it is chamfered to a quarter of an inch or less where it fits into the groove. Characteristic Colo-

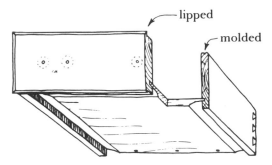

128. Colonial drawer construction, tongue-and-groove and dovetail.

129. Good Colonial drawer construction. Note the molded tops of the drawer sides and the open dovetails that join the drawer blades to the side of the carcase. The outside (primary wood) is all maple, but the internal construction (secondary wood) is chestnut on this particular piece.

nial dovetails are shown in figures 129 and 130. Dovetailing becomes finer in the Federal period, and one can say, in general, the finer the dovetailing, the later the piece (fig. 131). The lipped, thumbnail-molded drawer fronts of Colonial times give way to flush drawers again in Federal times. Beading usually adorns the edges of the late flush drawer fronts.

Making dovetails is a lot of work, of course, and efforts to mechanize the process began in the nineteenth century. The peg-and-scallop fastening of drawer sides is an early attempt at such mechanization (fig. 132). It appears on semiantiques made about 1860 to 1890.

131. Narrow dovetailing found on some Federal and later drawers.

130. Widely spaced stubby dovetails on the back of a good Colonial drawer, also shown in figure 129; the wood is chestnut. Note the score mark for the depth of the dovetail cuts.

132. Peg-and-scallop "dovetailing" on the drawer of the commode in figure 93. About 1860 or later.

PINS

Wooden pins of all sizes are essential components in early furniture construction. They are made of the tougher hardwoods (oak, hickory, maple, cherry, beech, or walnut), shaped in a roughly polygonal section, and slightly tapered toward the point. When driven into a round hole of the proper size, the pins bite into the wood and set firmly. Even if the pins were cut off flush right after they were driven, they slowly begin to work their way out. With time, the wood into which the pin was driven shrinks, but the pin retains its length, for the shrinkage of hardwood is almost nil in the direction along the fiber. After some years the pin may project $\frac{1}{16}$ inch or more above the surface, as shown in figure 133. This is one detail that is hard to duplicate in a faked piece. Modern pins, driven into kiln-dried wood and cut off flush, will remain flush for years; but if the faker went to the trouble of using air-dried wood and if some years have elapsed since, the pin evidence now may be unreliable. Twenty years ago I made a Queen Anne chest frame from heavy air-cured maple, pinned in the old way with hickory. Some weeks ago I happened to see the piece again and was surprised to note that the pins now protrude nicely about $\frac{1}{32}$ inch. Underneath the frame, the wood is still fresh, of course, and nobody would mistake it for being very old.

THE MARKS OF PLANES

Early cabinetmakers used planes and scrapers for all their smoothing, and they made no particular effort to conceal the marks of these tools. When they wanted to dress down a board quickly, they used a long "jointer" plane with the blade ground to a slightly curved edge. This blade left its

133. Projecting diamond-shaped pin in the authentic American chair of Flemish style in figure 32 (HHT).

unmistakable marks (figs. 134 and 135), and if you have ever seen a connoisseur slyly open the drawer of a piece on exhibition and run a hand over the underside of the drawer bottom, those are the marks being sought. Careful scrutiny will reveal similar (but less pronounced) marks on the sides of chests and desks, on door panels, and generally on surfaces that have not had much wear and that have not been carelessly refinished.

The absence of plane marks does not necessarily mean that the piece is not

134. Plane marks on the pine drawer bottom of a chest of about 1750 (HHT).

135. Plane marks on the chamfered pine drawer bottom of a Sheraton stand of about 1820. The blade of the plane was ground a little flatter and the planing is a little rougher than in figure 134, but those are minor differences and not always consistent.

genuine, but it does call for closer inspection. The cabinetmaker may have smoothed the wood with unusual care, even on the bottom of the drawers, or the piece may have been altered at a much later time. We do not usually find plane marks on furniture made after about 1850.

SAW MARKS

Most of the early American furniture makers spent little time dressing the lumber intended for the backs of chests, the bottoms of drawers, inner frames of upholstered furniture, and other parts that were not intended to be seen. These parts were planed, as we have just discussed, or they were left rough, showing the kerf of the saw teeth.

The boards for cabinetmaking were usually cut by hand. A log was laid over a pair of tall sawhorses, one man stood below and another above, and between them they pulled a long ripsaw up and down lengthwise through the log (fig. 136). By the same tedious process board after board was cut off the log, the thickness gauged by eye. The saw was held at some convenient angle, and as it progressed through the log, the angle changed gradually. Every time the sawyers took up a new stance or stopped to rest, their saw started at a new angle again.

As a result, the marks of the hand saw —or the pit saw, as it is sometimes called, for the lower man often worked in a pit—are never strictly parallel, never perpendicular to the grain of the wood, and generally are quite irregular from place to place on the same board (fig. 137). The surface was often so rough that the cabinetmaker felt obliged to plane off most of the bumps and ridges, but the deeper grooves, made each time the sawyers changed position, are likely to remain.

It may be hard to believe, but the

136. The pit saw. (Woodcut used as decoration on the cover of a notebook printed in Philadelphia about 1815.)

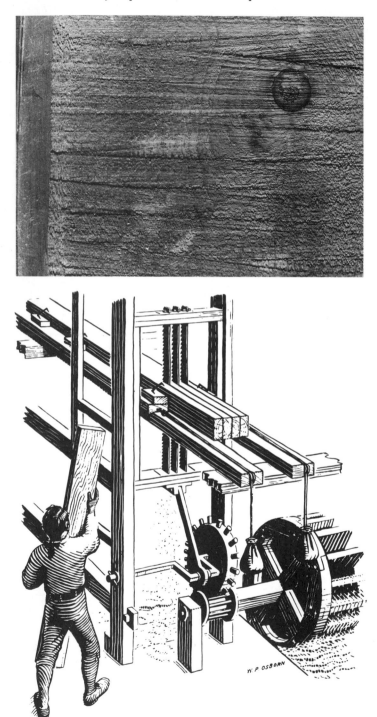

137. *Marks of the pit saw on the pine drawer bottom of a Colonial chest.*

138. *The basic working parts of a gash saw. These saws were driven by windmills or waterwheels and later by steam. (Original drawing by William P. Osborn, adapted from a diagram in John Evelyn's* Sylva *[London: 1670].)*

139. Marks of the old "up-and-down" or gash saw on the underside of a red oak floorboard of about 1780 (HHT).

primitive pit saw is still used in out-of-the-way places where "time has no hurry" (see *National Geographic* magazine, 115 [1959]: 575).

Mechanical saws were built in the New World from early Pilgrim days, but transportation was a problem all along so that it was usually cheaper to saw the logs by hand than to haul them to a distant sawmill. These mills were usually powered by waterwheels, but windmills in the Dutch style were not unusual, especially in New York. Early prints show them along the skyline.

As a rule, the lumber mills had several long saw blades bolted side by side into a frame, just far enough apart to cut boards of the required thickness. The gears and cranks of the mill,

whether wind or water powered, moved the frame up and down, and the log, mounted on a carriage, slowly advanced through the saws (fig. 138). These gash saws were large and cumbersome affairs, but one man could run one alone. We can still find this type of machinery in remote districts, basically unchanged after three hundred years.

Marks of the gash saw are regular, parallel, and perpendicular to the length of the board (fig. 139). The surface is fairly smooth, so that many of the gash-sawn boards could be left rough in concealed places.

Circular saws were introduced early in the nineteenth century but did not come into general use until about 1840, when the development of small

140. *The age of primitive pieces is often difficult to guess. The large burl bowl (21" in diameter) may have been made in 1750 or a hundred years later. The rude oak bench may seem very old to the inexperienced eye, but a glance underneath reveals the telltale marks of a circular saw—unquestionable evidence of nonantiquity.*

steam engines made the necessary high axle speeds widely available. The circular saw was so much faster and simpler and so much more easily moved as lumbering progressed that it soon relegated the gash saw to the backwoods.

The marks of the circular saw are un-mistakable (fig. 140). From what we have said, it should be obvious that circular saw marks are the last thing we would expect to see on antique furniture. In themselves, marks of the gash saw do not indicate great age, because some gash saws were still operated

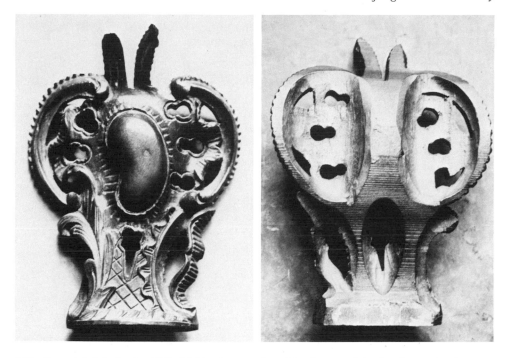

141. Central finial of a fine Philadelphia chest on chest. The lines are right, but the carving is not as crisp as it should be. On the back (horrors!): marks of the modern band saw.

long after they had become obsolete. Furthermore, marks of the modern band saw are also parallel and could be mistaken for the kerf of the gash saw (fig. 141). But the circular saw is strictly a development of the Industrial Revolution. Whenever we find the circular kerf, we can be quite certain that this piece of wood was cut after 1830— probably long after.

SHRINKAGE OF TURNINGS

Wood shrinks much less along the radius of the tree than along lines tangent to the tree rings (fig. 142). That is why

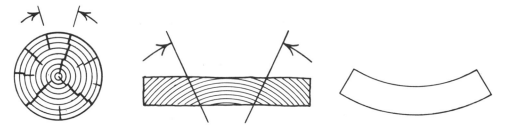

142. Shrinkage is greatest in the direction parallel to the growth rings. As a result, logs crack and boards warp.

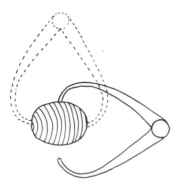

143. *Green turnings, originally round, shrink to an elliptical cross section, exaggerated in the sketch but easily measured with a caliper.*

radial cracks appear in the ends of logs soon after they are cut, and that is why boards warp. That is also why turnings, once perfectly round, become elliptical with time (fig. 143).

Early wood turners almost invariably used green wood to make chair legs and posts. A slat-back or a Windsor chair assembled from green turnings becomes firm and rigid as the wood dries and shrinks. At the same time, the cross-section of the turning changes from a circle to a slight ellipse—always detectable with a caliper, and often pronounced enough to be seen by eye.

Kiln-dried wood shrinks very little after it comes from the kiln, and a turning made from it will be almost as round after fifty years as the day it was made. Not that any of us would for a moment mistake a reproduction Windsor for the real thing; but if we ever have some doubt about the genuineness of a leg or a post, the caliper will tell.

SCOREMARKS ON TURNINGS

Much is made of the scoremarks that early turners made in chair legs and

144. *Scored lines mark the ends of the mortise chiseled into a chair post to receive the slat; similar marks are found for the holes bored to receive the rungs. Such marks do not necessarily prove great age, but the skillful restorer will preserve them if only to show that the chair has not been skinned.*

posts where they were to be drilled for stretchers or mortised to receive slats (fig. 144). These marks are not necessarily a sign of age. There are places in the Ozarks where slat-back chairs are being made right now, with scoremarks as pretty as you please.

But the scoremarks are useful to show at a glance that a chair has not been skinned. The overzealous refinisher who scrapes off the scoremarks might as well be chopping up the chair for firewood.

STRETCHER HOLES

The holes drilled to receive spindles, rungs, and stretchers in chairs were almost always made with the old spoon (or pod) bit, a style of drill bit that disappeared about the middle of the nineteenth century. The spoon bit made a hole with a rounded bottom, as seen in figure 145. Gimlet-point augers and the widely used modern flat wood-boring bits make square-bottomed holes with a little cone in the center.

The difference may be difficult to see just by looking down the hole, and the owner of the chair may not be pleased by the prospect of having its leg sawed lengthwise, as we did for figure 145. Fortunately, there is a scientific way out of the dilemma: X-rays. Any dentist with a sense of humor can make them, and dental films are not too small to catch the essential detail. Museum laboratories are often equipped to X-ray paintings and can do the same for chairs. A very fine pair of such pictures is shown in figure 146.

OLD PAINT

Paint remains soft for a very long time. The exact period depends on the type of paint, of course, but many paints are still soft enough to be nicked by the pressure of a fingernail after a year. When scraped, new paint comes off in ribbons. If a newly painted surface is exposed to the sun for long intervals of time, the paint tends to crawl, crack, and ultimately "chalk."

Genuine old paint, however, becomes hard and brittle just by normal exposure to air indoors. Again, it is hard to say just how long the process requires, but a dozen years is about the minimum. Such old paint will shatter and crack under the pressure of a small blunt point, like that of a screwdriver, for instance. It comes off in a powder when scraped, and may break into flinty slivers, almost like glass. I know

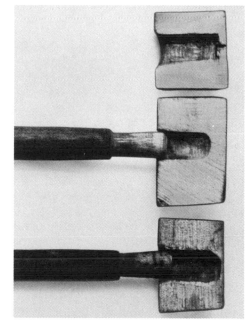

145. Stretcher holes in chair legs sawed lengthwise, to show the inside. Modern gimlet-point augers and flat wood-boring bits (top) make characteristic holes quite different from (center and bottom) the smooth holes made by the old-fashioned spoon bits used before the middle of the nineteenth century (HHT).

146. *X-rays of holes in Pilgrim chairs—genuine* (left) *and fake* (right). *These are positive contact prints made from the original negatives. Note the little cones in the flat bottoms of the holes in the picture at right. They prove that the holes were drilled with a modern bit.* (*Courtesy of the Conservation Center, Greenfield Village and Henry Ford Museum, Dearborn, Mich.*)

of no artificial way of aging paint quickly, so that any monkey business with paint is fairly easy to detect. Being of a suspicious nature, I always examine paint with the greatest of care. You never know what may be underneath.

WORMHOLES

One of the most popular fallacies told and retold about antique furniture is that wormholes are proof of genuine antiquity. Actually, the holes are made not by worms but by the grubs of small beetles—*Anobium punctatum* and the slightly larger *Xestobium rufovillosum,* among others. They are just as active today as they were a thousand years ago. They are busily at work in all parts of the world but are comparatively rare in North America, with the exception of the chestnut borer, *Agrilus bilineatus.*

Some years ago I was traveling in Holland and bought one of those lovely carved wooden gingerbread molds called *kokplanks.* I noticed that it was wormy, as many European antiques are, and I put it away in my suitcase, where it remained for a few days, wrapped in paper. When I finally unpacked it, I noticed a smidgin of fine wood dust in the wrapping paper. That seemed odd, and I put the *kokplank* on a sheet of dark paper on a high closet shelf and let it sit there for a week or two, undisturbed. When I looked at it again, sure enough, there were tiny piles of sawdust under some of the wormholes. The little devils were still at work! The wood must have become infested quite recently. I sprayed the plank with an insecticide, and the sawdust production stopped right there.

The beetles may attack any native American wood, but they prefer walnut, maple, and fruit woods. *Agrilus* likes chestnut and is distinguished by the particularly large holes it makes (about $\frac{3}{32}$ inch in diameter). Chestnut *(Castanea dentata)* was once a common forest tree in America, but early in the twentieth century it was all but wiped out by a fungus. The beetles went to work after the fungus had killed the trees but before the wood was cut. The "wormy chestnut" of the lumber trade is the product of these depredations, but I have seen very similar wood used in genuine eighteenth-century furniture, wormholes and all. Wood that was wormy when sawn can be recognized because some of the holes go straight through and others are cut lengthwise. Wood that was eaten by beetles after it was cut will have only round holes that go straight in and then meander about inside the wood. The worming may be so bad that almost all the wood is consumed and only the outer shell remains. Wood in that condition will seem spongy when squeezed, if it is not broken already.

For that reason alone, wormholes can never be considered an asset in any piece of furniture, and if it should be found that the beetles are still active, immediate countermeasures are indicated. The strong dusts and sprays used by gardeners to control Japanese beetles are most effective on the wood borers.

IMPORTED FURNITURE, MOSTLY ENGLISH

Enormous amounts of European furniture were brought to America by settlers, by furniture dealers, and (much later) by importers of antiques. This is a book on American antiques, and foreign furniture is of interest only insofar as it might be confused with authentic American furniture. In this respect, English furniture is the most important. English and American styles are similar, but the English pieces are far more common.

The British take good care of their property, and two hundred years ago England was a wealthy power whereas the United States was just a struggling little outpost with few refinements and little property. There is still enough antique furniture in England to be bought in wholesale lots and shipped to the United States for resale at a profit. And if we were to judge only by the appearance of, say, an unrecorded Jacobean piece, nobody could tell whether it came over on the *Mayflower* or in a container consigned to Macy's.

Once in a great while I have the chance to visit the big London antiques fair, and every time I am amazed by the "low" price tags on the good furniture. This is, of course, the finest antiques show in the world, and the price of a booth there is about the same as a very fine "bureau" (that's English for "desk"). Antiquity is strictly enforced, and the stalls selling real antiques are separated from those selling post-1830 material (like fabulous Fabergé and great big Victorian diamond jewelry) by a long corridor with the ladies' and gentlemen's cloakrooms. It's hardly the place for bargains, but the best English furniture there sells for about a third of what equivalent American pieces would bring at auction here. So if we see a fine English chest bring less than half the price of an undistinguished American chest in auction, it is not just blind chauvinism that accounts for the difference but simply the law of supply and demand.

Nor is it always easy to distinguish between English and American furniture. The very early chairs, stools (fig. 147), and simple chests are particularly perplexing at times, and we may even have to make microscopic slides of the wood if we want to be absolutely sure of the origin of some of them. Oak was

147. Late Pilgrim joint stool of maple. This one is obviously American, but earlier specimens, with less-pronounced turnings and made of oak, are very similar to the much more common Jacobean stools from England.

the principal wood used in Britain, and we find it in all interior construction. The woods of the English oak *(Quercus robur)* and the American white oak *(Quercus alba)* are quite different when cleaned off, but under a genuine patina (not to speak of dust and poor light) the difference becomes very slight indeed. If we are offered a really early piece, reverently advertised as "genuine Pilgrim" but made entirely of oak, we should scrutinize it minutely; chances are that it is English and therefore much less valuable than the extremely rare American equivalent.

White pine *(Pinus strobus)* and, to a lesser extent, the tulip tree *(Liriodendron tulipifera),* usually called poplar, were the common woods in early America. Whenever we see white pine in the interior construction of a genuine piece, we can take it as almost certain evidence of American origin. Even the earliest settlers, Englishmen though they were, soon switched from oak to pine because it was readily available in very wide boards and was easy to work.

It is difficult to say how much shipyard lumber was sent to Britain from Colonial America, but there is little doubt that some of it has found its way into furniture. Therefore, if we find a piece that looks obviously English but has a back of the typically American white pine, that would be no reason to doubt that the piece really is English, unless some other evidence points to the contrary. The same argument does not hold in reverse, for it is doubtful that much common lumber was shipped from Britain to the Colonies.

Chippendale furniture was often made entirely of mahogany, both here and in England, so that the origin must be decided on stylistic details alone. Comparatively simple English pieces, especially tables, may look very American, even to experts. I can recall several small mahogany Chippendale pieces which I examined with great care without reaching a conclusion "beyond reasonable doubt," as they say in courtroom dramas.

Recognition becomes easy when we come to Federal furniture. Here English and American styles diverge rapidly, and the expert can usually tell at a glance what is English and what is American. English pieces, as a rule, are more elaborate, both in design and in workmanship. The wood is usually richly grained, be it solid or veneered, and there is likely to be carving, fretwork, and fancy brasses. The admirable book by Cescinsky and Hunter, *English and American Furniture,* clearly illustrates the salient differences.

If the piece has drawers, a look inside will suffice. American full-length drawers usually have bottoms of pine or tulip poplar, rarely of chestnut, and hardly ever of oak. The drawer bottom is usually a single board, sometimes quite thick, and chamfered around the edges (fig. 128). Drawers of English pieces have thin oak bottoms, almost without exception, and with the grain usually perpendicular to the drawer front. A grooved cleat usually runs across the English drawer bottom, front to back.

7
HARDWARE

The brasses (or "mounts," as some sophisticates call them, though to me a mount is a horse), hinges, catches, pulls, latches, casters, screws, nails, and brads are the hardware that the early cabinetmaker had to buy. Most of it came from England, and it passed through many hands before it reached the cabinetmaker in the Colonies. It is not surprising, therefore, that the cost of hardware was almost prohibitive in Pilgrim times and that it continued high throughout the eighteenth century.

English pattern books of the late eighteenth and early nineteenth centuries show an enormous variety of brass hardware for the furniture trade. Any brass I have ever seen used on American furniture can be found in those catalogs. "Brass founders" are listed in Colonial America, but I suspect that they did much more importing than manufacturing. I have never seen an American hardware pattern book before 1830, but British books include some obviously "American" patterns (fig. 148), and that leads me to believe that almost all the brass "handles and

scutchions" found on Colonial and Federal furniture came from England, even during the Revolutionary War and the War of 1812. English brass exporters would not allow their king's military adventures to interfere with business.

Iron was a different story. The urgent need for tools led to the establishment of several ironworks in early Pilgrim times. In Virginia, the earliest effort came to a tragic end when the plant on Falling Creek near Jamestown was destroyed by Indians in 1622 in a massacre that took 347 lives (as reported in T. A. Rickard's *A History of American Mining*). A furnace was erected near Lynn, Massachusetts, in 1646, and another near New Haven, Connecticut, in 1662. At least a dozen furnaces were operating along the eastern seaboard in early Colonial times, but the official policy of Great Britain was aimed at stifling the working of iron in the Colonies and promoting the exportation of pig and raw bar iron to Britain. Although these regulations were only partly successful, they did impede development of the iron indus-

148. English brass stampers aimed to please everybody. In spite of the hostilities, their catalogs show patriotic designs intended for the enemy in France and America. Top, from a catalog internally dated about 1780–90; bottom, from another dated by watermark after 1801. (Both in the Victoria and Albert Museum.)

try in the Colonies, and their economic absurdity was a contributing factor in the discontent that led to the Revolution.

A small forge is something every pioneer settlement simply had to have, and good bar iron was not too difficult to obtain (at a price). The blacksmith made mostly agricultural implements, but an occasional order for a few pairs of hinges certainly did not stump him. I have seen fairly complicated locks and latches that obviously were made from bar iron by a country blacksmith with just a hammer, a pliers, an anvil, some bellows, and a little pile of hot coals.

Brass, then, with its golden sheen and high price tag was something spe-

149. Caption title of an Act of Parliament published in 1750.

An Act to encourage the Importation of Pig and Bar Iron from His Majesty's Colonies in *America* ; and to prevent the Erection of any Mill or other Engine for Slitting or Rolling of Iron ; or any Plateing Forge to work with a Tilt Hammer ; or any Furnace for making Steel in any of the said Colonies.

cial—one of the necessities of elegance. We shall find it conspicuously displayed on substantial furniture made for the folks who could afford it. Iron, on the other hand, was a common everyday material, and iron hardware was comparatively cheap. Wrought iron looks rare and handsome to us today, but in Colonial times there was nothing special about it.

ORIGINAL HARDWARE

Unexpected as it might seem, hardware is usually the first part of a piece of furniture to be damaged. Handles break or come loose and are lost. Hinges often suffer. Catches jam and are damaged or torn off, and locks are broken when people try to open them without benefit of a key. Brass is weak even when made well, and the old brass

castings were often unsound, full of flaws and bubbles.

When a few of the brasses were lost from the chest of drawers in Great-granddad's bedroom, he took the rest off, put them away for a rainy day, and installed a new set he had bought in town. The new brasses, of course, were in the pattern that was then in fashion and may have been a different size. It is not unusual to see early case furniture with the marks of three different sets of pulls on the drawer fronts, each in a different style and ending with wooden knobs.

I have often heard that the brass was taken to be used for cartridges in the Civil War. It is true that Europe was ransacked for every scrap of brass during the Franco-Prussian War and even more thoroughly during the world wars, but from what I have seen I would

150. Left, *English cast-brass catch in a brass founder's catalog in the Victoria and Albert Museum;* above, *a similar catch in use on a Philadelphia tea table of about 1780.*

suspect that in America much more brass fell prey to the Victorian fad for wooden knobs than to patriotic zeal during the War Between the States.

The Chippendale secretary in figure 6 had broad wooden knobs when I first saw it (fig. 152), but marks of the old brasses were clearly visible on the drawer fronts. That secretary had

stood for more than a hundred years in a house in Southington, Connecticut, when by a stroke of rare good fortune I was let loose in the attic just before the old place was sold. In addition to the secretary, there was a pair of Windsors, a blanket chest, two or three other chairs, a tip-top table, a smashed candlestand, a few good books, and a

151. *Iron latch on the underside of a simple tilt-top table made in Connecticut about 1780. This is a cheap catch; more elegant tables usually had brass catches. Note the narrow slots of the hand-made screws, some cut slightly off center.*

152. *The unmistakable marks of early hardware. Although the original brass was replaced by the broad Victorian wooden knob, we can easily determine the size of the original bails by the marks they left where they touched the drawer front and the diameter of the round rosettes by the circle they impressed into the wood. The restored piece is shown in figure 6.*

truckload of trash. The secretary was incomplete, and the better of the two Windsors lacked a spindle.

Now it is a well-known fact that Yankees throw nothing away, and I had a feeling that the missing pieces could be around the house. It was a hot summer, and under the eaves of the low attic the air was like an oven. After ten minutes up there, I looked like a coal miner with a derelict sense of hygiene, but I sorted through the piles of dust-covered junk, and sure enough, there in a corner was

the missing spindle, and under a pile of miscellaneous metal was a little box. From it I extracted half a dozen pieces of Chippendale brass, dark green with age. Hardly believing my eyes, I took the handles to the secretary, and they fitted perfectly.

Had the old ancestor taken the brasses off the secretary to help win the war, he certainly would not have hidden a few of them in the attic. It is far more likely that most of the brasses became broken and lost. Whoever owned the desk finally got tired of pulling the drawers out by their lips, so he removed the few remaining brasses, stashed them away, and installed wooden knobs in the highest fashion of the day.

Knowledgeable collectors usually prefer pieces with original brasses, if they can find them. Such pieces are, of course, rare, and it is not surprising that any piece labeled "original brasses" should bear a comparatively high price tag. Genuine old brasses (almost always in incomplete sets) may show up in shops and occasionally come up in auctions, and so we must distinguish between just old brass and really original brass. Many undiscerning dealers remove whatever original brasses remain on a piece they are refinishing and install a complete set of new reproduction brasses of some flashy variety. The old brasses ultimately appear on the market again, and I used to be amazed by the keen interest with which some of the better dealers bid on them. I suspect that some of those old brasses turn up as "original" on important pieces. However, there are thousands of patterns, and it is almost impossible to find two incomplete sets of brasses that could be mistaken for a matching set. So if we find a highboy with fourteen "original" brasses, of which seven are of one pattern, five of another, and two of still another—all similar, to be sure, but still not quite the same—our suspicions may well be aroused. It would be far more reassuring to find the plates matching exactly, but a few posts and some bails replaced by modern reproduction brass.

There are no hard and fast rules for recognizing original brasses with certainty, but two factors usually apply. First, the square bolts were originally driven with a hammer into round holes

153. *Genuine early Colonial punch-decorated ("engraved") escutcheon on a genuine early Colonial highboy—the two unfortunately united rather late in their respective careers. The scar of a willow brass underneath proves that the present escutcheon could not be original on this piece. A closer look at the fastening pins shows that they are modern.*

drilled undersize on purpose; consequently, the posts are tight if they have not been disturbed. Second, the edge of the metal plate, with time, makes a corresponding scar in the board underneath; no trace of any other scar should be discernible.

If our brasses do indeed turn out to be original and not just old brasses with the same posthole distance, then we should leave them undisturbed and take special care not to obliterate the evidence of their originality.

DATING BY HARDWARE

Hardware can be a big help in estimating the time when an otherwise nondescript piece was made, but one has to be careful about ages based exclusively on pulls or hinges or fastenings. We shall discuss various hardware styles and the periods when they were popular, but we all know that the early settlers were thrifty. A set of brasses was a valuable parcel, and a handful of nails was worth more than a bushel of fruit. If, for some unforeseen reason, the hardware was not needed immediately, it was stashed away until the time when a use for it developed, and that may have been thirty years later. Henry Taylor writes of a desk he found with

> some of its original brasses still in place. These brasses were of the bail-handle type, with two round plates held in place by bolts and nuts. Judging by these brasses, this desk could have been made as early as 1760. Such is not the case; for I found written in ink, on the under side of one of the drawers, this notation:

> *September, 19th day, 1801.*
> *I bote this deske of Lewis Burton of Stratford, Connecticut, for 4:—15.—6—paid all down by me.*
>   *Isaac Booth.*

Lewis Burton, who was a cabinetmaker of Stratford, Connecticut, had, for some unknown reason applied to this "deske" brasses which had been rather out of fashion for a long time.

THE SEQUENCE OF STYLES

EARLY WOODEN KNOBS

The earliest handles on furniture of the Pilgrim period were simple knobs turned from hardwood and driven into slightly undersize holes in the fronts of the drawers (fig. 155). As a rule, the knobs were small, rarely more than an inch in diameter and an inch and a half long outside the drawer. The shank extended another inch or less into the drawer front. We shall see them on simple furniture throughout Colonial times. The Shakers revived this kind of

knob long afterward, and we find it on their chests of drawers, even very late ones. (However, the usual nineteenth-century knob was quite different in design, as we shall see.)

DROP PULLS

The first metal drawer pulls were drops in the style of William and Mary, held to the wood by a single cotter pin pulled through and clinched in back (fig. 156). From an engineering point of view, this was a poor device, impractical and fragile, so that it went out of use fairly quickly. The heyday of drop pulls was about 1690–1710.

The plates of the drop pull were always cast from light brass. The pattern was occasionally plain but more often "engraved" or pierced, and the drop itself was round and solid in the early styles but made half-round and hollow toward the end of the period. Outside of museums, I have never seen a piece with original drop brasses still in place. Not that such pieces could not be found, it is just that I have never been that lucky. However, I have seen hundreds of pieces with fake drop brasses —almost all of them installed incorrectly. There was a vogue for the William and Mary style early in the twentieth century, and we shall see all sorts of pseudoantique abominations with that kind of pulls. Even genuine early Colonial furniture, originally drilled with two holes for the bail–cotter-pin brasses, is often wrongly restored with drop brasses, although new holes must be drilled for them, and the old holes show. Any piece originally made for drop pulls will have just one hole for each pull, with the unmistakable clinch marks on the inside of the drawer. The drawer front will show semicircular scars made by the drop as it swung

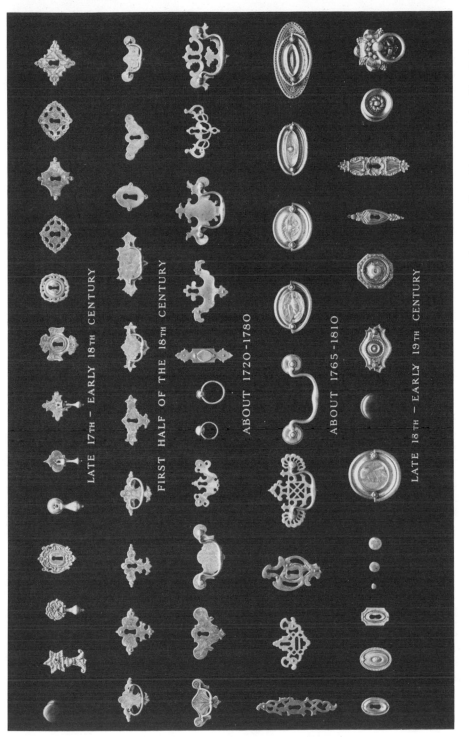

LATE 17TH – EARLY 18TH CENTURY

FIRST HALF OF THE 18TH CENTURY

ABOUT 1720-1780

ABOUT 1765-1810

LATE 18TH – EARLY 19TH CENTURY

154. Hardware used on American furniture, arranged as the styles changed with time. (Display at the Metropolitan Museum of Art, New York.)

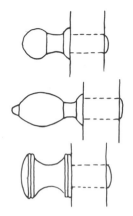

155. *Early wooden knobs.*

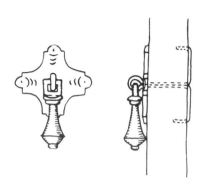

156. *Cotter-pin drop brass.*

from its cotter pin. On genuine pieces the scar is usually quite deep.

COTTER-PIN BAIL PULLS

The cotter-pin bail brass was a great improvement on the drops (see fig. 154, first brass in second row). A thin brass bail was held with two clinched cotter pins through a light cast plate that protected the drawer front. The

plate was usually "engraved," and the cotter pins were of brass or iron. Without being too dogmatic about it, we may date the period of thin-bail cotter-pin brasses as 1710–40. Some experts may prefer 1730 for the upper limit, but Howard Reifsnyder had a tall chest with this kind of brass, and the chest is dated 1737. (See no. 242 in Nutting's *Furniture Treasury.*)

The "engraving" on the plates was

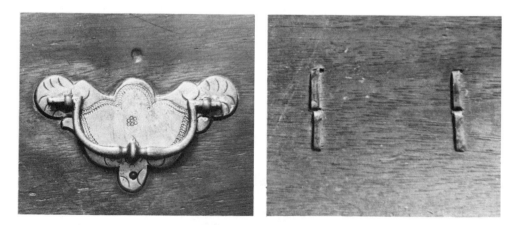

157. *"Engraved" brass drawer pull of about 1750, mounted on the inside of the drawer with clinched brass cotter pins. Actually, these brasses were not engraved but punch-decorated to imitate engraved designs.*

not really chased but stamped with steel punches similar to those now used for leather tooling (fig. 157). The pattern was made by combining a number of strokes with various tools—straight lines, dots, circles, semicircles, S curves, and so on. Naturally, the pattern will show slight variations from plate to plate.

After about 1740, the bails become thicker and more elaborate in profile and engage the cotter pins from the inside (fig. 157). These later cotter pins are made of thick brass ribbon, better than the old wire but still rather weak. The "engraving" disappears about 1750–60, but cotter-pin handles were still being offered—to archconservative cabinetmakers, I suppose—as late as about 1785 (fig. 158).

All cotter-pin brasses are relatively weak, and pieces with a complete original set of them are extremely rare. The original cotter pins are easily recognized by the clinching inside the drawer, as seen in figure 157. Few restorers bother to clinch the cotter pins of reproduction brass, and even if they did, they could hardly hope to imitate the appearance of undisturbed, clinched, rough wire in a time-darkened board.

BOLT PULLS

Bail handles held with bolts made their appearance about 1730 or a little later (fig. 154). At first, the bolt heads were pierced clear through, in the manner of the eye formed by the old cotter pin, but before long the bolt became standardized in the approximate shape it

158. *Willow and bat's-wing brass patterns, about 1785, in a brass founder's catalog in the Victoria and Albert Museum. Note the two patterns at the lower right, showing that cotter-pin brasses were still being offered.*

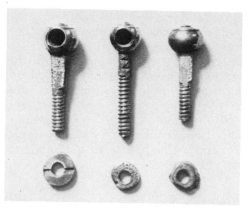

159. Cast-brass bolts and nuts, 1780–1820.

retained for almost a hundred years. The shank of the bolt was usually cast in a square cross section, so that the bolt would not turn in its hole (fig. 159). The head was round, drilled about three quarters of the way through, and the threads were rough and coarse—usually not too far from the nonstandard modern size 8-24 but highly variable. Reproduction bolts are hardly ever cast but are usually machined from stock. They are generally round, for it is cheaper to make them that way, and they have modern threads (8-32, 10-24, or other standard sizes).

The original nuts may be round, square, roughly hexagonal, or just irregular bits of cast brass, tapped to fit loosely on the crude threads. Each nut may fit only the bolt it was made for, and the parts may not be interchangeable even within the same set of brasses. This individuality of thread depth and pitch is characteristic of early hardware.

Once I was called upon to provide nuts for an original set of brasses from which all nuts had been lost. The owner was justifiably afraid the posts might pull out and be lost without the nuts. This apparently simple request

turned out to be quite a project. I pulled out one of the posts, measured the thread with a gauge, obtained blank nut castings from one of the reproduction brass makers, made a special tap according to my measurements (standard taps would not do), and drilled and tapped the nuts. About ten of them fitted the posts without difficulty, but the remaining six had to be fitted individually by scraping the thread to the right size. That is a tedious process, and by the time I had squeezed the last nut on the last post, I had learned to appreciate the advantages of modern standardization.

WILLOW PULLS

At first, the plates used with the bolt pulls were much like the plates of cotter-pin brasses, but the ornaments gradually disappeared, and the characteristic *bat's-wing* pattern evolved into the complicated shape of the *willow* design, which was popular all through the second half of the eighteenth century (fig. 160). The plates were always cast, so that the grain of the sand mold will be visible on the back. The edges were beveled with a file, often a rather coarse one, and the front was scraped smooth.

160. *Willow brass patterns from an undated anonymous brass founder's catalog in the Victoria and Albert Museum.*

Marks of the file and the scraper will be evident where the plates have not been polished too much with abrasive brass polish. The style of the plates gradually evolved through the years. The rather small (two- to three-inch posthole distance) designs with fairly plain outlines were in fashion about 1740–60. With time, willow brasses became larger and their outlines more elaborate. Pierced designs reflecting Chippendale ornaments appear on some of the finest furniture, mainly in Philadelphia before the Revolution. Newport pieces of 1760–80 often carry enormous brasses, as much as 6 inches wide (fig. 161).

Plates of reproduction brasses in the willow style are almost always cut from sheet brass, smooth on the back. The cheaper reproductions will have plates of very thin brass, embossed to simu-

late the beveled edges. Original bails have roughly squared ends and shoulders and may show marks of the scraper, for that is how they were smoothed (fig. 162). This scraped tex-

161. *Large willow brass on the drawer of a fine Newport desk of about 1770–80.*

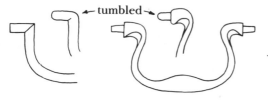

162. Top, *reproduction brass bails are rounded from tumbling;* bottom, *old brass was filed and scraped so that the corners are sharp.*

ture of old brass is a little difficult to describe. It is a slight rippling caused by irregularities of the rough surface as the scraper is drawn across to smooth it. (We shall find this same texture on the underside of cheap brass ashtrays from the Orient.) Reproduction bails will have the ends rounded from tumbling in a barrel, which is the modern method of smoothing small brass parts.

FRENCH AND ENGLISH PULLS

French and English pulls of Colonial times were larger and much more ornate than the pulls made for the American market. Some of these fancy brasses appear occasionally as original equipment on good American furniture. They may be seen, for example, in Downs (nos. 181, 183, 195, and 198) and in Nutting (nos. 247, 249, 253, 324, and 375), but such pieces are very rare. Whatever the piece, we should never install such fancy brasses unless we have very good evidence that the original brasses were of that kind.

ROSETTE PULLS

The brasses most frequently shown in the designs of Thomas Chippendale are what I here call rosette pulls, for lack of a better term. The bail of this pull was generally identical with the shaped bail of the late willow styles, but the bolt was fancier, with a shaped ornamental head (fig. 163). Instead of the plate, each bolt passed through a small round or elliptical rosette made of cast brass with grooved or beaded edges. The hole in the rosette was square, to fit the square shank of the bolt.

The secretary in figures 6 and 152 originally had rosette brasses. Reproduction rosettes are almost always stamped from thin sheet brass, and I had to make the missing rosettes for the secretary from rough blank castings furnished by a dealer in reproduction brasses. They look convincing from a distance, but a close look will quickly disclose the mechanical concentric surface texture produced by the modern metal-cutting lathe (in a friend's basement). The hand-scraped surface and slightly irregular outline of the original rosettes cannot be duplicated with modern machinery.

Rosette brasses can be seen on English furniture dating from as early as 1720. In the Colonies they were in wide use by 1760. Their popularity continued to the end of the eighteenth century, for they are simple and good looking and can be installed on a wide variety of furniture designs without detracting from the clarity of the lines.

HEPPLEWHITE PULLS

The advent of the Hepplewhite style after the Revolution called for entirely new brasses and an abrupt change in design (fig. 164). These brasses were widely used from about 1790 to 1820.

The posts remained similar to those of the rosette brasses, but the plates

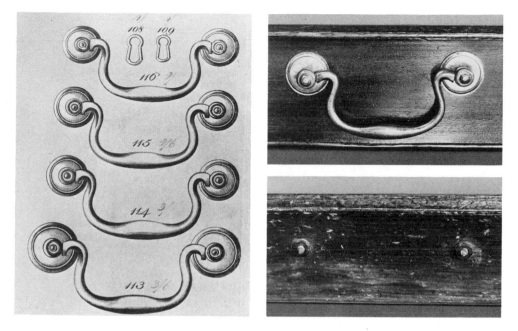

163. Left, *rosette pulls and keyhole inserts from a brass founder's catalog, about 1780, in the Victoria and Albert Museum;* Right, *a rosette pull installed on the drawer of a table of about 1760–80. Note that the holes for the posts are drilled above the center line of the drawer front to balance the proportions. Willow or Hepplewhite brasses would look off center in those same holes.*

were now die stamped with delicate patterns from thin, rolled-brass sheets. The bails became wider and hooked onto the posts from the outside. The patterns of the elliptical plates were either geometric (medallions, sunbursts), patriotic (mostly eagles and snakes but occasionally crossed cannons), or symbolic (beehive, dove, thistle, rose, acorn, grape, conch shell, sheaf of grain, horn of plenty). The variety is almost endless. The diemakers of the day were skilled in their craft, and their designs are usually sharp and clear. The more expensive plates are fire gilt. Some bails are marked with initials, probably of the maker (fig. 165).

Reproduction plates are cruder, fuzzier, and will lack the patina of age on the back, but they may be difficult to spot if they are well made and slightly corroded. The old posts were always cast, but reproductions are almost always turned from round stock, as we have already pointed out.

ADAM, SHERATON, AND EMPIRE PULLS

In the early nineteenth century, furniture was produced rapidly and styles diversified at increasing speed. We come now to such a multitude of patterns that I hesitate to go into them in detail. Perhaps we can skim them once over lightly.

The period is 1810–30, and the Adam influence shows itself in urns, Roman temples, and other neoclassic motifs in place of the earlier decora-

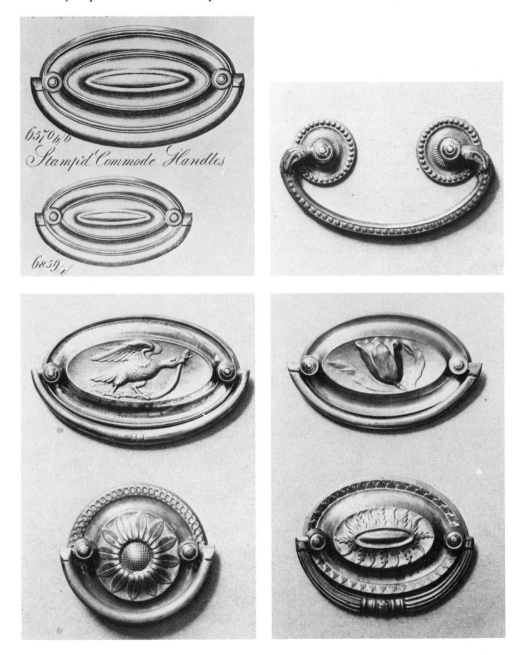

164. Hepplewhite handles, about 1780–1810. **Top,** *by far the most commonly seen is the simple concentric design (from a brass stamper's catalog in the Victoria and Albert Museum, indirectly dated about 1780–90). The photographs show a few of the many fancier designs, including* (**top right**) *a Hepplewhite adaptation of the Chippendale rosette pull (cf. fig. 163).*

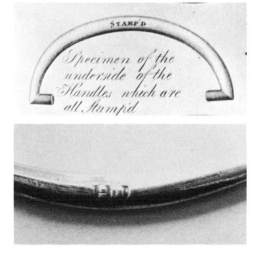

165. Top, *some brass stampers marked the bails with their initials, and the dealers' catalog called attention to the marks without disclosing the identity or even the initials of the maker. (This thoroughly anonymous catalog is dated by internal evidence about 1780–90; Victoria and Albert Museum.)* Bottom, *an enlarged view of the mark on a bail from a Hepplewhite brass, 1780–1800.*

tions on the elliptical plates. Sheraton furniture calls for a more angular effect, and so we have rectangular plates with clipped corners or quarter-circle cutouts and polygonal bails to match. Otherwise, the basic design is unchanged from the Hepplewhite pulls.

Some designers, beginning with Hepplewhite himself, preferred round pulls, and so we have a whole spate of knobs of thin stamped brass attached to a wood screw, all in one (fig. 166). Separate posts fall into disuse, and instead of the bail we have a ring, fastened at the top and hugging the outline of the plate. The lion's-head motif is common, and the ring may be in the beast's mouth.

That brings us into the Empire style, and here we find escutcheons and small knobs of ivory on dainty pieces. The wooden knob returns, but in a modern form—broad, flat, and usually fastened

166. *Knobs of stamped brass on a good Sheraton chest of about 1820–30. (Courtesy of Samuel T. Freeman & Co., Philadelphia.)*

167. *Pressed-glass knobs on a late Federal Shera-ton dresser. (Courtesy of Samuel T. Freeman & Co., Philadelphia.)*

to the drawer with a threaded hardwood dowel. Glass knobs are used occasionally—white, clear, or colored—cemented to steel screws and fastened with nuts on the inside of the drawers (fig. 167). Some of these knobs are cut, silvered, or delicately ornamented. Frankly, I think the best of them are corny, but if we find a good late piece with glass knobs, I would never advocate tearing them off and replacing them with willow brasses. On the contrary: here they are and here they belong. However, if one of a set is missing, we may have difficulty replacing it. The patterns are so varied that we can hardly expect the dealers to find an exact match in their stock. In that case I would still settle for a crude match in preference to replacing the whole set. Matching the late styles of hardware is troublesome at best. We are here at the end of the era of true antique furniture. The Industrial Revolution has started, and anything goes.

NAILS

Nails were used in American furniture from the beginning of Pilgrim times. Bible boxes, blanket chests, six-board chests, and early drawers are usually nailed. The popular notion that nails are somehow modern and that old furniture was put together exclusively with wooden pins is often heard, but anyone familiar with woodworking will know that pins are one thing and nails another. Each has its use, but the uses are different, and the earliest cabinetmakers knew that difference very well.

The earliest nails were imported from England, of course, but the equipment needed by a nailer is simple, and the making of nails soon became a widespread industry. A nail factory is recorded in the Colonies in 1731, and there must have been others.

The iron rod from which these nails

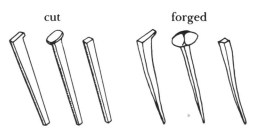

168. *The difference between cut and forged nails. Note the burrs left by the cutter on the cut nails.*

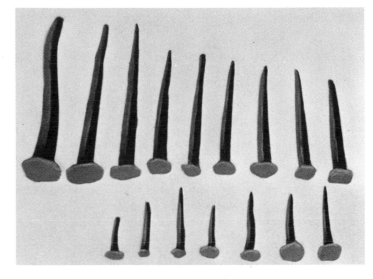

169. *Hand-forged nails and brads with rounded heads, slightly reduced (HHT).*

were made is said to have come mostly from Sweden and Russia via England, but much of it was undoubtedly made in this country. It was a material of high purity—soft, easily bent, but exceedingly tough and highly rust resistant. I have seen nails two hundred years old come out of old furniture with their blue scale entirely intact, as bright as the day they were made.

Early nails came in a variety of patterns and sizes, but they were almost always sharply rectangular in cross section and sharply pointed at the tip. Like any handmade product, no two of these nails are alike, but those in a set are all roughly the same length. Two styles of head were popular, as shown in figure 168. The nails with large, so-called rose heads were used mostly for hinges, but occasionally they serve to hold ends of flat moldings, to fasten end cleats on lids, and in a variety of other uses. The finish nails, with small heads, were used much more frequently in all phases of cabinetmaking. Small brads were often made with

roughly round heads or with no heads at all (figs. 169 and 170).

The cost of these nails was high, compared to our modern scale of values, but they were a product of very superior quality. The dense, work-hardened surface produced by hand forging, coupled with the ductility and toughness of the metal, combined to

170. *Hand-forged finishing nails, about actual size.*

give these early nails remarkable strength and serviceability.

Nail-making machinery was introduced about 1790; the issue of a patent for a nail-cutting machine to one Ezekiel Reed of Bridgewater, Massachusetts, is recorded in 1786. It did not take long for these machines to displace the tedious hand-forging process. The cut nails or "cold nails" were not quite as good as their hand-forged predecessors, but they were much cheaper. Made of the same soft iron, they lacked the toughness produced by forging, and they had square points.

Early cut nails may look like the hand-forged product at first glance, but a close examination quickly reveals the difference (fig. 168). For one thing, they are thicker and less tapered than handmade nails, and they end in a square tip quite unlike the thin, sword-like point of hand-forged nails. Furthermore, they show no hammer marks, but we may discern slight burrs made by the cutter all along two opposite edges of the nail. And, last, cut nails in one set are all exactly alike.

Obviously, then, nails can be a great help in setting a date on a piece of furniture. If a piece is made entirely with hand-forged nails it is most likely older than 1790, or 1800 at the latest. A piece made originally with cut nails is clearly of the nineteenth century. Many pieces made with hand-forged nails may also contain a few cut nails where repairs have been made long ago. In that case we shall look for holes of the earlier hand-forged nails. Once I was able to identify a fishy-looking base molding on a Colonial high chest as definitely not original when I found it to be fastened by cut nails and with *no older holes* to match those in the wood under the molding. Other moldings on the same chest were also refastened with cut nails, but neatly plugged holes of the earlier forged nails were clearly in evidence.

However, we may find nineteenth-century pieces made with hand-forged nails that some old codger simply happened to have around. Sizable caches of such nails still come to light every now and then. As usual, then, let us not be too dogmatic about isolated evidence. We must not judge a piece by a single nail but consider the nails along with all the other evidence that the expert examines in the process of reaching an opinion.

TACKS AND BRADS

Modern tacks are deceptively similar to the handmade product, and we may need a lens to make a clear-cut determination. We will consider the number and the placement of previous tack holes (especially in an upholstered piece) before we identify any tack as definitely handmade. However, the problem is not too serious—we shall see *very* few antique upholstered pieces with the original tacks still in them. Thin machine-cut brads may look a little like handmade brads, but again the lens will tell, and the burrs of the cutter will be visible.

WOOD SCREWS

The earliest wood screws appear in America about 1720, replacing nails as fastenings for hinges. These screws are crude, and their threads are rough. The shank is only roughly round, for it was forged, and marks of the hammer are often visible. The points of the screws were cut off square, the heads are not quite round, and the slot is narrow and usually off center. Only the flat-head style was made, and the length was rarely greater than half an inch.

With time, the quality of the screws improved, the threads became more regular, but the narrow slot persisted, and the point continued square. Making these screws by hand must have been a slow and difficult operation. It stands to reason that the product was very expensive, and so it is hardly surprising to see screws used so little in the eighteenth century. Their use on hinges was favored because nails must be clinched if they are to hold a hinge, and the clinching would disfigure the outside surface on drop-leaf tables, chest lids, and similar concealed hinge locations. We find early wood screws in a few other spots—securing table tops to their frames, holding cleats on lids and small tables, and fastening locks—but their use did not become widespread until after the Revolution. Screw-making machinery developed early in the nineteenth century, and screws became cheaper, but their appearance changed very little. The shank was now round, being made of drawn wire, and the threads were more regular but still remained rough (fig. 171). The head was still irregular and

the slot still narrow. Modern gimlet-point screws did not come on the market until much later, around 1860.

The wood screws used in repairs to the White House after the fire of 1814, shown in figure 171, are larger and better made than screws I have removed from early Colonial furniture, but I would be hard put to distinguish them from screws I have found in furniture of Revolutionary times. So I would say that wood screws are not very helpful for dating furniture. Rough, irregular screws are reassuring in that they are certainly old, but it is hard to say just how old, and even the presence of a few modern screws may mean no more than that the piece was repaired sometime after 1860.

The irregular threads of early screws do not cut a very good thread in the wood, and once they are removed they

172. An original cast-brass H hinge fastened by two iron screws and four brass pins (screws were expensive!)—one of a pair holding the door of a Colonial hanging cupboard made of pine. The skillful restorer will not disturb hardware attached with handmade screws. (The entire cupboard is shown in fig. 242.)

171. Three wood screws used in the repair of the White House after the fire of 1814 (removed in the 1952 restoration). Actual size.

cannot be expected to hold well when reinserted in the same hole. It is best to leave old screws alone, if at all possible, but if we have to remove them, we should mark them carefully so that we can put each back into its proper hole with a drop of white glue to help it hold. Old drop-leaf table hinges are often fastened with eight screws each, and the four screws nearer the hinge pin are usually slightly shorter than the other four. In general, old wood screws vary just enough so that the undersized ones will pull out and the oversized ones will split the wood if we do not get each back to its proper hole.

HINGES

The *staple* (or *cotter-pin*) *hinge* is the simplest and probably the earliest hinge generally used on American furniture (fig. 173). It consists of two forged staples, each about two or three inches long, linked together as shown in the sketch. Each half was pushed through a hole drilled at a slant through the board from the back, and the protruding points were spread apart and clinched back into the wood. This was neither the most elegant nor the most

durable arrangement, but it is simple and serviceable enough. After a time, the staples work loose and ultimately break. I would say that of the pieces originally equipped with staple hinges, perhaps four out of five have lost them by the time they reach us. The characteristic scars remain, however, and are a welcome mark of authenticity.

The staple hinge was popular from Pilgrim times almost up to the Revolution. We find it most commonly used on simple furniture of early Colonial time—Bible boxes, dower chests, blanket chests, and the simpler cupboards. As a consequence of its long period of popularity, the staple hinge is no great help in accurate dating, but an undisturbed pair of these hinges is—to me, at least—a very important plus for any piece of furniture (fig. 174). It is the kind of thing that experts notice.

More elaborate furniture usually carries more elaborate hinges. Today these hinges are called "ornamental," but the term is not particularly appropriate because early American hinges were mostly functional, and what decoration they provided was incidental. Five principal styles are usually distinguished: *butterfly, H, HL, rat-tail,* and

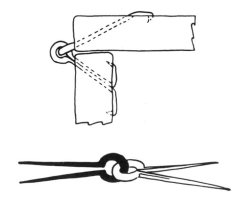

173. *Iron cotter-pin (staple) hinge.*

174. *Original cotter-pin hinge on the Hadley Bible box shown in figure 30. Such early hinges in this condition are rare.*

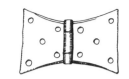

176. *Iron butterfly hinge.*

175. *Scar of a cotter-pin hinge on the lid of a high blanket chest made of sycamore wood, probably in Connecticut, in the first third of the eighteenth century.*

177. *Iron HL hinge.*

strap, all hand forged of soft iron, with the exception of the H and HL hinges, which sometimes come in cast brass.

The butterfly hinge is the oldest style, roughly contemporary with the cotter-pin hinge but going out of fashion a little sooner (fig. 176). We see it on drop-leaf tables and on cupboard doors, usually fastened with hand-forged round-head nails, clinched back or riveted over small iron washers. The hinge was made by folding two pieces of iron, properly cut out, over an iron pin, and hammering the folds together. For that reason, each leaf was tapered toward the edges, and the whole hinge was rough and irregular. Few of these hinges have survived intact, and they are mighty rare in any condition.

H and HL hinges, obviously named because of their shape, were used almost exclusively on the doors of cupboards, fastened with clinched nails, with rivets peened over an iron washer in back, with handmade screws, or with a combination of screws and pins (figs. 172 and 177). They are typical of Colonial times, but we find them on country

pieces of the Federal period as well. In general, I have seen them more frequently on Pennsylvania and New York furniture than on pieces from New England. They are rare (though not as rare as butterfly hinges) and seldom found in good condition. They are sought by collectors because they greatly enhance the charm of any cupboard and are (unsuccessfully) imitated by modern hardware manufacturers. If we ever need a handmade iron hinge, we shall have to order it from one of the small forges that are attempting to keep alive the ancient art of ironworking by hand. It would be treason to install trashy modern "Colonial" hardware on an original antique.

The rat-tail hinge is functionally quite different from the other hinges we have discussed (fig. 178). It is an indoor adaptation of the old hook-and-eye gate hinge, the hooks being fixed in the gatepost and the eyes attached to the gate. It is a demountable hinge: a door attached with rat-tail hinges can be removed by lifting it when it is open. These hinges are typical of Pennsyl-

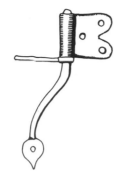

178. Iron rat-tail hinge.

vania, and their period is late Colonial to early Federal. Like all hinges, they are easily damaged, so that a good set is a rarity. However, let me add quickly that a good cupboard is quite a find in itself—hinges or no hinges.

Another very old style is the strap hinge, sometimes called *T hinge,* with a long tongue terminating in a circle or a spear point, like the ace of clubs (fig. 179). These are the strongest of old hinges and were preferred for sea chests, dower chests, and for the more substantial blanket chests. Occasionally we may see them on a cupboard, but their present-day decorative appeal was not appreciated by our ancestors, to whom this was just an ordinary strong hinge, like the one on a barn door. The older type of strap hinge did

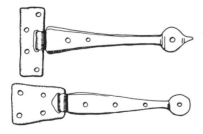

179. Early iron strap hinges.

not have a pin, but the tongue was merely pulled through a slot in the shorter plate and bent over. That makes a rattly connection, and from about the middle of the eighteenth century strap hinges were made with pins in the manner of modern hinges, and in that style they are still being made today (for barns, that is).

All the iron hinges discussed so far are of forged iron. The art of casting iron developed in the Colonies and flourished in the Republic, but cast-iron hinges did not reach the market before about 1820. They had the shape of modern rectangular hinges but were somewhat thicker and clumsier and often had only two holes in each half. The principal asset of these hinges was that they were cheap. We find them on all sorts of common softwood furniture of late Federal time, but cast iron is brittle, and the hinges went out of use when machine-made bent-steel hinges displaced them after the middle of the nineteenth century. Again, the presence of a pair of cast-iron hinges on a Colonial cupboard need not upset us, so long as we see marks of older hinges underneath or alongside. If the cast-iron hinges are original, however, then the piece is quite certainly late—probably after 1810 or so.

We have already said that brass was used for fittings on all high-grade furniture. Fine English cast-brass hinges with iron pins were available from early Colonial time. Most of them were rectangular, like modern hinges (fig. 180), but one sees brass H hinges occasionally on early Colonial pieces (fig. 172). Many of these hinges are well finished, and they were costly in their day. They are almost always attached with hand-made iron screws or with a combination of iron screws and brass pins.

Cast brass is not very strong anyway,

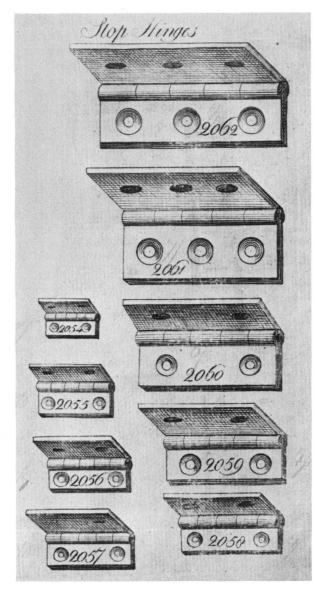

180. The cabinetmaker had no problem selecting just the right size of cast-brass "stop" (butt) hinges from the supplier's catalog. (Victoria and Albert Museum.)

and old brass was full of flaws, as we have already mentioned. For that reason old brass hinges do not last long in positions where they are strained, as on desk lids, for example. As a result, we now usually find nineteenth-century or modern brass hinges holding the lids of Colonial and early Federal slant-top desks, assuming that any hinges are left at all. There is always someone who forgets to pull out the slides that hold the desk lid, so that desk-lid hinges have one of the highest mortality rates among furniture parts.

The late brass hinges were made of rolled sheet brass, bent to receive the iron hinge pin. This manner of fabrication produces a much more serviceable brass hinge at a considerably lower price. Consequently, the cast-brass hinge quickly went into disuse when the sheet-brass hinge became available in the mid–nineteenth century.

LOCKS

If you have ever seen the complex and delicate locks produced by French blacksmiths of the fifteenth century, you may be less surprised by the precision and intricacy of the locks we find on the earliest American furniture. In a lock, of course, the inside is by far the most interesting, and one must remove the lock from its drawer or its cupboard door to see much of the inside.

The earliest locks are attached with clinched nails, and people who remove such locks just to peek inside ought to have their heads examined instead. Later locks are usually attached with handmade screws, rusted in place and often very difficult to remove. So it is that having handled hundreds of locks, I have seen only one or two from the inside.

Locks are usually mounted on drawers of chests and desks, on cupboard doors, and on desk lids, arranged in such a way that the bolt extends out and engages a slot when the piece is locked. Slightly different locks are found on dower chests: a notched or perforated tongue is mounted on the lid and extends into the lock when the lid is closed. The tongue is engaged when the piece is locked. The finer locks are mounted on a brass plate, which is the only part that shows on the inside of the piece, but most ordinary locks have iron plates. Modern cabinet locks, including those of the late nineteenth century, have broad thin bolts, but Colonial and early Federal locks usually have stubby bolts, squarish in cross section. The better locks may have double or triple bolts. Country furniture often has ingenious devices to extend the utility of a single lock, indicating that locks were expensive. Chests and desks may contain wooden bolts and various contraptions that "lock" all drawers and can be actuated only from the inside of one particular drawer, which has the usual metal lock. Some of these arrangements show great technical ingenuity on the part of the cabinetmaker, and in my own way of looking at these things they greatly add to the interest of a piece.

Locks were often smashed for reasons that are not too difficult to imagine, and a damaged or missing lock is (to me) a serious flaw. I much prefer pieces with the locks intact, even if the keys are lost, as they almost always are. It is not too difficult to make a key to fit an old lock, even without removing the lock from its place, unless, of course, the whole mechanism is rusted shut; that will be the case only if the piece has been kept in a damp cellar or outdoors.

If the lock is sound, any self-respecting locksmith can make a key for it in a very short time, provided suitable old-fashioned key blanks can be found in this cylinder-lock era. Most of the old cabinet locks require hollow keys that turn on a round post in the lock. Blanks for such keys are available from dealers in reproduction brasses. Those of us who have more than the average man's share of patience and manual skill, however, may actually enjoy cutting the whole key out of a piece of brass bar stock. There is nothing like the thrill that comes when an old lock finally

181. *Sturdy brass lock with four stubby bolts mounted on a fine Newport desk of about 1770–80 and held in place by large hand-made screws.*

182. *Small, comparatively inexpensive iron lock held in place by hand-forged nails on the 1760–80 chest in figure 129.*

183. *Small iron lock on a drawer of a plain Sheraton stand of about 1810–20. Note that the nails are less well made and the bolt is a little thinner than those in figure 182. Otherwise, one sees little difference, on the outside.*

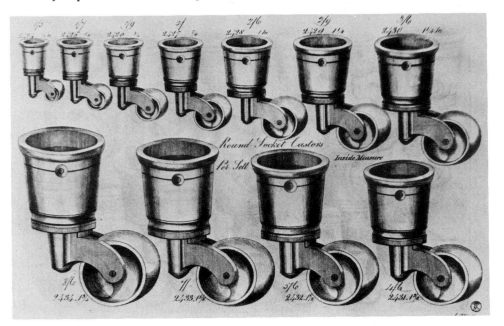

184. Top, *a page from a brass founder's catalog of about 1830 shows the wide range of caster sizes available* (Victoria and Albert Museum). Bottom, *an actual caster of the same type.*

yields to delicate persuasion. It is great sport—ask any safecracker.

CASTERS

There was a time in the gaslight era when everything had to roll on casters. Brass beds and chiffoniers, sofas and tables—all found themselves with little wheels at their feet, more for looks than for any useful purpose. The caster-borne Hadley chest and Brewster chair were so equipped in the nineties, but that does not mean that all casters are necessarily modern. Quite to the contrary, the idea of mounting wheels on furniture is rather old, but few specimens have survived. I am told that Colonial casters are known, but I have never seen them on an American piece. Among all the bizarre feet designed by Thomas Chippendale, none bear casters, at least not in his sketches published in London in 1754.

From about 1790 on, delicate metal casters appear on the slender legs of Hepplewhite and Sheraton furniture (mostly on stands and small tables), and casters become downright common on tables, chests, sofas—everything—when the Empire style takes over (fig. 184). The characteristic Empire lion's-paw foot, made of cast or stamped brass, usually carries a caster.

Casters break easily, and those that we see on antique furniture are often replacements. The style of pieces that are likely to bear original casters is so distinctive that we almost always date the furniture accurately without having to consider the hardware. It may be difficult to decide whether casters are original on a given piece, and I am usually guided by the style books in deciding whether a broken caster is to be replaced or the remaining three thrown away.

Part Three

8
THE
PHILOSOPHY
OF
RESTORATION

You always have questions when it comes to deciding what is to be restored and how. If there ever was ground for indecision, this is it. All aspects must be considered, the evidence is hardly ever clear, and a wrong guess means a botch.

By all means think twice or even ten times before getting out the saw, but once the decision is made, let's not worry about it too much. A successful restoration must proceed along a carefully considered path. It is my experience that whenever I have a bright idea in the middle of a job and quickly put it into effect, it usually turns out to have been wrong.

When it comes to the planning, each of us must work out our own philosophy. All I can do is outline the extremes of attitude that I have seen, present my own views, and leave the rest to you. I am, of course, quite sure that my way is the best—in fact, I have never known a restorer who did *not* think his way best. And as soon as you can prove to yourself that *your* way is better than mine, you will have become an expert.

There are some experts, notably including the dozen finest antiques dealers in the country, who summarily reject any piece that is not altogether (well, almost altogether) original. These are the people who buy the most important pieces at the most important auctions, and some of these shops contain more ultra-first-rate pieces than many a major museum. "Money is largely taken for granted here," one of the leading dealers told me, "but it is not enough. The customer must have impeccable taste and an appreciation of the quality we offer." On these Olympian heights of the collecting world, only brasses are freely restored. A new leg, a new drawer, or a patched-up desk lid simply would not be condoned.

It is true, of course, that the finest American furniture was always valuable, and even though it may have gone out of fashion, it rarely found itself relegated to the barn. Consequently, the damage one finds on block-front chests of drawers or on bombé secretaries will be, more than likely, the result of misguided upkeep or excessive refinishing rather than the usual "knocked off and lost" sort of mutila-

185. *The bottom section of the secretary shown in figure 6 during restoration. New wood is being glued into the lid where the hinges were ripped out, and a new foot and front base molding are being made. One of the drawer fronts has been cleaned of the crackled and discolored Victorian varnish to show the color of the cherry wood and to try new brasses in the old holes. The top bookcase section, curiously enough, required no restoration at all and is stored separately while this work is in progress.*

tion that plagues the ordinary stuff.

At the opposite extreme we have the optimist who drives out into the country and buys a cheap, semiantique chest from some picker—in the rough, of course—then spends two hundred hours repairing it and thinks he has something when he has finished. I know the feeling well, and it is not so terribly long ago that I did just that myself. The paint remover, steel wool, sandpaper, and lacquer all cost money, and figuring the restorer's time even at ten cents an hour, the price of the work may exceed the value of the piece. Furthermore, it always will be a cheap chest no matter how much skill and devotion may have been lavished on it.

So there we have it. In order to war-rant the expenditure of time, the piece must be of sufficient quality—not necessarily *best* on Albert Sack's scale in *Fine Points of Furniture* but at least good enough to rate *good.* The finer the lines and the rarer the type, the more worthwhile the restoration—except, as we have said, that the finest pieces are usually intact anyway.

When it came from its attic, the secretary in figure 6 lacked three quarters of one leg, a large piece of molding, pieces of the lid, and most of the brasses (fig. 185). The piece is not exquisite, but it is well made and the lines are clean. The type and size are highly desirable for modern living. Restoration involved no question of correctness of any detail. The cost of the work

186. Queen Anne tall chest on frame, about 1750–70.

was less than a tenth of the value of the finished piece. Very definitely, this is *minor* restoration.

The high chest on frame has quite a different story (figs. 129 and 186). It is a good piece, but it lacked all of the base. I bought it cheaply when the stock of an antiques shop in the Georgetown section of Washington was being dispersed after the owner's death. I am told that this chest stood in his shop for thirty years while the dealer tried to decide how to restore it. No marks of bracket feet could be found underneath, so it seems that the chest once stood on a frame, but the shape of the frame or its height could only be guessed. No matter how well I do my research before I restore such a piece, I shall never know whether I did it right. Only the comparative rarity of a seven-tier carcase (for another, see no. 613 in Miller's *American Antique*

Furniture), the fine workmanship on the drawers, and that bold and handsome cornice made me decide to go ahead. This is *major* restoration and just about as far as I care to go. The value of a heavily restored piece always will be restricted, no matter how skillfully the work was done.

RESTORING FOR USE

We are concerned here with restoration for use in the home. Authenticity may be important, but utility is essential. As a piece of art, the armless Venus de Milo leaves nothing to be desired, but a chest of drawers without legs is hardly the most practical thing, especially when you need something from the bottom drawer.

If we were restoring for a museum— and some of us may at some time be involved in such an enterprise—quite a different philosophy would be required. First of all, we would hardly expect to handle a piece so incomplete that it would require a *choice* of design for the restoration. A curator is not likely to accept such a piece. Authenticity is paramount in a museum, and utility counts for nothing. All the piece really has to do is stand up under its own weight. If you tried to sit in one of the fine Pilgrim chairs in the Metropolitan's American wing, the rush seat would almost certainly give way, and I am ready to bet that the superb block-front furniture in Boston's Museum of Fine Arts has drawers that stick.

How to make a piece useful without detracting from its authenticity is a dilemma that each of us will have to face according to circumstances. For myself, I prefer to bend in the direction of authenticity. I much prefer original brasses if I can find them (even if that means paying a premium price), and I severely discount even good pieces that are badly damaged or lack essential parts.

PRESERVE THE MARKS OF AGE

The aim of our restoration, then, is to make things useful without making them look new. The mellow quality of the antique piece is preserved only if we leave the marks of time on the slightly darkened outer layer of the wood. A chipped and discolored finish can come off, but wood must not be removed. A time-worn butterfly table may show imperfections here and there (fig. 187), but if the careless restorer tried to remove the rings that some ancient dishes have left on its surface, he would have to scrape rather deeply and would seriously damage the quality and value of the piece.

Henry Taylor wrote, "I have a secretary on whose slanting top some child once carved a rough ship and the name *Mary*. This secretary is more interesting to me with Mary's name on the lid than if the youthful indiscretion had been planed out. A banister-back armchair has the initials *I.H.* and *A.B.* deeply carved in the left arm. It is a pleasing touch, and we may wonder who I.H. and A.B. were, where they lived, and when. If I were the owner of the finest mahogany Chippendale armchair in existence, on the arm of which some old vandal had carved his initials, these initials would remain quite undisturbed."

Neither should we go out of our way

187. *Early Colonial butterfly table with ring stains on the top. The careful restorer will leave these marks, for they can be removed only by deep scraping, and such treatment would not enhance the charm or interest of the piece. (Courtesy Israel Sack, Inc., N.Y.; Taylor & Dull photo.)*

to remove evidence of legitimate wear, unless the wear seriously detracts from the esthetic appeal of the piece. A chair is not seriously damaged if it has lost an inch in height by normal wear, and a secretary is just as handsome when its finials are slightly chipped. The instances where wear can disfigure a piece are few. A Spanish foot, for example, looks odd if it loses an inch from wear, and such damage, natural though it may be, probably should be repaired.

Novices usually like their antiques skinned and brightly varnished, and many dealers cater to them. It is indeed a fortunate law of nature that they usually lack both the skill and the cash that would permit them to find and damage a really good piece. As collectors grow more discerning, they tend to lean toward less and less restoration. By the time they have learned to recognize the fine pieces—and by the time their resources have improved so that they can afford them—by that time they have also learned not to skin them.

About the time Bicentennial preparations were getting started, and museums were sprouting everywhere like mushrooms on a warm autumn night, a new fashion swept the tight little world of museum display art. The new idea was that exhibits should evoke a feeling of "reality" and that objects on display should look the way they did when they were first made—in other words, almost new. "A museum must speak to the public; it cannot be just a warehouse of musty relics," or so the story went, and a new era of skinning fine pieces was upon us.

In Philadelphia there is a deservedly famous highboy with a remarkable carving of Aesop's fox with the grapes on the low middle drawer. For generations it had stood there, getting darker and dustier, until it was brought out for the big show—very scientifically, of course, and photographed in infrared, ultraviolet, and every other color. The infrared picture showed a faint impression of two bands of fretwork, one under the cornice and the other in the moldings of the midsection. Apparently, some early owner had had the fret removed.

So, to make the highboy look properly contemporary (with George Washington, not with ourselves), they now carefully skinned it with alcohol down to the bare mahogany, glued on two fake bands of fretwork, buffed the brasses to a high shine, and sprayed the whole thing with several coats of lacquer, like a fine soapbox racer. It is still a superlative highboy, and it certainly does not look musty any more. It gleams!

Thirty years from now, museum laboratories will have gadgets that will make their present toys look antique by comparison. I can just see a learnedly outraged article in *Antiques*, a generation hence, bemoaning the Bicentennial skinning of important pieces. Future Philadelphia technicians will be stung by the rebuke of that respected journal. They will grab their late-model quantitative digital surface analyzer, aim it at the highboy, and the electronic readout will say ACETATE LACQUER CIRCA 1975—NO TRACE OF ORIGINAL FINISH.

EXCESSIVE REFINISHING

Once I saw an advertisement in the Sunday paper for a pine cupboard and other antiques, and as the people made sense over the phone, I went over to look at the stuff. It was a man and wife, and they were pickers, as a hobby. They would drive into the backwoods of Pennsylvania, pick up some broken-down tulip-poplar furniture, load it into their station wagon, and haul it home. Then he would "fix" it with a jim-dandy rotary sander she had bought him as a birthday present. He would attack the furniture like a fiend, and you can imagine what he did to it. The "finished" (and finished they were!) pieces had not a straight line or a square corner left in them. The wood was not only bare but plowed and furrowed with the circular marks of the sander. The formerly round spindles of plank-bottom chairs were now polygonal in cross section, and the cupboard moldings looked like quartered fence rails. It was such an incredible mess that I bought a cheap cupboard just to show people how completely a piece can be ruined by skinning.

Excessive refinishing ruins more antiques than all other causes put together. I know several large shops that buy old furniture from pickers by the van load—and have every stick of it skinned. I have seen row upon row of slat-back, plank-bottom, and Windsor chairs that looked as if they had been made yesterday and sloppily shellacked this morning. All the shellac in China will not restore the outer layer of wood, and nothing can repair the ravages of a rotary sander.

Any handmade piece of furniture will show marks of the plane on all flat surfaces (fig. 135). We may not always be able to see these marks, but sensitive fingers will feel them. Mortises, dovetails, carving, and difficult work in general will be marked by scored lines (figs. 131 and 144). Turnings will show the spiral marks left by the turner's chisel as it advanced over the slowly revolving wood (fig. 188), and scored lines will mark the spots where holes were drilled for chair stretchers. The sharp mark of the chisel, placed by eye

188. Lower corner of a turned butterfly table. Though refinished, it retains marks of the turner's chisel, old paint, wear, and evidence of age. An unwise use of the scraper and/or sandpaper would obliterate these guarantees of authenticity and ruin the antique "feel" of the table (HHT).

and moved in a decisive cut, identifies the skillful craftsman. The refinisher with any sense will preserve all these marks, not by working around them but by keeping the hand light so as not to dig below the surface of the wood. This goes for scraping, sanding, or what have you. We want to present the old surface, not produce a new one, for once the old surface is gone, the piece will look just like a reproduction. Deeply refinished pieces are untouchables in the best collecting circles.

FORMAL FURNITURE

People in the antiques trade have a general tendency to overrestore and overfinish. There was a time (around 1910) when even Pilgrim furniture was scraped, planed, and polished until it now looks as if it had been made in 1910. Similarly, an early Colonial tavern table, originally made to serve in the kitchen of that day, should not be swathed in eight coats of shellac buffed to a mirror finish, and a simple Windsor chair should not shine as if it were made of glass.

But when we find an elegant sideboard with herringbone inlays, medallions, and what have you, or a Duncan Phyfe table festooned with acanthus, then we can polish to our heart's content. These pieces were made expressly for a little friendly ostentation, and if there is a big ring where the old lady kept her potted fern, that stain adds nothing to the formal feeling and we should try to remove it. High gloss is proper here, and sharp corners are expected. In general, the formal character of elegant pieces should be preserved or restored, if it is obscured by a finish dulled through the years.

Formal pieces often have large, elaborate brasses. To some of us they may seem a little too rich and gaudy, but this is where they belong. We certainly would never mount such handles on a simple chest of pine.

IMPROVEMENTS ARE NOT ALLOWED

Perhaps I need not repeat that restoration means bringing back to the original condition. Under no circumstances should restorers take it upon themselves to improve the lines or add features that were not there. This is no place for genius! Even if no fraud is intended, embellishment is clearly faking.

Fancy scrolling on the chunky boards of an ordinary cupboard, elegant fluting on the formerly plain legs of a table, fine molding applied where there was none—these are standard tricks from the faker's bag. Unless they are done with superb skill, these changes are certain to be obvious to the experienced eye. No matter how good, they detract instead of adding. Once I saw spindly claw-and-ball feet carved out of the square front legs of a simple Colonial wing chair. This "improvement" reduced the value of the chair by more than half.

When a piece offers no internal evidence for the design of missing parts (as in the case of the missing frame of the chest on frame in fig. 186), then we must search for examples to find out how such detail was handled on other pieces of this type and style. A small but good reference library comes in handy here, and I refer the reader to the Bibliography in the back of this book.

Naturally, one cannot expect to find illustrated every single detail of every piece, but we shall find enough variations of every type to cover most of our needs. The correct scrolls and turning, the form of moldings, the shape of feet —all the essential details follow definite patterns, and we should not have much trouble finding examples.

"No collector who has access to these books has any possible excuse to

189. Old, crude, but effective repair of the post of an early slat-back chair. It detracts from the value, of course, but adds to the interest, in my opinion.

offer for bad mistakes of style or design in his work of restoration," said Henry Hammond Taylor. "No tavern tables with claw-and-ball feet, no turnip-foot chests of drawers with glass knobs, no inlaid mahogany chests with large ball feet will be allowed to add a high note of ghastly individuality to his collection. A sufficient production of such curiosities may be safely entrusted to our large furniture manufacturers."

OLD REPAIRS AND ALTERATIONS

Occasionally one finds an excellent old piece that was damaged and repaired long ago. These repairs may be fairly crude, but as long as they are still effective, I am inclined to leave them undisturbed. The Colonial candlestand in figure 78, for example, has a thin top that must have split perhaps within fifty years after the piece was made. Someone nailed two cleats across the bottom of this board to hold it together. The hand-forged nails that were used are evidence that the repair certainly was made before 1800, probably long before. I own a slat-back armchair with one of the back posts broken at the seat. The break is mended with three iron straps held by nails (fig. 189). It is a remarkably sturdy repair job, and I have no intention of trying to improve upon it.

Through the years, some old pieces have been altered for various reasons, and the alterations may have been less than altogether successful. For example, I have seen a scroll-top highboy with half the bonnet cut off to make the highboy fit into an upstairs room that had a low ceiling. Such mutilation needs to be restored, of course. Many good chairs were cut down and some of them converted into rockers. About the most striking example I know of this sort of abuse is the Lord armchair in the collection of the Connecticut Historical Society (fig. 190). This is a Flemish chair of about 1700 that was once straight and uncomfortable and did not suit the taste of some later owner. The feet were cut off, rockers installed, the old arms removed, the front posts cut down, and new, shorter, and more flaring arms installed. A thick squab (seat cushion) over a new and incongruous splint seat made up for the loss in height. Although the work was competently done and the change is interesting from a historical point of view, the result is offensive esthetically. One has to consider carefully whether or not such a fine piece should be restored to what we think was its original appearance. I would not presume to try to decide the question here.

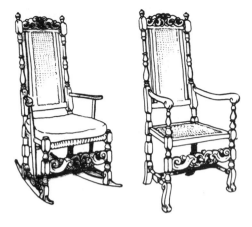

190. Left, *a Flemish armchair of about 1700 that has been altered and converted to a rocking chair.* Right, *the same chair as we think it was originally.*

WHO SHALL DO THE WORK?

Repairers and restorers of antique furniture advertise in magazines, newspapers, and classified directories, but don't be misled by the profusion of the ads. It will take a lot of looking and even more talking before you can hope to find one that meets your standards of quality and reliability. When you finally think you have found one, I suggest you start with some unimportant little job and work up. It might take several starts and could be a discouraging process.

For years I was on the lookout for a good wood turner, for example, but the best I was able to find was a friendly mechanic with a nice wood lathe buried under a pile of scrap lumber in a corner of his shop. Having moved the lumber we found that it was necessary to repair the motor. Then we had to find all the turning chisels, unused in decades, and sharpen them. When the good fellow finally took a piece of wood, started it spinning, and tried to demonstrate his "skill," I quickly realized that serious harm would soon come to him and (what is worse) the lathe if I did not manage to distract him somehow. I proposed, as a ploy, that he teach me. He seized upon the idea with enthusiasm, and with the help of a good book on wood turning, which I borrowed from the library and surreptitiously studied while the old boy was not around, I actually learned enough to make the post for a Windsor chair (fig. 42). What with the motor, the tools, and the library work, the post took just under twenty hours to make, but now I know how to make the next one.

We may be lucky enough to find a good commercial craftsman somewhere, but the odds are against it. Perhaps we may discover a retired accountant or postman or business executive who loves woodwork and has the tools in his basement. He may be devoid of imagination, but he has developed the skill and can do good work under tactful guidance. Alternatively, we may find a bearded craftsman of the counterculture generation who knows what he is doing, in spite of appearances. They are rare, of course, but a few of these former freedom fighters have become very good woodworkers.

Beware of the "expert restoration specialist" who boasts fancy credentials, drops a lot of names, insists that he knows best, and ignores your instructions. His talk is usually far ahead of his woodworking talent. After all, the piece is *yours,* and you will find it much easier to live with your own mistakes than with the goofs made by some loudmouth who thinks that he knows it all.

———

So we can conclude that no matter how the work gets done, the philosophy of our restoration shall be to bring the piece to a state that is most appropriate for the purpose for which it was originally intended. And when in doubt, we might better err by doing too little rather than too much. G. B. Shaw is reported to have said that people would be happier if they talked more and did less. That idea has merit when it comes to restoring good furniture.

9
TOOLS
AND
MATERIALS

The tool chest of the early American cabinetmaker was very simple, and the quality of his tools was miserable by present-day standards. When we consider the crudeness of his equipment, we can only marvel at the accuracy of the work he was able to accomplish. For our restorations, we might as well use the best modern tools available (if only to make up for our own inadequacy). Even so, our set of tools need not be much larger than that of our forefathers.

EDGED TOOLS

We shall need two planes: a small "block" plane and a "smooth no. 4" plane. A universal rabbet plane with a set of blades is useful for moldings and such. A spoke shave is handy for making spindles and legs. Three or four chisels (⅛, ¼, ½, and 1 inch wide) will round out our edged-tool department. We should select planes and chisels of good quality. For accurate work, edged tools must be kept razor sharp, and we

191. The names of planes have been the same since the Middle Ages. (Wood engraving from a nineteenth-century tool catalog.)

JOINTER

FORE

JACK

SMOOTH

will soon find that it is impossible to keep a keen edge on a poor piece of steel.

HAND SAWS

A ripsaw, a fine crosscut saw, a small backsaw (sometimes called miter saw), as fine as you can obtain, and a coping saw with an assortment of blades are all we shall need. A dovetail saw, which is nothing but a very fine, thin, small backsaw, is very useful but not too easy to find. In general, the thinner saws with more teeth per inch are the most useful in our kind of work, except, of course, for ripping softwood. That takes forever with a fine saw. Saws of the highest quality are a good investment.

POWER TOOLS

As for the arsenal of woodworking machinery one sees in many suburban basements these days, it may come in handy but not too often. Machines are very useful for production work, where the same operation is repeated many times. If I were to build a house, for example, I could hardly get along without a sturdy table saw. Furniture restoration, however, is a cut-and-try sort of job, and the time required to set up the machine for a certain operation may be longer than it takes to do the same job by hand. I have used table saws and thickness planers to dress down my lumber accurately and to rough out moldings, and a friend lets me use his enormous band saw to rough-cut cabriole legs, but if I were to divide the cost of this machinery by the number of times I had occasion to use it, the charge per job would be prohibitive.

Two machines, however, are particularly useful for the restorer of antiques:
a wood lathe and a vibrating (reciprocating) sander. The lathe should have a useful length of at least 30 inches between centers, to allow for the longest Windsor parts and ordinary table legs. It should be heavy and have a motor of at least $\frac{1}{3}$ horsepower. Cheap small lathes are not much help. They wobble and chatter and cannot turn fast enough to do good work.

The reciprocating sander is a great help in smoothing table tops, drawer fronts, and similar large unbroken surfaces—but I hasten to point out that the same work can be done just as well by hand with a little extra elbow grease. The machine is only useful for rough sanding; the finishing must be done by hand anyhow. We should select one of the makes where the sanding shoe oscillates in a straight line, back and forth. Some vibrating sanders describe a circular motion and they will leave a hardwood surface covered with little circles. The sander should be used only on unbroken surfaces. It will seriously disfigure moldings, corners, edges, carvings, or turnings. *Warning:* Belt sanders or rotary sanders, including the sander attachments often sold with electric drills, must *never* be used on fine furniture. I repeat: *never*.

DRILLS

A small, inexpensive, hand-cranked drill with a set of good carbon or high-speed twist-drill bits from $\frac{1}{16}$ to $\frac{1}{4}$ inch will do for the small holes we have to drill. I know that the reader is just itching to buy an electric drill, and perhaps already has one. They are very handy for metal, but in wood they have a way of going *bzzzt*—and suddenly there is a hole where we did not want a hole. Hand drills are slower but surer. A brace with a set of auger bits or an electric drill with wood-boring bits from ⅜ to 1 inch will do for the large holes, but we shall drill very few holes larger than ½ inch.

MEASURING EQUIPMENT

A good 6-foot steel tape, a common yardstick, and a carpenter's metal square will give us accurate length and right angles. An inexpensive 6-inch outside caliper is handy—and necessary if we try any turning.

FILES AND STONES

A professional cabinetmaker hardly ever uses a file, but to the amateur files are useful for rounding, smoothing, fitting, and many other delicate operations. I use an 8-inch mill file (medium fine), a 10-inch half-round bastard (medium coarse), two or three rat-tail files from 6 to 10 inches, and a shoemaker's half-round rasp, which I find more convenient than ordinary wood rasps. For cabinetwork, cheap files seem to do just as well as expensive ones. There is a new kind of rasp, made of perforated steel with all the edges sharpened, that is useful for rough forming. Contrary to the advertising that comes with it, however, it is no substitute for a plane or chisel.

To keep edged tools sharp, we shall need a combination sharpening stone, fine on one side, coarse or medium coarse on the other. Vitrified silicon carbide stones give the best service. Chisels and planes should not be ground with the edge perfectly straight; with time we should impart a slight convex curve to the edge, in the manner of the old cabinetmakers. We shall find that the planes in particular will handle much more easily on large surfaces when ground that way.

BRUSHES

We shall need only one good brush— for applying shellac. I prefer a soft 2-inch brush of very good quality and with long bristles for this task. A good ½-inch artist's brush is useful for touching up, but all the rest of our brushes can be of the dime-store variety. We shall use them for paint remover and for lacquer, both of which will eventually ruin any brush because they attack the compound with which the bristles are set.

MISCELLANEOUS SMALL TOOLS

In addition to the usual pliers and screwdrivers, we may use a small hammer (smaller than the usual carpenter's hammer); a rubber-tipped or plastic-tipped hammer; a small rawhide mallet; a 6-inch locking pliers, 4-inch diagonal cutting pliers, or 4-inch end nipper (for extracting stubborn nails); a couple of double-edged scrapers; a 1½-inch and a 3-inch putty knife; a couple of small nail setters; a hand sanding block of the type that holds the paper securely clamped; and a special glue-injecting syringe.

All these are standard items with the exception of the syringe. We use it to shoot glue into stubborn joints, and the specialty houses sell syringes for that particular purpose. However, an ordinary 2-cc glass or plastic syringe with an extra thick hypodermic needle will do the same very nicely. These syringes are sold in drugstores, and they are exactly the same implement dope addicts use in their illegal activities. That makes it tough on the restorer of antiques, and the best I can suggest is that you make friends with some physician or try one of the laboratory supply houses. They might be willing to sell you a box of disposable plastic syringes without asking silly questions.

RUBBER BANDS

Much of our gluing can be set with a rubber band (fig. 192) or with a good tourniquet. The rubber I use is the same as sold by hobby shops officially for model airplane motors and clandestinely for slingshots. The thickest rubber (slingshot grade) is best for our purpose. If your town is so well policed that slingshot rubber cannot be found, pick up a blown-out inner tube along the highway and cut it into long strips.

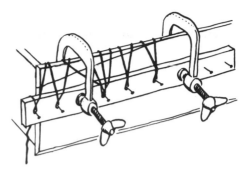

192. Two boards, each with a row of nails, are clamped on the two sides of the drawer front. A long rubber band holds the splice while the glue sets.

CLAMPS

When it comes to clamps, we might as well have what seems like too many. The first veneer job will convince us

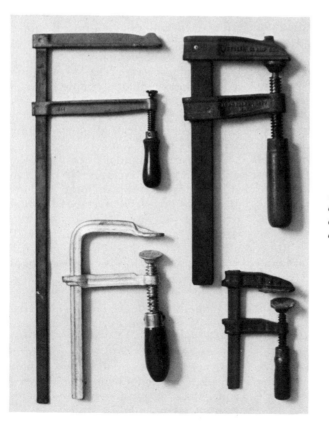

193. Slide-bar clamps are quickly adjustable over a wide range. They come in a variety of weights, sizes, and constructions.

that we do not have enough. It is useful to cement small patches of untempered hardboard or plywood to the jaws of metal clamps so they will not mark the wood.

Deep-throated aluminum C-clamps with a 4-inch or 6-inch opening are good, but quick-action slide-bar clamps are better, for they are easier to set and more flexible in use (fig. 193). Spring clamps are inexpensive and quick (fig. 194), and ordinary clothespins are handy for little jobs. For spanning large pieces, a couple of pairs of pipe-back adjustable gluing clamps will take care of all but the biggest jobs. Old-line cabinetmakers prefer hand screws—the large two-screw clamps with wooden jaws—for they do not mark the wood and can be set on surfaces that are not parallel (fig. 195). Hand screws are fairly costly unless we make them ourselves, and they take up a lot of space in a small workshop. Somehow I have never learned to appreciate their virtues. I have a nice old pair of them, and there they hang, on the wall, adding to the professional appearance of the place.

GLUES

One of the trademarks of the old-time cabinetmaker's shop was the glue pot, kept warm all day and diffusing its none-too-subtle aroma throughout the premises. Like so many quaint materials of the "good old days," the hide, hoof, and fish glues have now been replaced by more modern (and much more effective) adhesives: polyvinyl resin white glues, aliphatics, phenol-resorcinol adhesives, and the various epoxy resin glues. The old gelatin glues have only one advantage: they are removable with cold water.

The white glues (Elmer's Glue-All is

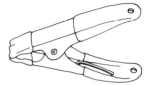

194. A spring clamp is useful for small jobs.

the most widely distributed, but there are many other brands of equivalent quality) are sold ready to use in liquid form. They keep well, are easily applied from their polyethylene plastic squeeze-bottles, require only a short clamping time (about an hour or two), and give a strong joint. They are elastic

195. Large, old-fashioned hand screws, all wood, marked *NATHAN BUTTRICK CARLISLE MASS.* on the end grain, mid–nineteenth century.

and transparent when dry and do not stain light-colored woods. I prefer them for most of my work. (*Note*: The white glues are not particularly water resistant but some are especially compounded to be water soluble, "for use in schools." The main purpose is to make them easier to wash out of Junior's clothes, but the washable glues are also weaker, and cabinetmakers avoid them.)

Much like the white glues in packaging, and distributed by many of the same firms, are the new aliphatic glues, also called "professional" by some distributors. They are yellowish to brownish in color and leave an inconspicuous glue line. Their main advantage over white glues lies in faster setting and much less slippage when first applied. One has to be quick with them, but they make complicated assemblies easier. That makes them worth keeping around for many jobs.

Casein glues, made from milk solids, were tops when I first started, but they have now been replaced by plastic-resin powders to be mixed with water for immediate use, like the old caseins. The plastics are very good, almost as strong as epoxies, and cheaper, but that is hardly a factor to us fine craftsmen, is it?

Phenol-resorcinol glues come as a liquid resin with a powdered hardener. They have to be mixed in just the right proportions and, once mixed, are good for no more than an hour or two. They give a very strong and totally waterproof bond, but who takes his antiques into the swimming pool? Anyway, many experts swear by them.

Epoxy glues come in many varieties and colors, but we shall use only the clear kind. The resin and hardener have to be mixed just before use in exactly the right proportion. Some set in a few minutes, but others need a day or two, depending on temperature. Premeasured packets are available and make the mixing much easier. The bond is extremely strong, and a good joint can be produced even if the surfaces don't fit too well. That is a great advantage in repairing old breaks such as you find in chairs and tables. The strength of the bond makes it possible to glue up very small surfaces, even chair rungs that broke straight across. Obviously, these are the best glues for small patch jobs. The only disadvantage is the gloppy mess they are until they set. They will not come off your hands with soap and water, and as for washing them out of your work clothes —forget it. They can be removed with acetone but only as long as they have not yet set.

Epoxy is the glue to use on oily woods like teak and yew, where white glue does not hold. Epoxy will also bond metals to wood, as in the kind of repair shown in figure 205-*A*. The material popularly known as fiberglass is a mixture of glass fibers and epoxy resin that offers enormous possibilities for small repairs, as long as you provide for the tiny amount of motion as the wood works with variable humidity while the epoxy part stays rigidly stable. Glass fiber and epoxy resins in any quantity are sold by marine suppliers.

The various prepared brown liquid glues, fish glues, hide glues, mucilage, and the various types of acetate-base and styrene-base household or model-airplane cements offer no particular advantage in our work. We might as well stick with the white glue. Yes, I have seen those fancy electric glue guns in the shops, with neat packages of glue sticks to go with them, and some day I will have to buy one to find out what I have been missing.

PAINT REMOVERS

There are many brands of paint removers on the market, some more effective than others, some cheap and some expensive. All paint removers are poisonous, some more deadly than others but all very nasty. They must be used only with excellent ventilation, preferably outdoors. On the basis of their ingredients, removers can be grouped into three categories: flammable, nonflammable, and alkaline types.

Flammable paint removers have largely disappeared from the market. Usually they consist of two parts coal-tar-derived benzol, one part acetone, and one part alcohol. Dissolved in this mixture is about 3 to 5 percent high-melting paraffin wax to retard the evaporation of the volatile solvents. Toluene or xylene may take the place of some of the benzol, but this substitution reduces the effectiveness of the remover as well as the cost and the toxicity. I need not elaborate on the fire hazard associated with any such mixture.

In nonflammable paint removers the active ingredients are chlorinated hydrocarbons, primarily methylene chloride. A small percentage of phenol makes some of them more effective (and much more poisonous). Ethyl cellulose or cellulose acetate is added to give them a jellylike ("semipaste") consistency. Some nonflammable removers contain emulsifiers (sulfonated oils) and thus can be washed off with water. Advertisements may state that some removers do not have to be washed off at all. That may be so, but I always wash off the last trace of every remover with the greatest possible care.

Alkaline paint removers are mixtures of lye (sodium hydroxide), soda (sodium carbonate), and trisodium phosphate. They are very effective and widely used in industry (usually on steel) but rarely seen in the retail trade, except in the guise of alkaline oven cleaners. Read the fine print and somewhere it will say, "contains 4 percent sodium hydroxide," or something similar. The oven cleaners also contain materials that make them stick to vertical surfaces, good for cleaning ovens and for removing paint.

Soda is readily available, but lye, still an everyday household chemical in the country, may not be stocked by city stores because it is so dangerous in the hands of children. It can be found in disguise under some trade name having to do with clogged drains, but in this form it offers no advantage over the oven cleaners. The drain uncloggers in powder form contain ingredients that foam when water is added. That's dandy inside a clogged drain, but when you try to dissolve them out in the open the bowl gets very hot, the foaming spews lye all over the place, and you soon wish you had never tried it.

Not long ago I found a stoneware jug with several coats of latex paint on it, one of the hardest paints to remove, but the oven cleaner took it off one-two-three. But before you run out to get some, please read what we have to say about lye on pages 241–242.

The best thing to do is to buy small amounts of various removers that are available and try them one by one. Price is no guarantee of quality, and we must balance effectiveness against cost. Some brands of paint remover are very expensive, for no obvious reason.

STEEL WOOL

The grades of steel wool most useful to us are 000 or even 0000, if we can find it, for cleaning original old finishes, 0 for general smoothing, and 1 or possibly 2 for paint removing. Coarser grades are likely to scratch the wood, and they cut no faster than the finer grades. I can observe no difference between expensive brands and cheap ones except for the wrappings.

SANDPAPER

Each of the standard types of abrasive sandpapers is designed for a particular application, and we shall have occasion to use all of them sooner or later. Common flint paper is the cheapest and wears out quickest; garnet or cabinet paper is stiffer, more durable, and cuts better. Both will be used in the coarser grits on softwoods and in the finer grits on all woods. If the work at first still contains traces of paint, the paper will fill up quickly, and the cheapest flint paper is indicated. Once the wood is clean we switch to finer grits of garnet paper. Wet-or-dry silicon-carbide paper is the most expensive. We shall use it, in the finer grits (240 to 600), for final finishing of some hardwoods and of shellacked or lacquered surfaces. Emery cloth or aluminum-oxide cloth is used on chair legs, spindles, and irregular surfaces in general, where paper goes to pieces very quickly. Otherwise there is no advantage to the cloth.

The nomenclature of the various grits is confusing. Flint paper goes from 00 to about 3, or simply from "fine" to "coarse." Cabinet paper begins with 0000 (extra fine) and goes up to 2 (coarse) and beyond. The cloths and the silicon-carbide papers go by grit-mesh size, the finest for our purpose being 600 and the coarsest about 40. We should always keep a good supply of the various abrasives in the grits that suit the work. There is nothing more aggravating than to find on a Sunday afternoon that we are fresh out of just the grade of paper needed for the job at hand. The natural impulse then is to use the nearest substitute. I have done it myself more than once, and I always regret it later.

FINISHING MATERIALS

We shall need surprisingly few ingredients for all the finishing: linseed oil, shellac, lacquer, synthetic varnish, wax, and thinners. The secret lies in the rubbing; fancy chemicals and mysterious procedures serve well to impress the unlearned but have no other value.

"Boiled" linseed oil of the finest quality is sold in art supply stores. The oil is not actually boiled nowadays but consists of raw linseed oil with synthetic driers added to hasten oxidation ("drying"). The old varnish makers made a similar product by prolonged boiling of the raw oil, and many a shop went up in smoke as a result of that dangerous procedure.

Shellac is a solution of lac resin (produced by the female scale insect, *Tachardia lacca*) in alcohol. It comes in various strengths ("four-pound cut," or four pounds of resin to a gallon of alcohol, is standard) and in two colors, white and orange. The white is really a cloudy, colorless-to-brownish liquid, but the orange is usually a dreadful gaudy hue, loud enough to stop traffic. For most of my work I prefer the darker varieties of "white" shellac. Labels mean little here—we must simply open the can and peek in. Shellac in flake form is sold in some art supply stores, and purists may want to mix their own in pure ethyl alcohol. It is expensive and takes time, but the bouquet is delightful.

Clear brushing lacquer is a solution of nitrocellulose and other plastics in an acetate solvent. The good grades of lacquer have about 30 percent plastic and 70 percent solvent. Lacquer is fairly expensive, but it is wise to buy the best quality. Cheap lacquer is almost all solvent so that, in terms of what we deposit on the furniture, it may turn out to be quite expensive. Read the label carefully; the composition should be there, somewhere, in fine print. In general, stay away from paint products of unstated composition.

Polyurethane "varnish" is a solution of urea-derived plastics and other ingredients in petroleum-derived solvents. It comes under various trade names, and you just have to look for the word polyurethane among all that fine print telling you not to drink the stuff or feed it to babies. It is probably the toughest finish available in the trade. Its only disadvantages are that it is very difficult to remove, if you ever want to remove it, and that it may tend to yellow with age.

High-grade yellow paste waxes are mixtures of beeswax, carnauba, japan, and petroleum-derived waxes with a volatile petroleum-derived solvent. These waxes turn white when they dry, particularly in cracks and corners, and that is something we want to avoid. A little burnt umber, about a teaspoon of the dry or oil-ground color to a pound of wax, will give a nice brown wax of just about the right shade. The can of wax should be warmed in hot water and the color stirred in and blended thoroughly. (*Note:* Never, *never*, NEVER try to heat a can of wax over an open flame or even on an electric stove. You are in for some lively doings when the whole mess catches fire.)

SOLVENTS

We shall need a solvent for each of the finishes: turpentine for the linseed oil and the wax, alcohol for the shellac, and acetate thinner for the lacquer. We can buy "genuine steam-distilled turpentine" or the cheaper petroleum-derived paint thinner called Tirpolene, Varsol, or other trade names. The distilled turpentine smells better, but that is its only advantage so far as I can tell. Shellac can be thinned with denatured (ethyl) alcohol or with wood alcohol (methyl or methanol). Methyl is a deadly poison, and I don't want it around the house for that reason, so I use the denatured ethyl variety. Several old recipes suggest strong whiskey as a good thinner for shellac, but I consider the practice wasteful.

We shall use the lacquer thinner only to clean out brushes, so that any kind will do. Acetone is good, but very volatile and highly flammable.

FILLERS AND SEALERS

The coarsely porous woods (oak, chestnut, some mahogany, walnut, and even some birch) may require a paste filler. The purpose of the filler, needless to say, is to plug up the pores in the wood and so give a smooth surface for the final finish. Genuine antique surfaces are usually filled with the remains of paints and varnishes, and the restored parts should be filled to match. We can use commercial fillers, but I prefer to mix my own for each particular job. The ingredients are very finely powdered silica (called silex in the paint trade) and a liquid that consists of five parts boiled linseed oil, two parts japan drier, and two parts turpentine. As a rule, I mix just enough for the job at hand, making the paste thicker for coarse woods and thinner for finer woods such as birch, for example. I tint the filler with oil colors until it matches the color of the filling in the pores of the old surfaces.

We may be offered one of the many

penetrating liquid sealers intended for interior woodwork and available on the market under a whole flock of trade names. These materials have their virtues, but ordinary shellac diluted with alcohol (about one part shellac to two parts alcohol) will do very well.

STAINS AND COLORS

Artists' or decorators' oil colors are useful for touching up and tinting new parts. We shall use more burnt umber than anything else, but a small tube each of white, raw umber, yellow ochre, and lampblack will come in handy. We need not be fussy over the quality of the colors, but let us make sure they are ground in oil. Signpainters' colors are ground in japan and are a sticky mess, at least for our purposes. Acrylic colors are good on dry wood but will not stick to oiled or waxed grounds.

Occasionally we may have to stain a large new part to bring it into harmony with the rest of the piece. Here we do not want to use pigmented colors, for the pigment tends to obscure the grain of the wood, which is the reason, of course, why we used it on small patches. On large surfaces, the pigment produces a strangely artificial appearance with no depth. Therefore, it is best to use clear dyes on these large areas, dissolved in water, alcohol, or oil, depending on the surface. Water stain is best for new and clean surfaces. We make it by dissolving water-soluble stain powder in hot, preferably distilled, water—about an ounce of powder to the quart. Alcohol stain dissolves in denatured or ethyl alcohol in similar proportions. It works reasonably well even on not-so-clean surfaces and does not raise the grain as much as water stain does. Some restorers use nothing else. Oil stain is best for surfaces that

are not entirely new and where gradual blending with old areas is necessary. Other than that I try to avoid it, for it does not penetrate as evenly as alcohol or water stain. Anyway, oil stain is made by dissolving about an ounce of oil-soluble stain powder in a liquid consisting of 1½ pints turpentine and ½ pint boiled linseed oil. The various prepared liquid and spray stains offer no particular advantage in our work, and they have various disadvantages, so that is that.

Stain powders are available in the paint trade and from cabinetmakers' suppliers in small quantities, and there is an almost interminable variety of shades. "Dark walnut," "brown maple," "red maple," "dark oak," "light oak," "brown mahogany," and "nigrosine jet black" stain powders will give us a more than sufficient palette to allow blending of any tone we might need.

NEW WOOD

For internal repairs, and for jobs that require turning or steaming and bending, we need new wood. I have often found to my dismay that wood of good quality is not always readily available. We can always find a lumber yard with a few wide boards of western sugar pine (*Pinus lambertiana*, but don't ask for it by that name), perhaps as much as 30 inches wide and without a knot. Western white pine *(P. monticola)* and tulip poplar *(Liriodendron tulipifera)* also may be available. We must expect to pay a price for the high grades of these woods, especially for wide boards. True white pine *(P. strobus)* is hardly ever seen in lumber yards at any price because the old stands are almost all gone. If you are lucky, you may find some at remote sawmills in northern New England.

196. *Stash of fine cabinet lumber. The heavy plank in the middle is black walnut—worth more than you might think.*

Hardwoods will be much more difficult to find. Only a fool would buy wood he has not seen, so our purchase of high-grade hardwood may have to include a trip to the country. Maple, birch, cherry, walnut, and oak may be available in various sizes, and again, the price may seem surprisingly high. Hickory and ash, the woods necessary for restoring Windsor chairs, may be the most difficult to find. We shall need 2-foot and 6-foot lengths for splitting. They must be straight grained and absolutely flawless to make spindles, combs, and bows, the most frequently damaged parts of Windsor chairs. We should stock up on this material if we intend to repair many Windsors. Do not try to substitute oak for ash or hickory in the bent members of a Windsor. You might get away with it for a straight piece, like a spindle, but it will never do for a bow.

With a little searching we may find a commercial woodworking establishment where scrap wood is sold to the public. Some of the "scrap" may be just what we need for restorations, but the stock is, of course, highly variable, depending on what particular jobs are in process. The price is usually much less than for new wood, and there is the added advantage that the pieces are likely to be planed so that we can see the grain.

True mahogany *(Swietenia macrophylla)* grows not only in Central America (especially Honduras) but also in northern South America, and appears in the trade as "Amazon mahogany." I have found some very wide and nicely figured boards in a hardwood yard at reasonable prices.

The soft, light, straight-grained, and often highly porous red wood sold as "mahogany," "African mahogany," or "Philippine mahogany" today comes from several large trees and bears little similarity to the true mahogany in antique furniture.

The best way to find figured maple is to ask around country sawmills. Many of them operate in remote locations, serving some industry downstream. Once in a while they come across a log of spectacular curly maple (also called tiger or fiddleback), or bird's-eye, and they lay it aside, partly because they like it and partly because industrial users consider it a nuisance. You might even be lucky enough to find a few rough planks that were put aside a few years ago so that they are now nicely air cured and ready for use.

All dressed lumber will bear the marks of the modern thickness planer: a series of shallow straight ridges and troughs perpendicular to the length of the board. These marks may not be obvious to the eye, but they can be felt with the fingers. When the wood is incompletely smoothed and then stained, the marks will suddenly stand out like the stripes of a zebra. On hardwoods it may be quite a job to plane out the mechanical planer marks, but letting them show is one of the marks of shoddy work.

OLD WOOD

I try to use old wood whenever possible. It is well seasoned, there is no question of warping, and the old worn surfaces often can be placed on the outside to avoid the sharp contrast between new and old, restoration and original. Old wood is also much cheaper. I have bought odd leaves or even whole tables in auction at prices much lower than I would have to pay for the same quantity of undressed lumber. A perfect monstrosity of a piece may have many board feet of fine lumber in it, and these things often go for very little in auctions. Most serious restorers of antique furniture will have a fair stock of odds and ends of such wood, picked up from junk shops, garage sales, auctions, and wrecked old houses, not because they just then happened to have a need for it but because it was cheap and might come in handy. This may seem like a silly way to operate, but I have found just what I needed in my own stock so often that I heartily

recommend gathering a little pile of old wood if you can find a place to keep it.

PINE AND TULIP POPLAR

We shall have no trouble finding useful boards of these softwoods, usually in the form of dilapidated six-board chests, wobbly tables, or old building lumber, but the price may be a problem. When I started restoring, I never paid over $5 for an old chest of clear white pine, but think of what they bring today, regardless of condition! Still, there is nothing like a chest lid or an old kitchen table to make a new top for a great old tavern table frame. New wood would be almost impossible to blend in in a pleasing manner. Perhaps we might find some old wide shelving from a wrecked house, making sure it is white, not yellow, pine or spruce. Smaller pieces, such as one needs for miscellaneous patching, are never difficult to find, and we might as well have lots of them to permit careful matching of the grain.

MAPLE

Wide old maple boards are almost impossible to find. I have seen them here and there, but never have I been able to induce their owners to part with them. I am speaking here of plain rock maple. If we have to restore a piece of curly or bird's-eye maple, our task may be almost hopeless, simply because matching wood is not to be found. The figure in maple is so variable that it is difficult to match under the best of conditions. As a consequence, we may have to resort to new wood, and even so the task will not be easy.

Smaller pieces are comparatively

easy to find. Old bed rails and tables can be picked up occasionally. Industrial flooring may be of maple. In general I would say that any old piece of good maple is worth saving.

CHERRY, WALNUT, AND MAHOGANY

Boards of these three hardwoods are fairly easy to find in the tops of old tables, but it may be very difficult to find a piece more than one inch thick.

Each of these woods is enormously variable within itself. Very old cherry *(Prunus serotina)* has the growth rings close together, whereas wood cut in the middle of the nineteenth century or later is likely to be much coarser, even if the color matches the old "first-growth" wood. The color of walnut *(Juglans nigra)* varies enormously, from dark brown to an almost purplish hue, and mahogany has a great variety of colors and densities. We must keep these things in mind when picking up odd bits of these woods. Of the three, cherry is about the easiest to match in color.

Old junk is the best source for the proper kinds of mahogany needed in our work. The finest early American furniture was made from the wood of *Swietenia mahagoni,* a large tree that grew in comparative profusion in the islands of the West Indies. The Santo Domingo variety was the most highly regarded, but the supply of the wood was almost completely exhausted in the nineteenth century. The slightly inferior wood of *Swietenia macrophylla,* a species native to Central America, is known as Honduras mahogany in the trade, and much of the Victorian furniture was made from it. It is a fair substitute for the Santo Domingo type but

may not be adequate for patching fine pieces.

ASH AND HICKORY

Spindles from wrecked chairs and old tool handles will furnish small pieces of ash and hickory. Pick up any old rakes, picks, shovels, and such. They will serve for the rungs and spindles of Windsors, slat-backs, and simple chairs in general.

VENEER

A small stock of old veneer, particularly mahogany, is essential if we restore any veneered pieces. Quite frankly, restoring veneer is one thing I try to avoid. On a good piece, the veneer is bound to be selected and matched, and it is virtually impossible to replace missing pieces satisfactorily. Perhaps it is just a matter of patience, plus a sufficient stock of old veneers to pick from. At any rate, junk furniture often carries good veneer, if it is old enough. Late veneer is likely to be paper thin.

WRECKING LUMBER, OLD NAILS, AND GLASS

Very old houses and barns are occasionally torn down, and from the wreckers we may obtain not only lumber but old nails, screws, and pieces of uneven, bubbly old glass. When the White House was refurbished in 1952, tons of such materials were carefully collected, labeled, and sold to souvenir hunters. If we are in luck, we may benefit from similar operations on less famous old houses, but we have to keep our eyes open. Henry Taylor was an expert at this sort of salvage, and he wrote, "But it is an excellent plan, before obtaining any material from even the most dilapidated house, to secure the owner's permission for such procedure. Nothing is harder to explain in a nonchalant and convincing manner than one's presence with axe and crowbar in a house owned by a complete stranger."

10
THE
BASIC STEPS
OF
RESTORATION

When we have decided that a piece is to be restored and have determined the best size and shape for all missing parts, we are ready to start. Whatever the piece and whatever the damage it may have suffered, the basic procedure is much the same:

1. Taking apart and cleaning.
2. Repairing or replacing damaged parts and refitting.
3. Gluing.
4. Final shaping and leveling.
5. Removing the old finish and preparing for the new.
6. Coloring and blending in new surfaces.
7. Refinishing.

Before we go into too much detail on particular problems, perhaps we should discuss the basic procedure in a general way, step by step. Whether we do the whole job ourselves or farm out part of the work to a professional, we cannot hope to achieve a satisfactory restoration without careful planning. We must decide in advance exactly what we intend to do and where.

Before I start a complicated job of restoration, I often spend weeks or even months poking at the piece, looking it over inside and out, finding the exact kind of wood I shall need for the repairs, and looking up similar pieces in all the books I can find, searching in museums and private collections if necessary—just generally deciding what needs to be done and trying to figure out the best way to do it. Even if we finally hire someone to do the work, our instructions will have to be well thought out and clearly presented to the workman. We should not expect the hired hand to do the thinking for us.

TAKING APART

If a piece is shaky and rickety, if all the joints are loose, and if it all shifts with a creak when we push it here and there, then it must be taken apart. If, on the other hand, the piece is firm and sound, no matter how badly damaged it may be, then we shall repair it without taking it apart, as best we can. Dismantling a tight piece is risky and may produce more damage than we set out to repair.

191

The careful restorer must be doubly meticulous in removing pins to disassemble a piece. A punch of the correct diameter (slightly smaller than the pin) is used to nudge the pin out of its hole. A nail with the point filed off will do nicely. Each pin should be wrapped with masking tape and numbered. That way it is less likely to be lost and can be reinserted into the same hole in the same position when the piece is reassembled. Early cabinetmakers rarely glued their pins, but a drop of white glue now may help lubricate the pin and set it, if it is loose.

One of the quickest ways to split an old piece of wood is to drive a new roughly polygonal pin into the old undersized hole, hoping that it will bite into the wood as the original pin did two hundred years ago. It is quite difficult to make new pins that fit old holes. They must be fitted with care, and it helps to steam them a little before driving them in.

Some pieces will come apart right off. We push out the pins, mark them and put them away, remove an occasional nail, pull the joints apart, and that's that. Yet other pieces, just as wobbly, can resist with exasperating tenacity all efforts to disassemble them.

Much of the inexpert repairing of old furniture is done with nails. Strictly makeshift, such repair is short lived at best. If the nail heads are deeply set and the holes well concealed, we may have trouble taking the piece apart for more permanent repairs. A small boy-scout compass can be handy in searching for concealed nails, so long as they are of iron and therefore magnetic.

Once the nails are found, there remains the problem of getting them out, and that may be no joke. If the head is on the surface, we can usually dig around it enough with a knife to be able to grip the nail with the small diagonal cutting pliers we have for the purpose, or we can modify a small pair of electrician's pliers in the manner recommended by John Rodd in his remarkably lucid and thorough book on furniture restoration. If the nail is contemporary with the piece, it should be marked and later put back into the same hole in the same orientation. But if it is a modern finishing nail set with a punch perhaps ⅛ inch below the surface, the pliers would do more damage than we can tolerate, and we must resort to other tricks. We might get a long punch, no thicker than the nail itself, and drive the nail through the wood until the point sticks out on the opposite side. The nail can then be gripped with locking pliers and carefully pulled through, in reverse. If we then soak the hole with warm water, it will close up quite well.

Some joints are set with wedges driven so that they expand a split member in a direction parallel with the grain of the receiving piece. When the joint is loose, the wedge is either lost altogether or it also is loose and will come out easily with a little prodding from a knife or a small screwdriver. We must mark the wedge immediately and save it for reinsertion in the same slot. If the wedges are firm, that is quite a different story—perhaps we did not want to take that joint apart anyway.

Screws can be bothersome. If they are the old, blunt-ended, hand-cut screws, then they have irregular threads and a narrow slot, so that they resist turning and are hard to grip. The tip of a hot soldering iron, applied to the screw head for a moment, will heat it and sometimes help start it. Screws are mechanically much stronger than the wood they are in, so that when the joint is strained, the wood splits and the screw pulls out. These splits have to be found, spread apart, and glue forced into them with our syringe. They are then clamped, the screw holes plugged, and let dry. We then carefully redrill the holes to fit the old screws (or new ones, if the original screws are lost), and if we are lucky the old joint will hold reasonably well. I am thinking particularly of such typical screw fastenings as hinges, latches, locks, and some handles.

When all the pins, wedges, screws, and nails are out, the joints should yield to persuasion with a small mallet. A few light but sharp blows, followed by a little rocking and jiggling, a few more taps, and in all probability the joint will come apart. If it does not, and if it looks as if further efforts to break it would risk smashing the piece, then the wise restorer will give up trying to dismantle the stubborn joint and will resort to the glue-injection technique discussed further along.

Those joints that did come apart now must be cleaned of old glue. The old-fashioned hoof glue dries to a hard, brittle, almost flinty substance that may be difficult to remove when dry but that brushes off easily if it has been soaked in cold water for half an hour or so. The modern waterproof glues have to be scraped off as best we can.

REPAIR AND REFITTING

Most of our repair will consist of healing splits and splicing in new wood where parts have been broken or weakened. If we were restoring for a museum, we would never replace any part with new wood, no matter how far gone or unserviceable it might be. However, we are repairing for use in the home, and ultimate strength must be considered. Therefore, if an original but patched-up part is likely to jeopardize the overall utility of the piece, we shall replace the whole part with a new one, matching the wood as best we can. The decision of what to repair and what to replace is often quite difficult, but it is ours to make, and we should not leave it to a repairman, even if he is to do the cabinetwork. Especially if we have the work done by a professional, we should understand the principles involved and know what is easy, what is difficult, and what we should not ask for. We shall get much better work if the craftsman realizes that we understand his problems.

It is very difficult to heal a bad split so that it will stay healed. A wide board splits because stresses accumulate in it as it goes through its cycles of expansion and contraction with varying humidity from winter to summer. Even a narrow board may split if it is rigidly constrained in a way that does not permit it to shrink across the grain when it wants to (fig. 197). Once a board has cracked, it usually becomes deformed so that the two sides of the split will not come together again even if clamped.

It will do no good to try to fill the split with plastic wood or some such

free   constrained

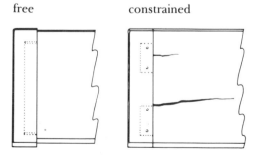

197. Left, a board left free to shrink will not crack. Right, a rigidly constrained board will surely crack with time.

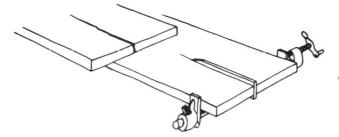

198. To repair a wide crack, a new piece is glued into a sawed slot.

filler. The job may look good for a week, but soon a crack will reappear, and in a few months the gap will be bigger than it was originally. The now rigid filler merely acts as a wedge to pry the split farther apart.

Somehow, we shall have to bring the two sides together and then glue them. We can do that by carefully chiseling and refitting the surfaces by a carbon-paper routine I shall describe. That is a very tedious process but the most satisfactory in the long run. Or we may try two saw cuts along the split and splice in a strip or a wedge just large enough to fill the gap (fig. 198). Or we may decide that the split is not so bad after all and leave it strictly alone. That's just what I have done with the lid of a blanket chest that had cleats fastened with clinched, hand-forged nails and had cracked as a result. I could not have removed the cleats without damaging them.

There is no denying that scarfing is a difficult part of furniture restoration. We must find wood that matches exactly; it is not enough to take just any piece of cherry to patch a cherry table, for example. The wood must have similar grain, be cut from roughly the same part of the trunk and in the same orientation as the part to be patched (fig. 199). Finding the right wood may be difficult and is likely to take more time than a repairman can afford if he is to earn a living. Therefore, the selection of the wood for repairs should be the collector's job; we are bound to be disappointed if we try to delegate the responsibility.

The damaged portion is cut away and a new piece, matching along as well as across the grain, is glued on. When the glue has dried, the new piece is shaped and polished until the part is as good as the day it was made. All this may sound easy, but it takes much patience and a little practice to produce a satisfactory splice. The cut we make must not deviate from the line of the grain by more than about 20 degrees, for cross-grain glue joints will not hold. A straight cut may be possible on some pieces, and that is by far the easiest, for all we have to fit then are two plane parallel surfaces. We make the cut with a fine-toothed saw and then plane and chisel the two surfaces until they fit.

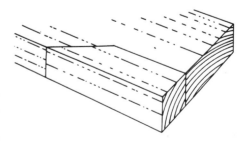

199. Properly matched wood fits both with and across the grain.

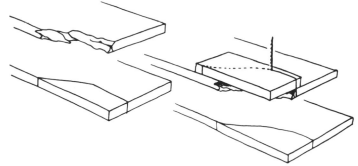

200. *Two methods of scarfing on new wood to repair a broken corner.*

More often, however, two or three cuts may be necessary, positioned for best appearance and strength. All these surfaces must fit accurately if the glue joint is to hold. A similar result may be obtained by a single curved cut made with a saw in both pieces of wood simultaneously, as shown in figure 200. A thin, fine-toothed blade should be used, and an electric jigsaw or a band saw with a good flat table is recommended. Even with great care, however, the sawed joint will not fit as well as one carefully fitted with a chisel.

I can hardly exaggerate the need for accurate fit. If the pieces do not make a tight joint, the glue line will show much more than it should, and the joint is likely to be weak. The dry surfaces must not rock, one on the other. When most of us try to chisel a really flat surface, we actually produce a slightly convex surface, especially if we finish with a file. Two such surfaces rock on each other, even though they seem perfectly flat to the eye. I try to circumvent this trouble by purposely chiseling the surfaces very slightly concave (fig. 201), less than $\frac{1}{64}$ inch higher around the edges than in the middle. These tiny levees then pull together when the pieces are clamped and make for a very thin glue line.

Fitting is best done with ordinary carbon paper. We lay the paper between the two surfaces, clamp them firmly for a second, and the high spots will now show black on one of the pieces. We carefully chisel them off and repeat the process until all high spots are gone and the surfaces fit perfectly. If the chisel slips a little, or if, after ten squeezings with the carbon paper, a little bump still remains, we may be inclined to say the devil take the little bump, let's glue up anyway. In that case I strongly recommend a coffee break or a walk around the block. If the surfaces do not fit when dry, no amount of clamping will make them fit when glued, and the result is bound to be disappointing. Generally speaking, the harder the wood, the more careful must be the fitting.

When everything fits, I make my little levees by chiseling lightly in the mid-

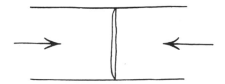

201. *Two parts lightly fitted for gluing should touch only on the outside if we want a barely visible glue line. The edges are less than 1/64" higher than the center of the fitted surface.*

dle, and the pieces are ready for the glue.

Gluing the splices is no different from the gluing we do to assemble the parts, so we may as well leave the discussion of gluing until we get to the assembly process.

When all the parts are made serviceable again, they must be refitted for reassembly. The fitting is necessary because the wood has shrunk and possibly warped with time so that some parts may not fit properly any more. Some members may have to be shortened slightly, some narrowed a bit, some straightened, and some bent. Steaming may be necessary, and we shall discuss this in chapter 11. All cutting should be done on interior surfaces if at all possible. We should not try to pound a piece together even if it did fit perfectly two hundred years ago. If we try to force things too much, something is sure to crack; a little paring here and there will do wonders for sticky drawers, ill-fitting desk lids, balky doors, and the like.

GLUING

Most early furniture was assembled without a drop of glue, the joints held together by accurate fit with a pin here and there to keep them from pulling loose. These dry joints allow the wood a little motion as it "works" with varying humidity, and a piece that may give a little under strain is, of course, much more durable than one that is rigid. For that reason, we should be sparing with the glue in assembling the larger pieces of furniture even now.

We must be particularly careful with long, cross-grain mortise-and-tenon joints like those that hold the cleats of desk lids (fig. 197). Here we should put glue only near the center of the wide board and leave the tenons toward the edge unglued. These tenons can then move a little in their mortises as the wide board works, and the spot of glue near the middle is quite enough to hold the cleat on. This motion may be surprisingly large—I have observed more than ⅛ inch from the center of a desk lid. When originally made, the lid of the desk in figure 4, for example, was ⅜ inch wider than it is now. There would be a gaping crack in the lid now if it had been rigidly glued to the cleats.

White glue will not hold on dirty, oily, or painted surfaces, nor can we hope to make a good joint without accompanying pressure from clamps or a tourniquet. When we first set the clamps, we must be careful to keep the joint from slipping as a result of the lubricating action of the glue. It is best to apply a little more glue than is needed, squeeze the joint lightly to distribute the glue, then add more glue where needed and clamp hard to squeeze out all excess. The final pressure should be enough to set the joint firmly but not enough to dent the wood, especially if it is soft, like pine.

The direction of the pressure should be as nearly perpendicular to the joint as we can make it. When irregular shapes are to be glued, we may have to make forms out of scrap lumber cut to the right shape specifically for each glue job (fig. 202). This may seem like a lot of unnecessary trouble, but it is the sort of thing that distinguishes the craftsman from the novice. It may take a few minutes to saw the forms out of an old piece of crate lumber, but we shall more than save that time when we set the clamps. The trick is to assemble and clamp the joint quickly once the glue is applied. The white glues we normally use set fast and will hold best if clamped minutes after they hit the

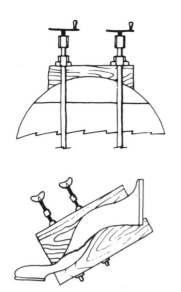

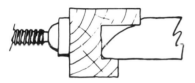

202. Scrap-lumber forms are helpful for difficult glue jobs.

wood. Therefore, we should have all the clamps and forms ready and know exactly how we plan to clamp the joint, even make a dry run on the more difficult jobs—all before the glue is applied.

Tourniquets are useful for gluing joined pieces like chairs, stools, and small tables. We tie a rope round and round and across the piece, insert a stick in a loop, and twist until the rope is tight. Or we may use the rubber band discussed in chapter 9 and wind it the way we did the rope. Although the rubber is weak in a single strand, a dozen turns add up to a respectable pressure,

and we can regulate the pressure by stretching the band or by adding turns.

In any case, we must make sure that the pressure has not distorted the piece. A chair, obviously, must have all four legs touch the floor. One way to make sure of this is to put a weight like a sandbag on the chair while we are tying it up on a level floor.

As soon as the clamps are set we must wash off with a wet rag or a sponge all excess glue that has oozed out of the joints. Dried glue resists paint removers and would cause trouble in the final cleaning of the piece.

EPOXY GLUING

With epoxy glue the procedure is a little different. The two glue components are first mixed in some disposable dish, just enough for what is needed for the next hour or two. Paper baking cups are great, but waxed paper or styrofoam are attacked by the glue and contaminate it. Just a sheet of plain paper is fine for small quantities. Very thorough mixing is essential or the glue will not harden properly. The surfaces to be joined need not be perfectly clean, nor do they have to fit perfectly, but they have to be absolutely dry. Some epoxies are said to adhere to moist surfaces, but I think I know otherwise.

The slow-setting epoxies are most useful for our kind of work because they penetrate the wood and hold like nothing else. If time is of the essence, an ordinary heat lamp will greatly shorten the curing process. Clamping is necessary only to immobilize the joint while the glue sets. Pressure is useful to distribute the glue and drive it into chinks and crannies but otherwise makes little difference. The joint has to fit well enough to keep the glue from running out of it, but no more.

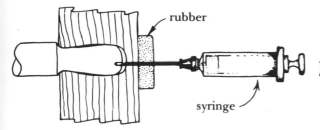

203. Glue injection with a syringe and a coarse hypodermic needle.

On very rough joints, where the glue sags and leaves voids, I wait until it has stiffened a bit and then plaster on some more to level out the surface. I keep the unused glue at the same temperature as the work, which shows me how the glue in the joint is progressing. At normal room temperature it takes about forty-eight hours for a full cure even though the glue may feel hard after ten.

GLUE INJECTION

When a loose joint absolutely refuses to come apart, then we perform a delicate little operation with the sinister-looking syringe I have already mentioned. First we take a very small drill, just a little larger than the hypodermic needle, and sink a hole into the joint from the back side (fig. 203). Now we fill the syringe with white glue diluted a little with water and squirt the thin glue into the joint until it comes out the other side. A piece of soft rubber like a small eraser or a piece of inner tube, speared on the hypodermic and pressed against the small hole, will keep the glue from coming out the wrong place. Then we rock and jiggle the joint as much as it will give and squirt again. Two or three repetitions

of the process will coat the inside of the joint with glue, and clamps may now be set wherever possible. An obvious variation of this technique is useful for healing small splits.

FINAL SHAPING AND LEVELING

All the new wood pieces have been left a little oversize, to allow for inaccuracies in the gluing. When the glue has dried, we shave the new wood down to size, taking along just the least little smidgin of the old wood along the edges. We smooth the new wood with sandpaper—medium on soft wood, fine on hard—and round off all edges and corners to match the appearance of the old parts. We should not be able to feel the glue lines as we run our hand over them, and all edges should feel unbroken where they are patched.

Only when all the paring, shaving, and sanding is finished do we begin to remove the old paint from the unrestored parts, and it is often helpful to smear the paint-saturated remover over the new wood. Some of the paint will lodge in the pores and tint the new wood just enough to make final coloring much easier.

11
MORE DETAIL
ON
RESTORATION

This chapter is bound to be a little personal and influenced by my own particular experiences, but that can hardly be helped. Quite naturally, I can write only about the jobs I have done and a few I have heard of. When I botch something, I usually remember the details more clearly than if everything went well because I want to be sure not to make that mistake again. Many details I know nothing about, important as they may be, simply because problems involving them have never come up. Clock cases, for example: I have never restored a clock case, not because clock cases never get broken but just because the only one that ever came my way needed little more than wiping with my special polish (see chapter 13).

WINDSORS

There's no use concealing the fact that I like Windsor chairs. To me they represent the highest form of utilitarian elegance and, at the same time, some of the most individualistic examples of the innate cussedness of inanimate ob-jects. They are remarkably graceful, amazingly durable, and simply hellish to repair. Every time I fix a Windsor, the engagement somehow becomes a contest—will it hold or will it not? Sometimes I win and sometimes I lose; it's a real sport.

Windsor chair makers carefully selected the toughest and most elastic woods they could find. They achieved great structural strength by combining seasoned and green wood so that the chair would tighten up as it dried. It is said that the holes in the seat were drilled by eye. Just take a look at a Windsor chair from straight above. There may be nineteen holes or more in the seat, all diverging, each at a different angle. Then look at the rail of an elegant Windsor, an arch-back armchair, for example. It may have fifteen holes, each drilled exactly at the correct angle to line up precisely with the corresponding hole in the seat. The spindles or the bow would break if the holes were not just right.

The underbody was usually made of partly seasoned maple, probably less than a year old when the legs and stretchers were assembled. Such wood may warp a little (and few Windsor legs are really straight), but it has a little more give to it, so that the slightly enlarged ends of the stretchers could be driven into the slightly undersized holes in the legs without splitting them. Further shrinkage then tightened the joint even more, so that it would withstand considerable tensile stress for centuries.

The seat was usually shaped of unseasoned pine, and the legs were set into the seat with wedges. The posts and the ends of bows were also fastened that way, but spindles are usually held only by the shrinkage of the seat. Hickory and ash of very high quality were most frequently used for the superstructure. The spindles are almost always straight on early Windsors but may be steamed and bent a little on the Federal types. The joint between an ash post and a hickory comb would not have held by itself, for both members are small, and shrinkage could not produce sufficient strength. Therefore, the tops of posts on comb-back Windsors are often pinned with a small nail, and one or two spindles may be similarly attached. The nails may be hard to find and even harder to pull out. The boyscout compass will help find them, but to pull them out we may have to dig a little.

WOBBALATION

The most common complaint about Windsors is that they are rickety. A cabinetmaker I know in Kentucky calls it "a case of wobbalation." A Windsor chair that is in constant use should be reglued every few years or whenever necessary. If allowed to go too long, the stretchers pull out as the raked legs spread, and first the stretchers break

and then the legs. For that reason I never put metal tips on the feet of Windsor chairs. The tips glide too easily on the floor and put an excessive strain on the stretchers.

To glue the joint, we first try to take it apart. A chair may be wobbly as can be, but the stretchers still may need a little persuasion with a rubber mallet before they come out. Considerable force may be necessary, but it must be applied with care if we are to avoid the sickening crash of splintering chair legs. I often use a lever arrangement made of two softwood pieces of which one must be cut to just the right length for this particular stretcher, as shown in figure 204. I pry with the lever and beat sharply with the mallet until either the joint gives or I acknowledge defeat.

When the stretcher end is completely out of its hole, I quickly swab it and the inside of the hole with white glue, guide the stretcher back till it snaps in, and then push it in as far as it will go. A light tourniquet or a few turns of the rubber band will hold it until the glue sets.

If the hole has been enlarged to the point where glue will no longer hold, a strip or two of glue-saturated canvas

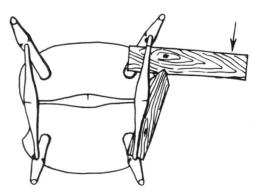

204. *Lever arrangement to spread Windsor chair legs for regluing the stretchers.*

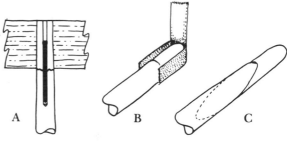

205. A, *a broken spindle can be repaired by setting a nail into the break.* B, *cloth strips help glue stretchers that are loose in their holes.* C, *a new end is scarfed onto a broken stretcher.*

over the end of the stretcher will help give a fair joint (fig. 205-*B*). The thickness of the cloth must be judged by the amount of play in the joint. If the cloth is too thick, it will tear when we try to push the joint together. If it is too thin, it will do little good. Do not use just a patch of cloth instead of the strips. The patch will wrinkle and rip.

A rickety joint may have been nailed at one time or another (enter the boy-scout compass). Be sure all nails and screws are out before you try forcing a joint. If it still holds, even after the nails are withdrawn, then use the glue-injection method discussed in chapter 10. It does not give as good a glue job, but it is the only thing to do.

Now you might properly ask: Why use white glue? Epoxy is so much stronger! Exactly. Epoxy is *too* strong. If you glue the underbody with epoxy, it is very likely to become too rigid. Instead of yielding a little, it will break under strain. Epoxy is great for replacing the ends of broken rungs and stretchers, especially if we use a nail as shown in figure 205-*A*, because it gives an excellent bond between the nail and the wood, but for the final assembly let's stick with white glue.

SPINDLES

One must take the back apart to replace missing spindles. Only the best wood is good enough. Selected handles from old garden tools may do, but new sticks split from perfectly clear hickory are better. The spindles are easily made with a drawknife and spokeshave or with a small plane, much as most early spindles were made originally. One can produce the bulbous shape of some spindles by bending them as they are being planed. A vise is a must, if we expect to have any skin left on our knuckles. Spindles of late Windsors are usually turned, but even the turned spindles are best replaced by careful whittling. One can approximate the original shape much better that way.

Broken spindles can be repaired, but hickory, ash, and oak do not hold too well with white glue, and epoxy is indicated. There are several ways to do the job. If looks are important but great strength is not required, we may drill in from the top through the break, put a drop of epoxy into the hole, and set in a finishing nail with the head filed off (fig. 205-*A*). The hole must be just a hair larger than the nail and should be well centered. As I said, this will not be a strong joint, but a neat one.

Scarfing a new end onto a broken spindle would be recommended if it could save the trouble of taking the whole back apart (fig. 205-*C*). The scarf must be well fitted, of course, but the new end must also fit into the old hole. When everything fits perfectly, the end is slipped into the hole with white glue, and the scarf is immediately cemented with epoxy and wrapped tightly with nylon thread. When the glues have set, the thread is removed and the joint shaved smooth. A fair amount of tinting with pigment is usually needed to mask such a repair.

SEATS

A split wooden seat will be difficult to repair if the crack has been mucked up with old glue and paint remover. Glue injection will be of little help, and it is probably best to force the split open till it breaks clear across, then clean the break thoroughly, splice in new wood from the back if necessary, and glue up. In time, however, the chair will probably crack again.

Some Windsor armchairs have had a hole cut from the center of the seat, to convert the chair for toilet purposes. If the hole is original, then it might as well stay. If it is a later addition (or rather subtraction), as is more likely, not much can be done to fix it. If the chair is fairly elaborate, we may want to plug the hole roughly, pad the seat, and cover it in leather with brass tacks all around. A seat that fancy would look a little silly on a simple chair, but the more elegant styles were sometimes finished that way (fig. 43). Then what shall we do with a simple chair with a hole in its seat? My advice is to let someone else bid on it.

BOWS, RAILS, AND COMBS

We have already said that a crack in one of the long bent members of a Windsor chair is a serious flaw. Patching a bow or a rail is not particularly difficult, and it may even be preferable from the antiquarian point of view, but chances are that the patch will not hold if the chair is in daily use.

The piece for the patch must be steamed and bent to the right shape. When it is dry, it can be scarfed, fitted in place, and glued down with epoxy (fig. 206). Some recommend reinforcing the joint with small brass screws, but that is not a good idea because any metal is likely to split the wood. I usually wrap a small band of nylon thread tightly near the feathered edge of the scarf, much like the wrapping one finds on old laminated bamboo fishing poles. The bands can be made quite inoffensive, and they do add a lot of strength to the joint (fig. 206). The break usually occurs where a hole has been drilled for a spindle. This hole is best redrilled in the patch piece after it is bent but before it is glued in. In that way one can set in the patch without disturbing any of the other members.

However, the only permanent way of restoring a broken bow is to replace it. Let us not fool ourselves—it is a difficult job. The wood must be steamed and bent to the right shape, and with arch-backs that means building an accurate three-dimensional form. Drill-

206. Repair of a broken Windsor bow. The ends are secured with narrow bands of nylon thread.

ing the holes in the bow and fitting the chair together may seem like an insurmountable task the first time we try it. However, if it is one of those handsome braced arch-backs with a finely turned underbody but with the arch smashed, as it often is, then the job is probably worthwhile. An ordinary bamboo-turned bow-back would hardly seem worth such trouble, unless it is part of a set or unless you are the kind of worker who enjoys rehearsing difficult jobs.

Henry Taylor wrote, "To the beginner in the restoration of Windsor chairs, I would say, 'Do not become discouraged if your first efforts seem rather unsuccessful.' Most of the methods and processes employed on Windsors are very different from regular cabinetwork. Even expert cabinetworkers, sometimes, are not at all successful when they attempt to treat wrecked Windsor chairs. I frankly acknowledge that some of my own early efforts in restoring Windsors appeared very much as might those of the manual training department of a summer camp for small boys."

STEAMING AND FORMING BENT PARTS

Hickory, ash, and oak are easily bent once they have been made pliable by steaming. The bent wood will retain its shape quite well if it is clamped wet and allowed to dry in the bent shape. The wood should first be soaked for a day or two before it is steamed. We can rig up two types of steaming apparatuses: a wooden steam box or a long boiler.

The steam box should be long, narrow, and tight. It should have a few transverse cleats in the bottom to lay the wood on so that the steam can circulate around it. A small boiler and a piece of tube to bring the steam into the box complete the arrangement. The boiler need not be anything special—an old teakettle or a large fruit-juice can will do. A small box can have the steam hole in the middle of the bottom and two small vent holes, one on each end, as suggested by John Rodd (see Bibliography). Such a box would be put directly on top of a water pot on an electric hot plate, all neatly balanced, as shown in figure 207. However, I need not dwell on the fact that the whole affair is a little tricky, and even the best makeshift boiler is not exactly safe and must be handled with caution. If you should forget and let it run dry, you may soon find yourself calling the fire department.

Henry Taylor used another arrangement for steaming Windsor parts. He made a boiler of a piece of 4-inch pipe, tightly capped on one end and just long enough to take the longest piece he was

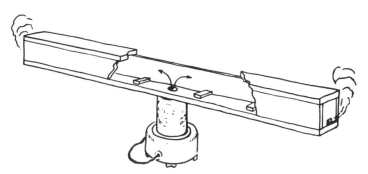

207. A quickly made steam box: a large tin can, an old electric hot plate, and a long, tightly nailed wooden box with cleats along the bottom and vents in each end. One end is removable for loading.

likely to want steamed, which makes it about six feet. Any pipe will do—a section of galvanized gutter downspout with a suitable tin can soldered tightly on one end, for example, or a piece of large water pipe with a cap screwed on. The rig will serve as a container for soaking the wood (do not count on the bathtub—it is too short), and when we are ready to steam we put the whole affair upright on top of a small electric hot plate, secured in some way so it will not fall over. Actually, the water in the pipe need not really boil, but it should be very hot.

The steaming time depends on the size of the wood, just as cooking time depends on the size of the potatoes. About an hour should suffice for the largest Windsor parts, either in the steam box or in the boiler.

Each bending job requires a special form. A bow, a comb, or an arm rail can be bent over blocks nailed to an old bench top or to a basement wall, as shown in figure 208, clamped, and allowed to dry. A paper pattern will help place the blocks just right, but one should allow for a little rebound when the wood comes off the form—in other words, make the bends a little tighter than the ultimate shape you want to achieve. The bow for an arch-back armchair bends in three dimensions, and we shall have to find some lumber and build a fairly elaborate form to the dimensions of the original bow. The form must be rigid and accurately cut, if the finished bow is not to look like the crooked branch of a tree.

The steamed piece should be left on the form for a few days, depending on how dry the weather is. Even so, it will spring back a bit when we release the clamps, and that is why I suggested exaggerating the curves a little. Final shaping is best done after the piece has

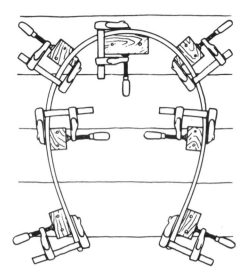

208. *Making a new bow for a Windsor chair.*

dried. The holes are drilled at that time, too, and we are ready to assemble the chair again. This time let us try to keep our temper.

LEGS

The legs come clear through the seat on early Windsors and are set in with wedges from the top (fig. 209, *left*). The wedges are always perpendicular to the grain of the wood, for otherwise the seat would split. The holes on Federal Windsors are drilled only partway through the seat, and the wedges are concealed (fig. 209, *right*). The ends of

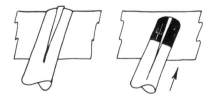

209. *Wedges in Windsor chair legs.* Left, *an early open wedge;* right, *a late "fox wedge."*

210. *Late rocker, crudely attached to the shortened leg of the slat-back chair in figure 16. Restoring the leg to its original length is not an easy job.*

the legs were sawed lengthwise, the wedges lightly inserted, and the legs then driven into the holes. The wedges hit the bottoms of the holes and spread the ends of the legs to give tight joints. The reader will understand why these joints are so difficult to take apart.

Chair legs are often cut down for one reason or another (fig. 210). If the loss in seat height amounts only to an inch or so then I suggest leaving it alone. However, if the chair has lost several inches, as many of them have, then we have to restore the legs if the chair is to be of much use.

First square off the ends of the legs and then drill a ½-inch hole into each of them from the bottom; a hole ⅝ inch in diameter can be drilled in the legs

that are thick enough to take it. In any case, the hole must be at least an inch deep and must not touch the stretcher (fig. 211).

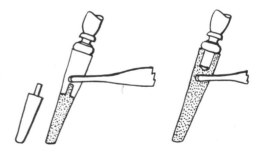

211. *Repairing a shortened leg.* Left, *the splice may go below the stretcher, but,* right, *if the leg is worn right up to the stretcher, then the leg must be cut off and the splice made above the stretcher.*

If we have not enough room, then we must cut the legs off just above the stretcher, or perhaps at the first shoulder of the turning, and make the splice there. The new ends then must be drilled to receive the stretchers in their former position. All in all, that makes for a rather drastic restoration.

Next we turn new pieces from matching wood, as shown in the sketch, forming dowels that will fit the holes we drilled. It is best to taper the end of the dowel a bit so that it will distribute the glue better when it is pushed in. Now we line up the grain in the new part with the grain of the leg and fit the two parts together, by which I mean, of course, that we whittle and pare until the two fit tightly. The fitting will be easier if the shoulder of the new part has been undercut a little in turning. (Figure 233, new foot for a tavern table, clearly shows the taper of the dowel and the undercut. These are exaggerated in the sketch to make them obvious. In actual practice each would slope no more than 2 degrees.) The operation requires more than routine care. The dowel must fit loosely enough to allow room for the glue yet not so loosely that it will rattle in the hole. The proper clearance is what machinists call a "slide fit." If the fit were too tight, all the glue would wipe off as the dowel is pushed in, or, worse yet, the leg would crack.

When everything fits to our satisfaction we glue it all together with epoxy and let it set. Sometimes I clamp the joint with one clamp set parallel to the growth rings in the wood—in other words, perpendicular to the direction of the likeliest split—but it is more from force of habit than for any technical reason. This kind of job has become much easier since epoxy glues came onto the market.

The turnings for the new feet are made a little too large on purpose, and when the glue has hardened, we shape them to their proper size with a spokeshave. One must be careful to remove no more than a hair of the wood above the splice. It is almost impossible to drill the dowel hole exactly in the center of the old leg, and that is the reason for the final shaping. When everything is done, the joint should be barely detectable when you run your hand over it. To the eye, however, the glue line will show, unless the chair is painted. Any repair like this, made on all four legs in the same place, is bound to be noticeable, and that is the reason why experienced buyers severely discount the price they are willing to pay for a cut-down chair.

EARLY CHAIRS

Slat-back, banister-back, and other early chairs often lose a few inches at the bottom, and the damage can be repaired much the same way as with Windsors. Occasionally a slat or a banister may be missing, or the finials may have been knocked off. Slats can be replaced easily with thin oak boards. Finials can be restored with dowels, just like legs, but I seldom bother with such a repair. One would have to guess at the shape of the missing finials, the result would be patchy, and simple chairs minus finials probably are not worth restoring anyway.

Missing half-round banisters can be split-turned, but it amounts to a bit of work. We find two flat, rectangular pieces of wood that match the present banisters. We glue these strips together with water-soluble glue and a sheet of paper in between and then turn the glued piece on a lathe to the right contour. If all the split banisters are missing, then we adapt the contour to match the outline of the back posts. Soaking in water will separate the two halves after turning.

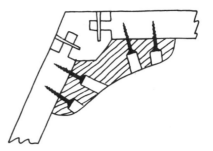

212. *Corner block for wobbly framed chairs.*

FRAMED CHAIRS

A good Chippendale chair is worth fixing even when it has been smashed to smithereens. The mortise-and-tenon construction of these framed chairs offers no particular problem to the repairer who knows how and where to glue on new wood. Their design makes it possible to conceal the scarfing reasonably well, so it is really just a matter of patience to clean out the joints, repair them where necessary with new wood, and then glue them together again, with all the pins in their proper places.

It is not unusual to find these chairs fixed with nails and screws in a makeshift manner, but as in all good restoration we shall rely on the glue to do the holding. Metal screw plates and angles will not produce a permanent repair, for wood is not strong enough to join with metal that way.

The seats of framed chairs may be strengthened with corner blocks, as shown in figure 212. Such blocks are used regularly in modern chairs but were usually smaller on antique chairs, which derive their strength from the framing (fig. 213). The corner blocks are glued and fastened with four wood screws of just the right length. They must fit the corners perfectly if they are to do much good.

WOVEN CHAIR SEATS

A woven seat on a frame is a very ancient device for pampering the posterior. Many antique chairs were made to receive seats woven of rush, splints, or cane. The seat is often worn out by the time the chair reaches us and may be covered by later upholstery or even by a board. Whether or not a given seat is "original" may be of interest to a museum curator, but the question is purely academic if the chair is to be used to help furnish a home. Cane, rush, and splint become very brittle with time and soon disintegrate under normal conditions of use. My favorite manual on reseating is Marion Burr Sober's *Chair Seat Weaving for Antique Chairs.*

There is no mistaking the frame originally intended for cane. It will have a line of little holes about ½ inch apart all around the seat. Many of the early Flemish chairs have caned panels in the back as well. Rush and splints are woven on a frame of rails, usually oval or pear shaped in cross section. They are interchangeable (a frame will take either rush or splints without alteration) and were most frequently used on country furniture. We can usually tell whether a frame ever carried splints by the slight grooves that splints wear into the frame where they rub against it. Rush is soft and leaves narrower and less pronounced marks, but even clear splint marks are no guarantee that the original seat was splint. It means only that a splint seat was there at one time

213. *Original corner blocks on a fine Philadelphia Chippendale chair, about 1770. They may need regluing but should not be replaced.*

or another. We are, I think, quite free to use either rush or splints in such a chair. Either of them is better than falling through.

Weaving chair seats is a method of occupational therapy, and many institutions for the blind will take care of our chair-seating requirements at a modest fee. When we place our order, we must make doubly sure that our job be done with proper materials. Paper "rush" (fig. 214), cardboard "splints," and plastic "cane" are widely sold. They are useful for manual training purposes but are neither as durable nor as pleasing as the real thing. We certainly would not use any of them on a good antique frame. Sea grass is a fair substitute for rush but rather expensive. Flat rattan reed may be used instead of splints, but the splints are more durable and look better, at least to my orthodox eye.

For those readers who like to do everything themselves, the following is a brief outline of the weaving procedures.

RUSH SEATS

Cattail rush (*Typha latifolia* to the botanist but "flag" to early chair makers) grows in swamps and ditches from Maine to California, and experts tell me the best quality comes from upstate New York, around the Finger Lakes. That may be so, but I have seen perfectly good rush growing in Grand Junction, Colorado, near Amarillo, Texas, and many other places too fierce to mention. Rush is available in the trade, but it is bulky and difficult to ship so that the price for a small quantity may turn out to be prohibitive. I find it much simpler to cut my own. It makes a good outing.

The best time to cut is late summer or when the tips turn brown. Choose the tallest stand you can find and cut near the base with a small sharp butcher knife, picking only the barren stalks, without the brown, bushy cattails. Strip off the lower (outer) short leaves and spread the stalks in the sun for a day or two, to dry off the sticky gelatinous gook exuded by the fleshy part of the stalks. After that, the rushes can dry indoors, but it takes about a month, even in dry weather, before they are ready.

Just before use, the rush is soaked overnight—in the bathtub, of course. It has to be bent double to fit, but that

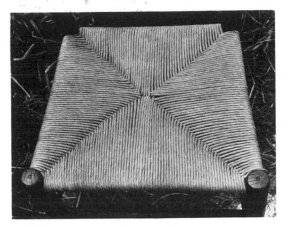

214. A seat of paper "rush." It is strong, relatively durable, and devoid of character.

215. Cutting rush in western New York state.

does not harm it if it is put in tips first and allowed to soak a while before it is bent over. I soak only what I expect to use in the next two or three days—wet rush starts rotting within a week. For weaving, the rush should be damp but not dripping wet, and I keep it in a long fold of polyethylene sheet as I work.

As they come from the tub, the stalks of rush must be separated into individual leaves and "broken" to make them flexible. The best way to do that is to run them through one of those old-fashioned roller wringers, if you can find one. Pulling them over a towel rack, or the dull edge of a table, bent at almost a right angle so that they crackle as you pull, will accomplish the same purpose. The object is to make them limp so they will not break as you weave.

Old-time weavers usually split each leaf of rush lengthwise into three or four strands. I have no idea how they did it. I use one of those multibladed gadgets fancy cooks use to split french-cut green beans. They come on the end of some potato peelers, and I clamp mine to the bench and pull each leaf through, butt end first. Then I run the split leaf through my fingers again, bent so it crackles, and I am ready to weave.

Taking enough of the strands to give me a rope of the thickness I want, butt end first, I pinch and twist them into a smooth flexible rope, twisting always toward the middle of the rail to be covered. The pattern is shown in figure 216. The end is taped to the side rail to start. Most seats are trapezoidal, and more turns of the rope will be needed to cover the front rail than the back. I make up for that by taking two turns around each front leg every second time around the seat until the bare gap on the front rail is exactly the same width as on the back rail. Any irregularity in the lengths of the side rails can be compensated for in the same way. New rush is added to the rope from underneath, every time it rounds one of the inside corners that are forming in the pattern. The rope must be tight and the corners flat and square. As the weaving progresses, the exposed portions of the rope get longer, and it may be necessary to splice the rope between the corners. The form of the splice is shown in figure 217, and one always places it in a spot where it will get covered up by later weaving. All the loose butt ends are pulled downward and allowed to stick out the bottom, to be cut off later. One twists the rope just enough to bring it twisted over the rail but to leave it straight underneath. Twisting a smooth even rope is a skill to be acquired, but it is nowhere near as difficult as learning to play the violin, for example.

The rush rope relaxes a little when it

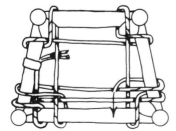
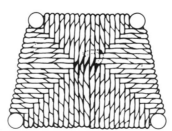

216. Weaving pattern for a rush seat. Note that the strands are always twisted toward the center of the rail.

217. Splicing a new leaf into the twisted rope of rush.

dries, and it is useful to let a seat dry out before it is quite finished. Eight pockets have formed in the weaving; they are now stuffed with loose rush to take up some of the slack produced by drying and to give the seat a cushiony contour. Then the last few turns are put in place, and the end of the rope is pulled from underneath around the two middle ropes of one of the sides and tucked in. Toward the end, as the hole in the seat becomes smaller and smaller, a small hook made from a coat hanger is needed to pull the rope of rush through, and a stout flat hardwood stick is helpful in stuffing the pockets. That is all there is to it, apart from the mess in the bathroom and little bits of rush all over the house.

Rush seats are most comfortable left bare, but they go to pieces very quickly that way. In Hitchcock's time, the seats were soaked with dilute shellac to make them more durable, and some finishers today prefer synthetic varnish. My own choice is acetate lacquer, not only for strength but also because acetate shrinks vegetable fibers and makes the seat a little tighter. When the seat is absolutely dry, I coat it liberally, on top and underneath, with lacquer diluted one to one with lacquer thinner or acetone. Unruly strands are smoothed down and odd ends tucked in before the lacquer hardens. A few weights may

help keep the seat flat as the lacquer dries.

SPLINT SEATS

Splints are made of green ash or hickory wood, in strips about $\frac{1}{16}$ inch thick and about $\frac{1}{2}$ inch wide. The standard length is about 12 feet. They should be soaked in water overnight to make them pliable for use. Even so, they are fairly stiff, and a twill weave is required to make a good seat. Splices are made by interlocking the splints as shown in figure 218, but they split very easily, and the splices will not hold unless they are firmly woven in, usually underneath.

To begin with, we splice one end of the splint back on itself to form a loop around the back rail of the frame. Now we begin winding under the front rail, up front, over the back, under the front again, and so on round and round the frame, laying the splints as close together as they will go, until the back rail is full. Since most seats are trapezoidal, the front rail being longer than the back, there now remain two triangles not covered with splints, one on each side. Do not fret; we shall attend to them presently.

First, however, bring the end of the last turn around the back post over to one side and start weaving side to side: over two, under two, over two, and so on in a twill pattern both on top and

218. Splicing ash or hickory splints.

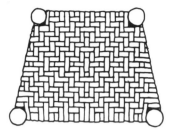

219. Splint seat woven in a cross twill pattern.

underneath the seat. The next strand goes over one, under two, over two, and so on, and the next again over two, under two, over two to make the twill. We can make a fancy twill like that shown in figure 219, if we have the urge; it is not particularly difficult. When the seat is covered, we secure the end by doubling it under itself, and now it is time to attend to those triangles. With what short pieces we have left we complete the pattern in the triangles, doubling the loose ends under as tightly as we can. A narrow dull knife, something like a letter opener, is very useful in manipulating the splints toward the end.

The finished splint seat may be rubbed lightly with linseed oil, but shellac or lacquer make it stiff and brittle. It will creak and groan when sat upon, but all things considered, it is really the most durable of all woven chair seats.

CANE SEATS

Cane seats are durable, but that does not take into account the frequent misuse of cane-seated chairs as stepladders. Stepping through the caned seats of chairs was a particularly successful item in slapstick comedy of early motion pictures, and I have seen it done by many great artists in excruciatingly funny ways. At any rate, I now know exactly why the caned seats of so many chairs have a big hole in them.

Before we start replacing such a seat, we must make sure that the frame is not cracked parallel to the line of holes. Any such cracks must be repaired very well if the seat is not to give way under the first sitter. The crack may be simply glued by the hypodermic method, but it is probably wiser to splice on new wood underneath and redrill the holes.

The names of some cane suppliers are listed in the Appendix. The width to be used depends on the spacing of the holes in the frame. The chairs with holes about ½ to ⅝ inch apart will take *medium* cane for the usual pattern. Chairs with holes about ⅜ inch apart are best woven with *fine* or *fine-fine* cane. We shall need some wooden pegs, slightly tapered and about the same diameter as the holes in the frame; old golf tees do nicely. A big needle with a wide eye is helpful, and special caning needles are available.

The weaving process is a little complicated, so let me number the steps for convenience:

Step 1. Starting in one corner (fig. 220, *left*) secure one end of the cane in a hole with a temporary peg and run the cane to the corresponding hole in the opposite member of the frame, parallel to the front of the seat. Thread it through the hole, come up again through the next hole, and run back to the hole next to the starting hole. Go in, under, up the next hole, and back again—back and forth—until you have a *warp*, which is a set of parallel lines running across the seat. Set all lines finger tight. When a piece of cane gives out, go to the nearest hole, twist the end of the old piece and the end of a new piece lightly together, and pull the

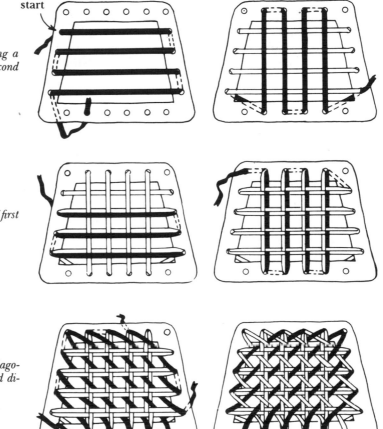

220. Left, *first step in caning a chair seat (warp);* right, *second step (woof).*

221. *Third and fourth steps (first weave).*

222. Left, *fifth step (first diagonal);* right, *sixth step (second diagonal).*

twisted pair through two holes. Friction will hold the ends together.

Step 2. Now start across, on top of the warp and at right angles to it, back and forth in parallel lines until the *woof* is formed (fig. 220, *right*).

Step 3. Repeat first step (backward) and start on the second line of the warp, parallel to the first, using the same holes used before, and this time lay the lines on top of all the previous caning (fig. 221, *left*). So far we have only strung our loom. The weaving is now to begin.

Step 4. The second strand of the woof comes next, except that this time weave back to front and back again—over one, under one, over one, and so on— as the basic pattern begins to emerge (fig. 221, *right*). By this time we may have trouble getting the cane through the holes, and an awl or an ice pick can be of great help for that.

Step 5. Now comes the trickiest part of the caning process: the first diagonal strand (fig. 222, *left*). Begin in the same old corner and go diagonally across the pattern, weaving over two, under two, and so forth. The difficulty arises from the fact that few seats are strictly rectangular. Curiously enough, a perfectly regular pattern can be woven on any shape, even a round frame, but we must be careful with the diagonals to maintain the pattern.

Step 6. The opposite diagonal is woven over three, under three, and so on (fig. 222, *right*). Again, great care is required to keep the pattern regular at the edges, but that may not be as difficult as before, for we either have got the knack by now or have given up in disgust.

The caned seat is finished off with a thicker strand of cane ("binder") laid over the holes and stitched on with thin cane looped from underneath through all the holes, rather tightly. All caning is done with the cane damp, but the binder may be stiff and may have to be soaked a bit. All this may sound like a horrendous procedure, but most weavers learn it the first time they try.

UPHOLSTERED FURNITURE

If an upholstered chair is a little wobbly, but the old or even original covering is still in good condition, then I recommend we let it wobble. Almost any repair on the basic framework of an upholstered piece requires the removal of the old covering, and it is usually most difficult to put it back. This is one thing that restorers find very hard to explain to a customer: a good glue job on the frame may have taken thirty minutes, but the covering took an hour to remove, and six hours to put back again. Furthermore, it ripped in two or three places, oi, oi, oi!

The upholsterer's craft has never been displaced by mechanized production, and so we should be able to find a good upholsterer. The best antiques dealers in town will be able to recommend a man who is reliable and experienced with antique pieces. The cost of upholstery is high, both for labor and for materials, and must be considered when we contemplate bidding on a wreck. There are few jobs I am not willing to tackle; upholstering is one of them. All the good intentions in the world are no substitute for experience—knowing just how much to stretch a piece of a given material over a given padding and get the shape we want and not have the thing rip.

I can say with confidence that upholsterers earn what they get, but the price they are likely to charge simply means that condition is a most important consideration in selecting upholstered antiques. A Colonial wing chair may be valuable (fig. 223), but let us not forget that extra slice for the fellow with the tack hammer.

BROKEN LEGS

Chair and table legs get broken, and the difficulty of repairing such damage depends on circumstances. If the break is due to a split, then we can usually glue it up again, even though we may have to add a little wood to replace lost splinters. If, however, the break is clean, right across the member, then epoxy may do the trick. Failing that, we have to do a little artful scarfing, as shown in figure 224. In any case, we should leave no stone unturned in searching for all the missing pieces, for it is much easier to glue up a shoebox full of fragments than to make a leg that matches three others.

TABLES

When old tables went out of fashion, they were commonly relegated to the

223. Very fine "stockinged-slipper" trifid-foot Philadelphia wing chair, about 1740–60, sold for $85,000 in 1977 just the way you see it. The upholstery is certainly not original. Internal construction is what counts here, and the old cloth was ripped off to show it. Soon after this photograph appeared in newspapers, antiques dealers were besieged with calls from people who had torn-up armchairs and wanted to sell them. (Courtesy of Sotheby Parke Bernet, Inc., New York.)

kitchen or to the barn, and their owners often thought nothing of cutting them up to suit some purpose of the moment. After all, they were just old tables. Someone may have thought the tavern table that lost one of the cleats would look much better with an oval top, and out came the saw. Or someone took a leaf off a drop-leaf table to fix a crack in it, but somehow the leaf never was put back. Or Grandma needed some shelves to put her jelly jars on,

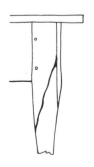

224. Typical repairs of broken table legs.

and there was that old table in the cellar, just the right length. In other words, tables fall prey to all sorts of handy arrangements, and that is the reason for the alarmingly high divorce rate of early table frames and their tops.

A mutilated top severely detracts from the value of any table, even when it is properly restored. We should first decide whether the base is interesting enough to warrant restoring the top. Good Pilgrim and early Colonial tables are probably worth restoring no matter how badly damaged, but simple tables of the Federal period are almost certainly not worth fooling with. The high-grade Federal tables are normally in fair to good condition anyway.

DROP-LEAF TABLES

Missing leaves are not too difficult to restore, once we have found the right lumber. Sets of spare leaves for late tables often come up in auction without any table to go with them, and they are by far the best material for this sort of repair.

When both drop leaves are missing, we can get a good idea of their former size by considering the proportion of the whole table. The leaves could not have been wider than about 26 to 28 inches if the table is of usual height (28 to 30 inches). Wide leaves had supports that reached far out to brace them, usually almost the width of the leaf. Narrow drop leaves had less substantial underpinnings. The shape of the drop leaves can be reconstructed from the outline of the short sides of the central leaf (fig. 225). If the sides are straight, then the whole table was almost certainly rectangular, possibly with the corners rounded or cut out, as shown in figure 226. I show these adornments

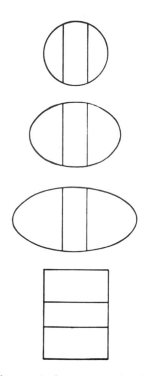

225. *Shapes of the tops of drop-leaf tables (HHT).*

only as extremes. Most rectangular tables are simply that, with no fancy treatment of the corners. If the short sides of the central leaf are curved, then the table was either round, elliptical, or serpentine, and we can divine the shape by projecting the curve of the

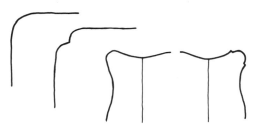

226. *Ornamental corners on rectangular drop-leaf tables and serpentine Pembroke (small drop-leaf) tables.*

sides, assuming the shape was a true ellipse, which is usually correct. (A true ellipse, in case you have forgotten, is a figure easily drawn with the aid of two nails, a piece of string, and a pencil, as shown in figure 227.)

The joint between leaves usually follows one of the three styles shown in figure 228. The simple butt joint was rarely used, except on very simple tables. The tongue-and-groove joint is often regarded as a sign of great age. It seems to have gone out of fashion about 1720–30 in favor of the obviously superior rule joint, but this opinion is not universally held, and my own experience is not conclusive on that particular detail. The rule joint, of course, is much neater and safer in use than any of the others.

A good rule joint requires careful fitting. It is not enough to match the shape of the molding, but the boards also must be straight and the hinges placed correctly, so that the center line of the hinge pins coincides exactly with the geometrical center line of the quarter-cylinder part of the molding. I suggest careful measurement as the easiest way to accomplish the task, for hinges

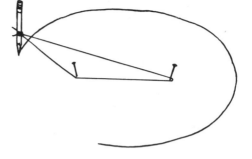

227. How to draw an ellipse.

are not easily moved once they have been screwed in place. A proper rule joint will fit when the leaf is either up or down and will not bind in between. A warped or poorly fitted joint will strain the hinges until they break.

The thickness of table tops varies from ⅝ to 1 inch, but in the absence of evidence to the contrary I rely on the usual ¾-inch boards for my restorations. We should pay particular attention to the edges of the restored leaves. If we can find old boards for the replacement, then we should arrange to use the old, worn edges on the outside wherever possible. Lacking that, we

228. Drop-leaf table joints. 1, butt; 2, tongue and groove; 3, rule (HHT).

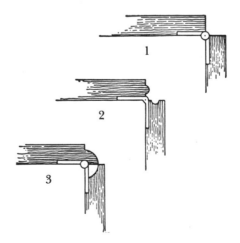

should shape the edges with care to give the typical outlines shown in figure 229. Cheap reproductions often have a peculiarly wrong outline of the edges, which makes them immediately obvious. The thumbnail-molded edge in particular must have a low shoulder if it is to look right (fig. 229, *bottom*).

TAVERN TABLES

The tavern table, a basic necessity of the Colonial kitchen, went into almost complete oblivion during the nineteenth century but has now come to occupy a position tantamount to minor aristocracy among American antiques. I have never quite understood the great popularity of these rough tables, but one should not worry over the public's taste. The fact remains that early tavern tables, even rather plain ones, are well worth restoring.

Tops. Tops of tavern tables are often damaged or missing. It really does not make a whole lot of difference, for if the top is badly cut up, it must be replaced anyway. From my own experience I am tempted to say dogmatically that old wood is necessary to make a convincing restoration, and I do not just mean old wood planed down but old wood with a usable old surface. I know the usual tricks for making new wood look old, even the one that involves beating the surface with old tire chains, but all that anyone can hope to accomplish by that treatment is to produce a table top that looks as if it had been beaten with old tire chains. There is no quick way of producing the pleasing appearance of age on a surface as large as the top of a tavern table.

Old pine is fairly easy to find, and we should look for boards that show wear on the surface and on the edges. Such boards can be taken from the plain kind

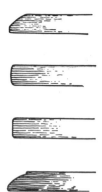

229. *Correct edges of table tops (HHT).*

of six-board chest or from shelves from old houses. For almost all such jobs we shall need two wide boards and two cleats to make a table top. If we do the thing right, then the ends of the cleats will be the only places where new cuts will show on the surface. I admit that we may have to search a little before finding the wood that permits this happy solution.

The two boards will have to be joined to make the top. The methods commonly used by old cabinetmakers for joining boards are shown in figure

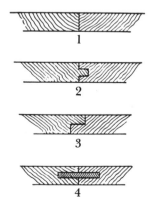

230. *The joining of boards of table tops. 1, butt; 2, tongue and groove; 3, lap; 4, spline (HHT).*

230. The butt joint is easiest but not particularly durable (1). The tongue-and-groove joint is standard technique (2), but I prefer the shiplap joint (3), because it can be cut accurately on a simple table saw with just two settings of the blade, clamps easily, and therefore glues well. The spline joint is also good but more difficult to make (4); nevertheless, I use it if I need the extra width. In any case, we arrange our cuts so that the nicely worn edges of the boards now form the outside edges of the top.

The cleats can be attached to the ends in several ways, as shown in figure 231. Wooden pegs (1) or hand-forged nails (2) most commonly held the cleats on Colonial tables. The nails are stronger, of course, and I prefer them. Handmade modern reproductions of Colonial nails are available, but if I could not find them I would get blue rectangular cut nails, hammer sharp points on them, and set them into holes drilled to receive them, leaving the head flush with the surface. In pine, the holes can be much smaller than the nails that go into them. There is no point in gluing the cleat down, for the glue will not hold on the end grain; besides, we do not want an excessively rigid joint. Other, less common ways of fastening the cleats are the tongue-and-groove method (3), and the mortise-and-tenon construction (4), both usually held in place with small wooden pins. These joints are very strong—too strong, in fact—and they are likely to make the top crack. I recommend the tongue-and-groove cleat to those who like to be fancy and to those who are afraid the boards may warp. However, the joint should be glued only in a 2- or 3-inch spot near the middle. The cleat would hold so well if the whole joint were glued that the boards would surely crack as they work with time. A 20-inch pine board will shrink and swell ⅛ inch in the course of a year, and that is more than enough for a big crack if the board is rigidly constrained.

If we live right, we may be lucky enough to find a single board wide enough for our top. One always prefers table tops made of a single board, although the advantage is purely esthetic, modern glues being as strong as they are. The tongue-and-groove cleat is probably best for single-board tops,

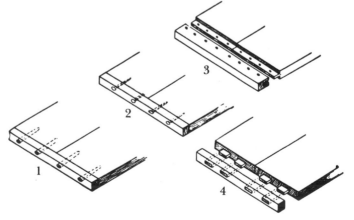

231. End cleats on old tavern table tops (HHT).

for they are more likely to warp, but we must be doubly sure to attach the cleats loosely enough so that they will not crack the wide board.

Feet. The next thing most usually missing from tavern tables is the feet, and we may see them restored in some mighty peculiar ways. Yet the choice is very simple here: The portion below the stretcher almost always reflects the shape of the turning above the stretcher, as shown in figure 232. Plain rectangular legs had plain rectangular feet. Fancy turned legs were symmetrical with respect to the stretcher—in other words, distance *a* was almost always equal to distance *b*. This is one of those ironbound conventions that pervaded early American cabinetmaking.

If the feet are lost to line *c* and the table now rests on its stretchers, then the restoration is bound to be difficult. The dowels of the new feet will interfere with the mortises of the stretchers, and a lot of recutting will be necessary. It is the same sort of trouble we discussed when we talked about restoring the shortened legs of chairs. Things are easier if there is a stub left, but the repair will be rather obvious no matter how well we match the wood. Only if just the tip of the foot is missing can we hope to conceal the glue line in one of the crevices of the turning and thus make a presentable restoration.

The restoration procedure follows the same pattern already outlined for the legs of Windsors, except that the dowels can be larger, perhaps ¾ inch in diameter, and the need for accurate positioning of the dowel hole is greater if the foot is nicely turned. Figure 233 shows a new foot. I prefer to do the drilling in a large drill press with the leg rigidly clamped and the drill accurately squared off. This is the kind of drilling where mistakes are not al-

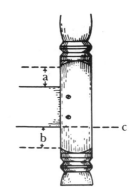

232. *Foot and stretcher of a tavern table (HHT).*

lowed, and the extra work in setting up can be written off as worthwhile accident insurance.

Replacing feet, then, may be easy or difficult depending on how much was lost. Tacking on four button feet is no strain, but making four large turnings, doweling them on, recutting eight mortises, and refitting all the stretchers may be more of a job than we bargained for. One can tint the wood to match, but the glue lines of this patch job will certainly show.

Perhaps I have made it clear that a tavern table is no bargain when more than just the tips of the feet are miss-

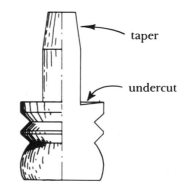

233. *New foot for a tavern table.*

ing. Yet the average auction buyer pays no attention to this very important detail, and a wrecked table often brings the same price as one in good condition.

Missing drawers. A missing drawer is the third serious defect of many a tavern table. We shall discuss drawer repair later under a separate heading, but now I refer only to the drawers for tavern tables. Some of them may have been dovetailed and others simply nailed. Now you may be a whiz at cabinetwork, and I can think of many ways you can exercise your talent with profit, but making dovetailed replacement drawers for tavern tables is not one of them. Whatever you do, the drawer will be "fake," and a fake drawer is a fake drawer. For that reason I would just rabbet it and nail it together and spend my time on some other job where precision is essential.

The proper pull for a tavern table is the long kind of wooden knob (fig. 155) —one for narrow drawers and two for wide ones. Few tavern tables had brass pulls, so we should not use brass unless we have good evidence that the original drawers had brass on them.

SAWBUCK AND TRESTLE TABLES

Pine tables with sawbuck or trestle underbodies were popular in the country from Pilgrim times to the end of the eighteenth century, but few of them have survived to this day. They are simple tables, easy to make, and frequently faked for that reason. Most of these tables we see on the market today are of dubious ancestry, but one does see a genuine one occasionally, and that is the kind we shall talk about in the rest of this section.

These genuine tables are rare and deserve a good deal of work if they are not too crudely made. Usually they reach us via some barn, and the mortise-and-tenon joints will be loose and wobbly. We should take the pieces all apart, mark them carefully, and soak them in water for a few days. Then reassemble them wet without glue or pins, and clamp lightly across all the mortises, using blocks under the clamps to distribute the pressure. When everything is dry, after a few days, take the joints apart again, glue them, pin them, and clamp again. One can make a passably firm table out of a trembling skeleton that way.

This method will not work if the wood has suffered. Then we have to cut out all rotten or splintered pieces, scarf in new wood wherever necessary, recut mortises and replace tenons, and in general do much work that we had not expected. When the top is in poor condition, then we use the same approach already discussed in the section on tavern tables, except that this top will be much larger, and old wood for it may not be easy to find. The tops of these country tables are often quite thick, as much as 1½ inches. Personally, I like these tables, but a cordon-bleu cook tells me that they are too narrow for proper setting.

TRIPOD TABLES

Considering how fragile tripod tables are, I never cease to wonder that so many of them have survived. Their fragility lies in their basic construction (fig. 234). Each leg is set into the central column by means of a long dovetail, so that the weight of the table tends to pull the base of the column apart. The pull is across the grain, in the direction where wood is weakest, so it does not take much of a jolt to split the wood. Many tripod tables have a

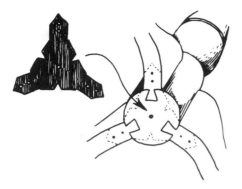

234. Bottom of a tripod table, and the iron contraption (spider) that holds it together.

three-cornered metal contraption underneath, sometimes called a spider, consisting of three straps radiating from the center. Each strap is screwed or nailed into the bottom of the leg. The purpose of this gadget is to take the weight off the column, and it does so effectively as long as the nails or the screws hold.

A broken tripod table will not stand, of course, so that we are most likely to find it tied up in a bundle or thrown into a box. A good top with a bundle of sticks can add up to a nice table, assuming that all the pieces are there. So before we get too excited over a find in that condition, we should make doubly sure that all is present. A missing splinter usually means a complicated scarfing job, what with the dovetailed legs and all.

The rest is just a matter of thorough cleaning inside the joints, followed by glue and making suitable forms for the clamping. The rubber band may come in handy, too, and when the glue has set we should attach one of those three-cornered whatdoyoucallits (spiders?) underneath—the original one if we have it, a new one otherwise. Any welder or blacksmith can make one

235. Unusual two-tier tripod stand (dumb waiter), held together by an iron rod that passes through the column and is fastened with a wing nut against the usual spider. Made in Philadelphia about 1770.

without much trouble, and if we can lay our hands on a piece of 16-gauge sheet steel or brass and a hacksaw, we might even whittle one out ourselves. Each strap should have two or three countersunk screw holes—there is no use in making more than that—and the piece should fit snugly.

CARCASE REPAIR

I have been using the word carcase to mean the four wide boards, usually dovetailed together, that form the main part of chests, desks, and cupboards (fig. 236). I follow the spelling used in John Rodd's *Repair and Restoration of Furniture,* and it seems to me explicit as well as elegant. Its meaning and pronunciation are exactly the same as *carcass,* but without the meat-cutting implications.

Split sides are the most frequent difficulty with carcase goods. The split is usually caused by the drawer runs, moldings, and other members fastened to the sides across the grain. In order to heal the split, the whole piece must be taken completely apart and each split opened up, cleaned out completely, refitted, and glued up. Then the carcase may be reassembled, and that may take a little fitting, for the sides may be hardwood while the bottom is almost always pine, and it would be unlikely to have these different woods shrink just the same amount.

All this adds up to a passel of work, but such is life. We may have worked all day and healed the split beautifully, but the casual bystander will hardly notice the difference. Only the expert will know the importance of the repair. On a slant-top desk, for instance, split sides cause the lid to fit badly so that the lips are likely to get knocked off the lid. A cracked side is a fundamental weakness, and we might as well get it fixed.

If it looks as if the crack would not hold with glue alone, then we can attach glue blocks—short pieces of hardwood about ½ inch thick and 2 to 3 inches wide—inside the carcase between the drawer runs. The grain of the block must be parallel with the grain of the sides. Carcases with corner pilasters usually have enough room for the drawers to clear the blocks, but the design of simple carcases may require that the glue blocks be made thinner, perhaps ⅜ inch, and let into the sides flush from the inside, as shown in figure 237. Healing a crack thus

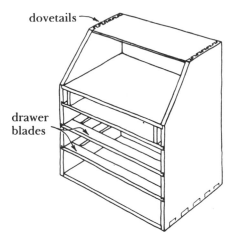

236. *Carcase of a slant-top desk.*

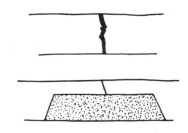

237. *Healing a split in the side of a carcase. The new piece is set on the inside.*

becomes advanced surgery, but I know no simpler way of achieving the same result with any degree of permanence.

DRAWERS

We have discussed the various styles of drawer construction in chapter 6; now let us consider the repair of the usual kind of damage on Colonial and Federal drawers. This damage is not caused by abuse. It is merely the natural consequence of shrinkage of the wood and normal wear from use. The bottom of the drawer—usually a wide pine board—may shrink so much that it falls out of the groove cut for it in the drawer front. It will then drag on the drawer blade and wear excessively when the drawer is pulled open. The bottoms of the drawer sides gradually wear by friction against the runs, until they wear off and the drawer bottom is laid bare. This wear may be severe when all pieces are dry, and we often find little piles of fine wood dust lying on the drawer runs of old pieces.

These difficulties are fairly easy to correct, and I suggest, if you have never scarfed wood, that a broken drawer may be a good piece to learn on. First make sure that none of the dovetails are nailed across. Then knock the drawer apart with a rubber mallet. Plane the edge of the front tongue of the drawer bottom until it is straight and even, and glue on a strip of matching wood just a little thicker than the width of the edge and wide enough to restore the drawer bottom to its original width (cross-grain dimension). When this new tongue extension is shaped down to the thickness of the old tongue, and the bottom is returned to its place in the drawer, the new tongue should fit into the groove in front and the back edge should line up flush with

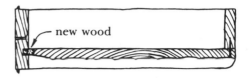

238. *Cross section through a repaired drawer showing the new piece (dotted) glued onto the drawer bottom to restore it to its original width.*

the outside edge of the drawer in back (fig. 238). That is job number one.

Now plane down the bottoms of the sides until they are straight, which means that you have to plane off the old groove if the drawer is badly worn. Next, glue on a strip of matching wood to bring the sides back to their original width, and then recut the groove for the drawer bottom. The old-timers used a router plane for that, but you have my permission to use the table saw. Now refit the sides to the front and back, slide in the bottom, and nail it in back with two or three small nails. If we have made no mistakes in measuring, everything ought to fit. The bottom should not be glued in place, but we can glue the dovetails if they seem to need it. Be sure the drawer is square before you let the glue dry. Burning a solid layer of paraffin wax onto the bottom of the drawer sides is a good finishing touch. An old electric iron is just right for that.

Drawer runs are the pieces of wood, usually pine, on which the drawers slide. They are fastened inside the carcase, nailed in back, as a rule, and fitted into slots in the drawer blades, but they may be just nailed to the side boards in two or three places. They are often worn to the point of uselessness, but it is easy to remove them, and they can be replaced with new runs without too much trouble. In that case I do not throw the old runs away, but I usually soothe my conscience by fastening them somewhere inside the carcase where they are out of the way of the drawers but where they may be found by those who look for them as signs of authenticity. The real antiquarian would not replace the runs. He would merely scarf in new wood to build up the worn places to their former level and then return the runs to their original places, fastening them with their original nails. Again, a coat of hot wax on the runs will make the drawers slide easily and minimize wear in the future.

Most of the Colonial and early Federal drawers were made with thumbnail-molded lips, which become chipped through the ages. I leave the chipped corners alone if the damage is small, but if larger pieces are missing then I scarf on new pieces of wood, taking the greatest possible care to match the grain and color of the wood. The repair will look a little patchy even then, and many collectors seriously downgrade pieces with chipped drawers. Some restorers prefer to plane off the whole top of the drawer front and glue on a new strip clear across. That means removing the lock, if there is one, but I cannot deny that such a repair looks better than two patched corners. Nevertheless, I usually hesitate about making such drastic restorations just for the sake of appearances. In general, I like to take off as little of the original wood as is consistent with making a sound joint.

SELECTING THE PROPER BRASSES FOR REPLACEMENT

If the piece we found still bears some of the original brasses, our problem is simple. We send a sample to one of the better dealers (those that I know are listed in the Appendix), and he can ei-

ther select the nearest matching pattern from his regular stock or duplicate the sample quite closely, if we are prepared to pay for the extra hand work involved.

Most pieces, however, have lost all their brasses, and here we have a chance to do a little fine detective work. The old postholes will be easy to find, even if one of them has been enlarged to receive the threaded wooden shank of a Victorian knob. Marks of the clinched cotter pins will be clearly discernible inside the drawers of early Colonial pieces, where the cotter pins were bent and driven back into the wood (fig. 239). A minute examination of the drawer front will produce additional evidence: If we look closely, we are likely to find scars left by the original plates. The marks may be quite prominent (as shown in figs. 152 and 153), or they may be very faint, just barely visible when the clean wood is moistened lightly with turpentine.

In any case we should select a style that corresponds closely to the marks we find. This is no place for original ideas; any desire to put on some other "better-looking" brasses should be nobly but quickly sublimated. We have

239. Wrong brasses in the right holes. The posthole distance is correct, but the scars make clear that this drawer was originally equipped with cotter-pin brasses.

already agreed that our purpose is to *restore,* not embellish. Only if the drawer fronts have been so deeply refinished that no trace of the old plates can be found are we free to select any brass that suits our fancy, guided only by the general style requirements of the piece and leaning on the side of simplicity.

Perhaps it goes without saying that the brasses we use should fit what we think are the oldest holes in the drawer fronts. As a rule, it is not difficult to tell which holes are the ones drilled for the originals. Scars of the old brasses, or the places hollowed out in back to receive nuts, or the remains of clinched cotter pins—any of these will tell the tale (fig. 240). Often these holes may be much enlarged by wear.

A good way to set new posts in oversize holes is to roll a strip of glue-soaked brown paper onto the post, just to the diameter of the hole, push the thing in, and tamp the paper in from the back. Where the brasses have been replaced by wooden knobs, the brown-paper treatment will not suffice and we may have to plug the holes properly.

To do that, we first drill the holes out to the next standard drill size. This must be done with great care to obtain a smooth, round hole without ragged edges. I prefer to work on a sturdy drill press at a high drill speed and with the drawer front rigidly clamped to the table of the press. Now we cut plugs from matching wood with a plug cutter of the same standard size as the drill. These cutters are available from dealers in woodworking machinery, and the ½-inch size will do for almost all our jobs. The cutter makes it possible to cut an accurately round plug across the grain so that we can glue the plug into a corresponding hole and match the grain of the wood reasonably well. If we simply used a dowel to plug up the hole, the end grain of the dowel would look mighty peculiar on the drawer front, if any part of it should show, and the cross-grain position of the plug in the hole would cause it to work loose before long.

When the old hole is plugged, we redrill a hole for the new brass in the right place, not forgetting to make the hole just slightly smaller than the shank of the bolts. The size must be selected with care; if the hole is too large, the brass will soon become wobbly, and if it is too small, the old wood may split when we try to drive the bolts in.

ORNAMENTAL MOLDINGS

Early Colonial furniture is often trimmed with light molding applied

240. Good reproduction brasses correctly installed in the old holes.

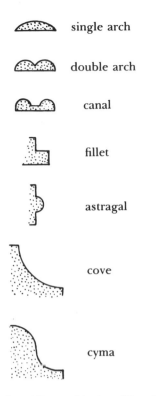

single arch

double arch

canal

fillet

astragal

cove

cyma

241. Simple moldings and basic molding elements.

with small iron brads (fig. 241). The single- and the double-arch molding are probably earlier than the canal molding, which is, however, most common. The blanket chest sketched in figure 53 might have canal molding along the edges of the front. The strips are thin and fragile, and some are likely to be missing on such an old piece.

Later Colonial and early Federal pieces may carry moldings of a multitude of designs, usually built up of several elements. The most common basic shapes are the quarter circle (cove) and the cyma, each sometimes combined with the fillet and the astragal. These moldings are all fairly difficult to make without special tools. Crenelated (dentil) moldings are even more difficult,

but fortunately they appear mostly in cornices, where they are rarely damaged (figs. 6 and 242).

The old craftsmen cut moldings with special planes, each shaped for a particular molding (fig. 243). This is the easiest way but hardly practical for the restorer, who would have to have dozens of planes to match even the most common shapes he might need. Modern moldings are made with rotary power tools, using special cutters for each shape. These cutters can be ordered from power-tool distributors to produce any particular shape we may need, but they are rather expensive. It is hardly worthwhile to order a special cutter to make just three feet of molding—it being the nature of things that the next job will require, if not a different shape, then at least the same shape in a different size. The variety of moldings used on antique furniture is almost endless. The famous Salem designer-carver-cabinetmaker Samuel McIntire (1757–1811) owned forty-six molding planes, according to the inventory of his estate (see Hipkiss, *Eighteenth-Century American Arts*, p. 361).

About a dozen or more modern shapes are considered standard now, and cutters for them are readily available to the home craftsman. Unfortunately, most of these shapes are not particularly useful to the restorer of antiques, but with the help of two of them (the cove cutter for the quarter circle and the ogee cutter for the cyma curve) we can approximate a multitude of profiles by making a series of properly spaced cuts and then scraping off the remaining edges. We may want to grind a special scraper from a sheet of hardened steel to help finish the molding to the desired shape, as shown in figure 244. This operation takes time, and I do not want to pretend that it is easy.

242. Colonial pine hanging cup-board (33" high, 30" wide, 14½" deep) distinguished by a bold crene-lated (dentil) molding forming the cornice; all original except for the lower molding. The thoughtful re-storer will be most careful to pre-serve the crisp outlines and corners of the molding.

In the absence of a molding cutter, I have found it easiest to reproduce small pieces of molding by rough-cutting on a table saw and then shaping with a small plane and a sanding block, with a touch of the scraper where necessary. Let me illustrate the procedure for a simple canal molding with the help of a series of sketches (fig. 245). First prepare a narrow board, perhaps 3 inches wide, and dress it to the thickness just equal to the width of the molding desired. Now adjust the fence to make the first cut with a fine-tooth crosscut blade exactly along one side of the canal. Now move the fence over just enough to cut the other side of the canal. A third cut may be necessary to give the canal a smooth, even bottom.

Each time the fence is moved, it is well to make a practice cut on a piece of scrap, for the cutting will have to be very precise if our molding is to look like the sample we are trying to dupli-cate.

Now bevel all the edges with a small plane and round them with a rough sanding block or a scraper ground to the proper shape. Then use fine sand-paper to remove the scratches, and we are ready to cut the molding off the board, as shown in the last sketch. We can make a fair approximation of al-most any molding that way, but it does take time and very precise setting of each cut. The rotary saw is a dangerous instrument, and every time I make a molding, I wonder how many fingers I

243. Special plane made to cut one particular molding. **Top,** *on the sides in four places it is branded* J. E. UNDERWOOD, *presumably an early owner.* **Bottom right,** *these planes are usually stamped with the maker's names on the front end grain. On the back end, this particular plane is also stamped ⅞* BY INCH & ¼, *the size of the finished molding.* **Left,** *Israel White's name in* Desilver's Philadelphia Directory *for 1835. He was listed from 1830 to 1840.*

shall end up with. So far I still have the original number, which is a great help in writing this book.

VENEER

Veneer was used on the finest furniture of the late Pilgrim era, then went out of fashion for almost a hundred years and returned with a bang in late Federal time. The early veneered pieces are, of course, very rare and worth every drop of the care and effort we can lavish on them, but I rather think that late pieces may not be worth repairing if too much veneer is missing (fig. 246). It is not

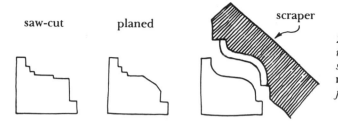

saw-cut   planed   scraper

244. Shaping a typical base mold-ing. Left, rough cut on a table saw; center, corners planed off; right, scraped with a tool ground for the purpose.

easy to match the color even when we use old veneer for patching, so that extensive repairs give a crazy-quilt effect. Small bits and narrow strips will go unnoticed, but patches of a few square inches and larger are difficult to hide.

We should try to find old veneer of the same thickness for our repairs, for it will be much easier to match and blend than raw, new veneer. Failing that, we can use modern sliced veneer, but the common rotary-cut veneer—the kind that is used in plywood—will be of no use in the restoration of an-

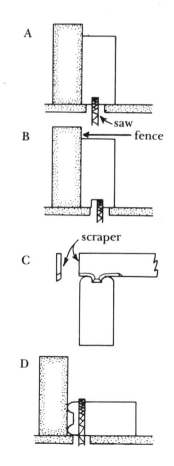

A

B

saw

fence

scraper

C

D

245. Making a canal molding. A, first cut; B, second cut; C, shaping with a scraper ground specially for the job; D, cutting off.

246. *Bits of veneer have come loose on this fine Queen Anne New England highboy at points where the stress in use is most severe. Once the veneer is lost, it is very difficult to match replacement patches with the original. The new veneer is likely to work loose again in the same place.*

tiques, for veneers were not made that way until after the middle of the nineteenth century. The edges of peeled areas must be cut sharp and square and the patch fitted in with the greatest possible accuracy. I make a rubbing if the shape is complicated. I stretch a piece of thin paper over the area to be patched and rub a flat point of a carpenter's pencil along the edges until the exact outline is clearly impressed, and then I transfer the outline to the patch with carbon paper. Old glue must be cleaned off completely before the patch is glued in.

Replacing a large area of veneer—on the top of a chest, for example— becomes quite a job. Courageous types should equip themselves with a sufficient number of sandbags and with a photographer's roller squeegee. Making sure all surfaces are level and clean, apply a coat of undiluted white glue to the backing, lay on the veneer, slide it in place, clamp one corner, and squeeze out all excess glue by rolling energetically with the squeegee in radial directions away from the clamped corner. Now wipe off the excess glue, cover with several layers of old newspaper, clamp all corners, pile on the sand-

bags, and hope for the best. Use fairly thick veneer (about $\frac{1}{16}$-inch) whenever possible. It is more durable and easier to apply evenly.

When a veneered piece is stored in a cellar or some other damp place, the veneer may separate from the base and form waves. Similarly, careless placement of flower pots or hot dishes may cause blisters. Small blisters can be reglued by moistening them, letting the water soak in for a while, then covering with several layers of paper and weighing down with a hot flatiron. The steam generated in the process may be enough to soften the glue underneath and heal the blister. In case this procedure fails, we may inject a shot of white glue, diluted one to one, by means of our fiendish syringe, and repeat the process. That ought to hold it.

The blisters may have cracked and gotten full of dirt. Then we must cut a flap around the blister, two cuts with the grain and one across, lift the tab carefully, clean out underneath, and then glue it back in place. When the veneer has separated in large waves, we lift off as much as comes off without straining, clean out, and glue it down again in the same way. If the waves are really curly, then I first only dampen the veneer, after cleaning out, and clamp it down so it will dry flat. Then I lift it off again and glue up. I prefer to take this operation in two steps because veneer may draw and warp the wood if it is glued on while wet. We shall need a pile of clamps and a supply of slightly curved, springy clamping boards for such a job. Sandbags are usually not enough to remove the waves.

INLAY

Inlay is probably the most difficult thing we are likely to be called upon to repair. I would say that we should give such jobs to a specialist if I did not know that the task of finding one may be much more difficult than learning how to do the job ourselves. Missing bits of line inlay may offer no particular problem beyond accurate fitting, but more complex borders or whole medallions can be quite exasperating. I use a rubbing to cut complex shapes for replacement, and when a medallion is missing I try to build it up piece by piece.

The woodworking specialty houses offer a selection of standard prefabricated borders and medallions, but the chance is small that we will find just what we need among the routine patterns. Modern factory-made inlays are crude compared to good antique ones, and the contrast will be obvious if we place the two side by side.

GOLD AND GILDING

Mirrors with gilt ornaments became popular early in the eighteenth century. The parcel-gilt Colonial mirrors may have a gilt bird at the top and gilt scrolls and other carving on the sides, highlighting the somber mahogany or walnut frame. Many of these mirrors were imported from England, and most American frames closely follow the English designs. Federal mirrors are often gilt all over. The gold on them is usually laid on wet ground over gesso on a base of soft wood and plaster, perhaps reinforced with wire here and there. That makes for a dreadfully fragile thing, and few such mirrors survive intact.

Early mirrors are rare, especially the more elegant ones, and well worth repairing. The best advice I can give about Federal mirrors is to steer clear of them if they are badly damaged. Any mirror can be repaired, of course, but the product of a complete regilding job will look like a new gilt mirror.

I should say, as usual, that any extensive gilding job should go to an expert gilder, but the trouble with that advice is that there are hardly any good gilders left. Gilding is difficult, but there is nothing magic about it, and the skillful amateur can do quite well once he has caught the knack.

The raw materials are plaster of paris, gesso, one of the three kinds of gold size, bronze powder of the highest quality, and tissue-backed 23-karat gold leaf (the kind made for "gilding in the wind"). Sometimes I think that the word size was coined by gilders especially to confuse the public. Burnish gold size (also called gilder's clay, gilder's bole, or red ground) is a mixture of litharge (a form of lead oxide), clay, and some red earth color to give a deep red tint. One old recipe also mentions oxblood, and I suspect that human blood might be even better, but so far I have not had the opportunity to try it. All the ingredients are ground to an extremely fine slurry in a very dilute glue solution, about 1 ounce of fine gelatin to 1 quart of water. The exact proportions depend on the kind of clay, so we may have to experiment a little. A good burnish size is smooth, sticks well, and does not crack when it dries. Prepared burnish gold size is not easy to find, but it is commercially available.

Oil gold size is a slow-drying type of varnish, and japan gold size is a quick-drying variety of the same thing. The third kind of size is a dilute solution of glue, and I shall refer to it as final size, simply to avoid utter confusion. The final size is made by soaking clear gelatin in cold water (about 1 ounce to the quart) for ten minutes or longer, until it swells to a jelly. The solution is then warmed (but not boiled), and the glue dissolves quickly. The solution is used warm, to keep it fluid. All these materials are available from good art supply houses, although we may have to go to more than one to find what we need.

Most of our gilding will be on mirror frames, some of them probably broken. First we replace any missing wood parts. The plaster parts are then built up in place and allowed to harden. Molds made of plasticine are useful for making casts if a model for a missing part is available elsewhere on the frame. I need hardly remind you that plaster sets very rapidly, so that we must mix a new little batch every ten minutes or so. When plaster parts are cast in place, they may seem to stick to the wood while still wet but may come off in our fingers when dry. This is no catastrophe—we simply glue them back with white glue and then carve and sand them into their final shape. Where the plaster has to be built up on wires, it will be easier first to wrap the wire with narrow surgical gauze soaked in thin plaster and then model with thicker plaster on that foundation.

Burnish gold size will not stick to raw plaster. Therefore, when all the shaping and rough sanding is done, it is well to give all plaster parts a thick coat or two of the final size as a primer. Two or three coats of gesso then go over the whole thing, both wood and plaster. Gesso, incidentally, is finely ground gypsum (hydrated calcium sulphate) and zinc white mixed in a glue solution. The usual proportion is half gypsum and half zinc white, and the glue is mixed about 3 ounces to the quart. Because it is the most expensive ingredient, some recipes cheat on the zinc white and may substitute whiting (precipitated calcium carbonate) for a "lean" mix or white china clay (kaolin) for a "fat" mix. The goo used with perforated tape in dry-wall construction is sold in powder form. It sticks well and makes a good lean base for the red burnish size. Fat grounds allow finer burnishing, but they crack and peel easily unless applied in many thin coats. All gesso grounds can be smoothed with the spatula or a modeling tool while still wet and sanded smooth when dry. The grounds should be dried slowly in some cool place. Once I was in a hurry and set some gesso panels out in the sun to dry. They cracked all to bits, and the gesso came off in curly flakes.

We can now proceed with the bronzing, if that was our aim. Oil size is best for that. We lay it on the gesso in a thin coat, preferably over a priming coat of thin shellac, and set it aside for ten to twenty hours to dry, depending on temperature. By that time it should be firm but still tacky, ready to receive the bronze powder. Japan gold size becomes tacky soon after it is laid on. For that reason it is useful on small surfaces, but it may dry unevenly on large ones.

Bronze is carried from its bottle on a little piece of velvet and is spread on

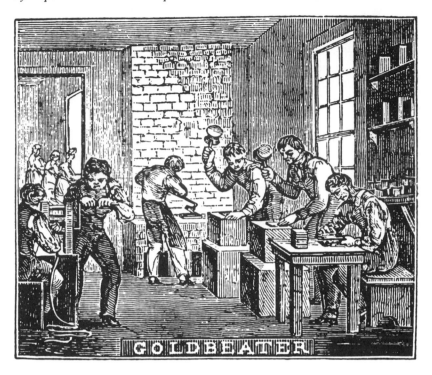

247. *For centuries gold foil for gilding was made by pounding bits of pure gold in books made of vellum with heavy hammers. (From Edward Hazen's* Panorama of Professions and Trades *[Philadelphia: 1839] in the University of Pennsylvania Library.)*

the tacky ground until a uniform coat results. A very small amount of powder will go a long way. Several tones of bronze are available: silver, light gold, dark gold, copper, and others.

Art supply stores may carry a "bronzing liquid," and the instructions on the label may suggest that bronze powder should be mixed with this liquid for gilding. Actually, such a mixture would be no more than the usual gold paint. It would produce a thick, dull coating, and certainly should not be used as a substitute for bright gilding or surface bronzing. Unfortunately, we shall see many Federal mirrors messed up with gold paint. The superior quality of proper gilding comes from the gold's

being right on the surface, with nothing over it. There is an enormous difference between bronze applied on the tacky surface of a varnish and bronze mixed into a varnish and applied like a paint. Perhaps I should add that, unlike leaf, bronze may be covered by a very thin coat of shellac, varnish, or clear spray lacquer. The coating will dull the finish, of course, but it will keep it from coming off on everything.

Bright gilding with gold leaf is much more difficult, but it gives a very superior product. The smoothness and brilliance of the gold depend on the smoothness of the ground. Gesso is not smooth enough, and that is where the burnish gold size comes in. At least three coats of the size are laid over the gesso or directly over the primed plaster, each coat quite thick and finely sanded before the next one goes on. The final coat has to be perfectly smooth, for the leaf greatly enhances all irregularities. If I want a bright burnish, I apply half a dozen coats of the burnish size and polish the final coat with 0000 steel wool and a clean wool rag. Leaf laid on such a surface can be burnished until it looks just like a highly polished piece of solid metal.

Now comes the final sizing. With a soft brush I quickly coat one small area at a time with the glue-water solution, spreading it carefully so that there are no puddles. Some gilders add a little sugar and a little alcohol to the final size, and I have heard tell that red wine helps a lot. Of this I have no doubt.

I lay the gold quickly while the size is still damp. The gold comes in sheets about 3 or 4 inches square, and the beginner may want to cut each leaf into quarters for easier handling. Leaf gold is extremely thin and more fragile than a spider's web. We must handle it carefully with its tissue-paper backing, cut it with clean scissors, never touch it with our fingers, and lay it down without crumpling it, with just a small overlap

248. Gilders at work in the 1830s. The man at the left is transferring gold leaf from the book to a "sized" carving, the man in back is preparing the ground on a carved picture frame, and the men at the right are carving ornaments. (From Edward Hazen's Panorama of Professions and Trades *[Philadelphia: 1839] in the University of Pennsylvania Library.)*

between sheets. We rub the tissue backing lightly with a small wad of cotton to make sure that the whole leaf adhered, and then we pull off the tissue.

Some experienced gilders prefer to use regular (unbacked) gold leaf. They slip it out of its folder onto a flat suede cushion, flatten it by gently blowing on it, cut it with a dry straight knife with a slight sawing motion, and pick it up with a wide, flat, soft brush (called the "tip") that they have made slightly (ever so slightly) sticky by passing it through their hair. Yes, their hair. I have no idea how bald gilders handle this situation.

Usually I size just enough for two or three sheets of the gold at a time. It is best to wait a few hours before burnishing with a highly polished stone (flint or agate). Burnishing is not strictly necessary, but it greatly enhances the luster and removes minor irregularities.

This kind of gold surface is not very strong, but it remains bright for a long time. It would be a mistake to varnish or shellac over the gold to "protect" it. Such coatings are less permanent than the gold—they dull its sheen and discolor it with time. If we need a surface that resists wear a little better, then we should use oil size or japan size, although neither of them can achieve the smoothness and luster one gets with the glue-water final size.

The newly gilded parts will appear new and bright and will contrast severely with the shabby old gilding. We can tone them down a bit with burnt umber, raw umber, and yellow ochre applied very thinly with an almost dry soft brush. A quick brushing of the old parts with thin shellac and a dusting with gold bronze powder will help soften the contrast.

It is difficult to blend the old with the new, and we might be tempted to regild the whole mirror. The purist will shudder at such a thought, but most of the later mirrors are cheaply made and eventually become terribly shabby— the very opposite of what their makers intended them to be.

The last such mirror I repaired was caked with the black dust of the nineteenth century, and a mud wasp had built a handsome nest right under the cornice. I could hardly clean these fragile surfaces except by wiping them with alcohol and a slightly damp cloth, and even that had to be done with the greatest care. I regilded some surfaces and left others as they were, more or less symmetrically, and the compromise did not come off too badly.

"RESILVERING" OLD MIRRORS

Original old mirrors may have spots and splotches where the old reflective coating of tin amalgam has come off the glass. These blind spots certainly detract from the appearance of a good looking-glass, but fortunately they are not too difficult to repair.

First, carefully remove the thin board that usually covers the back of the mirror. If at all possible, leave the glass in the frame. The earlier beveled glass is thick enough, but Federal glass is usually very thin and breaks at the slightest provocation. The spots to be "resilvered" are scraped clean from the back, washed with a strong solution of caustic soda, and rinsed three times with clear water. The last rinse should be distilled water, if we can find some. Now sponge off all water and let the glass dry. Cut a piece of clean pure tin foil (*not* aluminum foil) roughly to size, slightly larger than the spot to be covered. Lay the foil on a clean sheet of paper with the side up that is to face the glass. Mercury will stick to the foil and a small drop should be spread all over it with a piece of cloth until the whole foil glistens silvery bright. The surface must be absolutely clean and flawless. Now flip the foil over and slide it onto the glass, mercury side down. Rub it gently but firmly from the back to squeeze out all excess mercury, then cover with a piece of blotting paper or thin felt and a layer of foam padding. Support the glass from the other side with a felt-covered board and then apply gentle but steady pressure on the newly coated area with weights or a contraption of boards and clamps. The pressure should continue for a week or so. The mercury slowly diffuses into the tin, and the coating remains tender until all excess mercury has evapo-

rated. That may take a month or two. After that time the metal should be covered with a protective varnish with a little asphaltum in it.

This is essentially the same procedure as was used in the eighteenth and early nineteenth century for "silvering" mirrors, but I hesitate to suggest that we try coating a whole glass that way. It is difficult to produce a uniform reflecting layer with tin foil, the risk of breaking the old glass is rather great when we squeeze it as we must, and I need not remind you that mercury is a dangerous poison. For repairs, however, I find the old method quite good and not as difficult as it may seem at first reading. Finding the raw materials is by far the worst part of the job.

12
RESTORING
OR REMOVING
OLD PAINT
AND
VARNISH

DO NOT STRIP AN ORIGINAL FINISH

One school among collectors of early American furniture holds that the look of bare wood is the ultimate in beauty. No sooner do these aficionados get a piece home than out comes the paint remover and off comes the finish. Now it has often been said that this is a free country, and I do not want to belittle the scraping school. Removal of the finish may be indicated for most pieces in the rough, but I respectfully suggest that it may not be best for all of them.

Once in a while we may be lucky enough to pick up a piece with its original finish intact: a Windsor chair with just one coat of dingy dark green paint, an old pine chest painted red with buttermilk paint, or a desk with a graying and finely checkered coat of late Colonial varnish. At times it may not be easy to tell whether a finish is original or later, but even when I merely suspect that it *may* be original, that is reason enough for me to try to save it. I refinish only those pieces that bear an obviously later and clearly inappropriate finish.

FEEDING OLD VARNISH

The procedure for restoring old finish is called "feeding" in the trade. It is a simple if tedious process of infusing new life into a finish that has become brittle and dull with time. Different treatments are required for different finishes, so let us discuss them one by one.

First we must check whether we are dealing with a shellac or with a varnish finish. Shellac is soluble in alcohol, but varnish usually resists. A small cotton pad soaked in alcohol will make a shellacked surface soft and sticky within a few seconds. For the moment let us assume that the finish resists alcohol so that it must be varnish. We wipe the piece down with a damp sponge and let it dry. We might use a little mild soap or detergent if that seems to help or if the piece is unusually dirty, but too much water does more harm than good, and strong soaps, particularly those recommended for washing interior woodwork, are to be studiously avoided. Next we rub the surface down thoroughly with steel wool, grade 000

238

or 0000, soaked in turpentine. This ul-trafine steel wool removes all loose dirt but does not harm the varnish, and the solvent attacks any grease stains. When the surface is clean, the piece must be wiped with a soft, turpentine-soaked rag to remove every trace of steel wool, and now we can start with the feeding.

We mix up a small jar of our own special "secret" furniture feeder—two thirds turpentine and one third raw lin-seed oil. We rub the piece briskly with a small pad soaked in this mixture, carefully wipe off all excess, and let it dry for a week. I use raw (not boiled) linseed oil because it is highly penetrat-ing and dries slowly. However, the oil film must be very thin or the piece will become sticky, and the gathering dust will make the surface dirtier and duller than it was before. For that reason it is useful to keep the piece covered with cloth (not plastic) during the feeding process, although that may not seem terribly practical in a family household. At any rate, we may rub the surface with the feeding mixture about half a dozen times at two-week intervals, after the first coat, and the old varnish should now begin to show signs of coming back to life. The gray tinge should gradually disappear and the finish should begin to show the grain of the wood underneath. It·is a slow pro-cess, and even though each rub may take only a few minutes, the whole pro-cess cannot be hurried. One can just barely get the whole feeding job done in three months, and six months is a more realistic estimate.

Painted surfaces are easier. Here we use half boiled linseed oil and half tur-pentine, and three rubs about a week apart are usually enough to rejuvenate the colors as far as they are going to be rejuvenated. Now we can touch up with new oil color wherever that seems nec-essary, but I suggest that we go easy with the new paint. Most serious collec-tors prefer paint slightly faded to paint obviously touched up, especially where decorations are involved. Natural wear spots, where the paint is worn through to the wood—as it often is on the spin-dles of Windsor chairs, for example—should not be retouched at all.

If the decorations are important, they should be left strictly alone, but if retouching is absolutely necessary, one should use water-soluble colors formu-lated especially for the restoration of paintings. They are available in the art-supply trade and have the advantage of being removable without disturbing the oil-painted original.

To rejuvenate a shellacked surface we rub it lightly with a cotton pad moist-ened with dilute shellac, with two drops of olive oil on the pad. One such rub-bing is enough, but the results may not be very pleasing, for the surface often appears streaked, especially if our hand was not quite light and swift enough. A polish with very fine steel wool usually removes the streaks, but if it does not, then we may want to give the whole piece a coat of dilute new shellac and a polish with no. 500 silicon carbide paper with turpentine as the cutting fluid.

A coat of wax should follow on top of any restored finish, once it has dried thoroughly, to give it a dust-free sur-face. Wax in itself will not strengthen varnish or paint as linseed oil does, but it will protect it and make it easy to clean.

STRIPPING PAINT

In the course of years, a piece of an-tique furniture may acquire any num-ber of coats of paint. Windsor chairs and tavern tables usually end up painted white. Maple may be stained to imitate mahogany or painted brown to satisfy the Victorian desire for dark wood, and, believe it or not, I have seen even inlaid mahogany furniture covered with two coats of dime-store enamel with cute little decals plastered all over.

If the piece before us is covered with several layers of paint, then we shall have to strip it, of course. However, we have already mentioned that all repairs should be complete before we start stripping. The reasons for that sequence of steps are not hard to understand. First, paint remover runs into cracks and makes it almost impossible to glue them properly later. Second, the old paint will protect the piece from knocks, scratches, and dripping glue—the unavoidable hazards of normal restoration. And last, the old finish, smeared over any new parts in the stripping process, will tint them and may help a great deal in matching the colors later on.

The question now arises: What shall we do with the brasses? If they are original, then they shall have to stay on, and we shall have to work around them, which is a nuisance. There really is no choice.

One of the reasons there are so few pieces with original brasses is that they are usually removed for refinishing. Some of them may get broken in the process, some of them may get lost, and even if all goes well, will anyone believe the brasses are original with fresh finish underneath?

Reproduction brasses offer no such dilemma. We might as well put them on after the finish is complete, preserving, if possible, scars of the old brasses under the finish, so that our descendants may confirm that we picked the right replacements.

All refinishers have their own prescriptions for paint removal, and here is mine. I work in a well-ventilated spot, preferably a shady place outdoors. The fumes of most paint removers are noxious, and drippings (try to avoid them!) will severely damage any kind of flooring other than unpainted concrete. Mixed with air in just the right proportion, the fumes of the flammable paint removers make a splendid explosive, and the pilot light of a nearby hot-water heater or a spark in an electric motor could set them off with a bang you would not soon forget.

I start with the cheapest paint remover on the market (see chapter 9) and proceed according to the instructions on the label. The paint may come off as advertised, and that is good. Or it may staunchly resist and remain as hard as ever.

In the latter case I switch to one of the methylene chloride removers and try again. As a rule, that does the trick and the paint begins to soften. Apply the remover liberally with a large cheap brush, and let it soak in just enough. If we hurry too much, only the top layer of paint may be softened, but if we wait too long, the remover will evaporate and the paint may harden again. We should try to place our piece so that the surface we are working on is nearly horizontal. Liquid removers are best on large flat areas, but the jellies are better for chairs and irregular surfaces in general. On flat surfaces, a sheet of polyethylene, laid over the spread paint remover, will retard evaporation and improve penetration.

I should mention that ordinary shellac resists most paint removers. A coat of shellac between several layers of paint may pose quite a problem, for it will impede the action of paint remover on the paint under the shellac. In that case we may have to scrape or rub with straight alcohol and steel wool. Alcohol ultimately dissolves all shellac. Acetate lacquer also resists paint removers, but fortunately we are not likely to find it on old furniture. Acetone or lacquer thinner (*not* paint thinner) will remove it, with a lot of rubbing.

When the paint has softened, I peel it off the flat surfaces with a dull putty knife, or with burlap or coarse steel wool where the putty knife cannot reach. The emulsified removers can be washed off with water, aided by a stiff brush. When most of the paint is off, I apply a second coat of remover, let it soak in, and rub with medium steel wool right down to the dry wood. Reluctant patches get a third dose of remover and another rubbing with steel wool until all paint is off.

Steel wool is a very useful tool at this stage. It cleans without scratching and does not fill up like sandpaper. Generally I wear a heavy leather glove when I work with it, for the slivers of steel have a way of working into the skin. When I have finished with the steel wool, I wipe the wood with great care. Bits of steel do not take long to change into spots of rust in a damp climate, and the rust is almost impossible to remove.

Every trace of paint remover must be wiped off with synthetic turpentine or with water on the emulsified types. This cleaning must be thorough, even if the manufacturer claims on the label that no cleanup is required. Even for the emulsified removers, water soluble as they are, I prefer the mineral turpentine for cleanup. Water raises the grain, gets into crevices and crannies, and warps the wood just enough to make joints rickety and rabbets loose. All joined wood suffers from getting wet.

With some pieces it may be possible to strip only the outer layers of paint and save the original paint underneath. Perhaps I should say that this can be done on any piece, but the labor will be prohibitive on most. With luck, we may be able to lay bare the original paint by applying the paint remover uniformly and then carefully scraping and wiping the softened paint layer by layer. It is a very tedious and risky process but may be worth trying in special cases. Alcohol is a good solvent for this kind of work.

So far we have gone on the assumption that the paint will yield to some sort of remover after a while. However, every now and then we find a paint that resists any commercial remover. Some of these refractory paints may have been mixed with whey, and are often called buttermilk paints. They were made by farmers with the materials they had at hand but were never particularly popular in the cities, presumably because they are rather odorous when fresh. With time, however, they become devilishly hard and resist most removers. Once or twice I have also encountered something that looked like commercial enamel but resisted all solvents. Some latex paints also can be very resistant, but they are rarely used on furniture.

LYE

In these special cases we may either scrape dry—a tricky, dangerous, and tiresome procedure, as we shall see— or we may resort to lye. Now lye has a terrible reputation, but commercial refinishers use it as a matter of routine because it is quick and cheap. A careful professional restorer I know in California once told me why he rarely used lye. "It makes any wood look like mild steel," he said.

There is no doubt that lye discolors wood and gives it a dead gray tinge. For that reason, if I use lye at all, I use it only on the outer layers of paint. I make a strong solution, apply it with a cotton dishmop, and rinse it off as soon as the recalcitrant layer of paint starts to go. The rinsing must be thorough, and it is a good idea to put a pint of vinegar into the last gallon of rinse water to neutralize the lye that may have penetrated into nooks and crannies. When the piece has dried, I finish up with commercial paint remover.

I use lye on furniture only as a last resort. It is a deadly substance (a drop in the eye can blind a man) and will quickly remove not only paint but skin, fingernails, shoes, trouser legs, and shirttails with equal efficiency. It will completely destroy a bristle brush in a minute or two and will leave its mark on any wood it has touched. If you insist on trying lye, go ahead, but start with a piece that is not worth much.

DIP STRIPPING

In the early seventies a new cottage industry sprang up on the fringes of the antiques business: dip stripping. All you have to do to get started in business is plunk down a few thousand dollars, and one of several companies will set you up with a "hot tank," a "cold tank," and all the secret ingredients to go into them, including a "toner" or "developer" intended to "bring the rich original color out of the wood." The procedure is to dip a piece of furniture into the hot solution for a few minutes to half an hour, rinse it off with a high-pressure water hose, and then dip it again to stain the wood and neutralize the remains of the stripping solution. The secret solutions are easy to decode. Active ingredients are caustic soda (lye, sodium hydroxide) and TSP (trisodium phosphate). You already know my views on lye. TSP is a strong industrial cleaner, also used as a minor ingredient in domestic scouring powders and some laundry detergents. Would I recommend such treatment for antiques? Perhaps. What kind of antiques? Well, maybe a stoneware crock or an old horseshoe, but definitely not anything made of wood.

SCRAPING IS NOT EASY

People often talk about "scraping down" old furniture, but cold shivers run down my neck whenever I hear the expression. I remember, long ago, watching a man scrape an old table. He took a piece of window glass, laid it on the moist ground, and stepped on it so that it broke into a number of crescent-shaped pieces. These he would pick up in his fingers and use their slightly convex edges to scrape away at the paint. Before long he had cut himself several times, but he was methodical, and the neatly furrowed, plowed-field appearance of the table top would have made a regular pattern had it not been for the bloodstains. I was so awed by the gory procedure that I cannot recall what finally happened to the table, but if it had any antique value before, it certainly lost it that afternoon.

The cabinet scraper is, of course, much better than glass, but it is a tricky tool and will do more damage than good in the hands of a beginner. To work properly, the scraper must be very sharp and ground with a slight burr. To get this burr, we grind on a rotating stone from the back toward the edge and only in that direction. On a chisel we would grind back and forth and on both sides to get a smooth edge, but on a scraper we do just the opposite. Some cabinetmakers enhance the edge even more by burnishing it over from the back with a piece of hard round steel, like one of those old-fashioned round knife sharpeners that Grandpa used at table when he carved a roast.

The scraper requires great strength and a steady hand, so that it is a tiresome tool to use. Very definitely, it is no substitute for a good solvent. I scrape a piece once in a great while, but only when nothing else will do.

For example, a fine old pine table may have been stuck in a chicken coop somewhere, and you can imagine what the chickens did to the top. No amount of washing will clean it, and one may have the impulse to get out the plane. That would be a bum idea not only because the surface is sure to have a nail in it somewhere—and that nail would wreck the plane—but because the planing would remove more wood than is necessary and thus make the top look new. Original pine table tops are scarce, so we certainly do not want to make the real thing look like a replacement. Therefore, we shall scrape.

The surface must be completely dry before we start. We go only with the grain, using short strokes as we progress slowly across the surface, gauging the depth of our cuts by the depth of the stain we are trying to remove. It is a slow process, and we shall need practice before we learn to produce a smooth, even surface. However, a skillfully scraped table top will retain the appearance of age and will need very little sanding.

SANDING

We must keep in mind that we sand to *clean* the surface, not to remove it. It is quite possible to skin a piece by excessive sanding, especially if we use paper that is too coarse. On the other hand, the surface will be rough and lifeless if we do not sand thoroughly, for it will retain a film of the old finish. So we must use our judgment and sand just enough to bring out the sheen of the wood but not enough to damage the mellow outer layer.

Sanding requires neither great skill nor special experience but lots of patience. If the wood is perfectly dry and all traces of paint, varnish, or paint remover are gone, then we can use ordinary flint paper or the red cabinet paper. However, there are always some impurities on the surface in our kind of work, and all the dry sandpapers will clog up fairly quickly. Therefore, I have gone over to the waterproof silicon carbide papers. They are fairly expensive, but they stay sharp a long time and cut fast. They are brittle, so I would not recommend them for turnings or uneven surfaces in general. In such places we have to use emery cloth. As a rule, I use a petroleum-derived "turpentine" (Varsol, Tirpolene, and other trademarks) as the cutting fluid. I stretch the paper on a small sanding block, with a layer of foam padding between the paper and the block, and always keep liquid on the wood as I rub. A slurry soon forms and carries away the cuttings, so that the paper stays open and cuts evenly. The wet sanding effectively cleans the wood of grease stains as well as the waxy residue of paint remover. Always rub with the grain and wipe the piece dry whenever changing grades of paper. One can produce a remarkably smooth surface that way, and the cutting fluid on the surface will give some idea of what the piece will look like when it is oiled.

The choice of the proper abrasive depends on the type of wood we are working with and on the condition of the surface. The final sanding depends on the kind of finish we intend to put on the surface. Perhaps I can illustrate the process by a few examples.

A pine table top that is in bad shape but does not require scraping may be sanded first with medium-coarse flint paper until the surface is leveled, always taking the greatest possible care to rub only with the grain. A thorough sanding with medium paper will be necessary to remove the scratches, followed by prolonged smoothing with fine paper. Or we may start with no. 120 silicon carbide paper and turpentine, then switch to 240. Nothing else may be required, for the silicon carbide papers do not scratch as badly as dry-sanding papers. Steel wool will not be of much use once the paint is removed, for it tends to dig out the soft wood between the growth rings and catch on small splinters.

Mahogany or walnut may require a more thorough sanding—perhaps no. 180, followed by 240, and finished with 320. Shellac will be the next step, in all probability, so extreme smoothness will not be required as long as there are no scratches.

Cherry, maple, and other hard, dense woods can be scratched badly by a single cross-grain swipe with coarse paper. It would take hours to remove such scratches, and for that reason I like first to clean these woods with steel wool (no. 1 or 2 to start with). Then I take silicon carbide paper (no. 240 on most pieces, but 180 if the wood is very rough) and rub with long strokes, with the grain. A wipe with a rag follows, and then a thorough rubbing with wet no. 320 paper. Another wipe and still another rubbing with no. 400 paper, and the job is finished. A remarkably smooth, almost glossy surface can be obtained by this treatment on dense woods; and contrary to what you may think, it is not all a colossal waste of time. The wood must be very smooth if we are preparing for a wax finish (see p. 250).

FILLING

Some of the coarse, open-grained woods like oak, chestnut, coarse walnut, or hickory should be filled during the smoothing process. Take some paste filler (p. 185), diluted with turpentine if necessary, and a small shaggy rag. First brush all dust out of the pores of the wood. Then work in the filler, wipe off the excess, and let dry quite thoroughly. Usually the filling step follows a rough sanding, so we now continue with the intermediate and fine sanding. A polish with no. 400 silicon carbide paper and turpentine would be the last step if we intended to use wax, which is the preferred treatment for oak—but we are getting ahead of ourselves. We shall come to the finishing soon enough.

This whole process requires time. Proper treatment of the surface prior to finishing makes the difference between a good finish and a mess. If the piece still seems a little rough here and there, let us go back and rectify the oversights while we may. The final finish will not hide scratches and irregularities; on the contrary, it will make them stand out.

STAINS

We have already mentioned the stains on tables. The work space inside desks is another area that is often stained with inkspots, the drippings from tallow candles, and dabs of glue. The wooden seats of chairs and the tops of chests are often stained; we may, in effect, find stains on any horizontal surface, wherever candles or dishes or flowers are likely to have been placed.

Most of these stains are difficult to remove unless we are willing to scrape. Soap and water may help a little, vinegar or lemon juice may have a slight effect, and careful bleaching may serve to minimize the color differences. Hydrogen peroxide (concentrated commercial grade), household hypochlorite solutions (Clorox, Dazzle, White Sail, and many other trademarks), and oxalic acid are the common bleaches. One should always start with a very dilute bleach and increase the concentration to obtain the desired effect. Concentrated peroxide and hypochlorite are rather strong as they come from the bottle, but they will not damage the wood as far as I know. Oxalic acid can be used in a saturated solution. The peroxide sold in very dilute form for antiseptic purposes is too weak for bleaching wood.

Perhaps I should admit that I rarely use any bleaches, for they lighten not only the stain but also the color of the surrounding wood. Usually I prefer to leave a few small ink spots rather than produce a large blotch of light color on an otherwise time-darkened board. Once wood has been bleached, it will not return to its natural color for a long time.

Shellacked tables often show white rings where hot dishes have been placed, and I have heard the wildest old wives' tale about how the rings can be removed. One takes white cigar ashes, I was told, and rubs them into the stain with a piece of cork. That was obviously such patent nonsense that I never tried it myself, but when I repeated the prescription to a cigar-smoking friend whose Sheraton table was stained that way, he got a cork, flicked a little ash from his cigar . . . and it worked like a dream. Still, a little alcohol will do the same thing, but we have to polish afterward with pumice or very fine (600) paper to remove the streaks left by the alcohol. A small cotton pad moistened with alcohol (or dilute shellac) plus two drops of olive oil on the rubbing side makes a dandy tool for touching up all sorts of stains on shellacked furniture.

DENTS

The kicks and knocks suffered by old furniture often leave dents in the wood. Small nicks can be overlooked, but if the wood is severely crushed here or there we can restore it by steaming. Place several layers of wet cloth over the crushed area and let it soak thoroughly. Then apply a hot flatiron to the cloth and let the steam sizzle all around until the cloth is dry. We may have to repeat the process two or three times, but I have seen depressions half an inch deep swell out almost to their original contour after repeated steaming. It works best on soft wood, needless to say.

Small nicks, old nail holes, and minor blemishes may be filled with stick shellac, kids' wax crayons, or an acetate-sawdust filler (Plastic Wood, Softwood, and other trademarks). Stick shellac is the time-honored material, and it comes in a variety of colors to match any wood. One heats the end of the stick over a candle, presses the liquid shellac into the hole, and smooths the surface with the heated blade of a flexible knife.

Plastic Wood is a mixture of acetate cement and fine wood flour. Press it into the wood with a spatula and let it harden for an hour or so. It is then ready to sand smooth and color (with oil paints) to match the surrounding wood. I use both of these fillers, depending on the circumstances, but in any case I see to it that the hole is absolutely clean before I make any attempt to fill it. Any filler will pop right out of a hole that is dirty, greasy, or dusty. And we cannot hope to have a filler stay in the hole unless the wood is firm and everything is properly glued up.

The care with which we must fill a hole depends on where the hole is, of course. If we pulled four small nails from the middle of a cherry table top, the resulting holes will be very obvious unless they are carefully plugged and meticulously blended in. On the other hand, the hole left by a no. 10 wood screw will be barely noticeable on a carved surface, once the splits caused by the screw have been healed properly.

13
THE
NEW FINISH

All repairs are now complete. The piece is firm, and all moving parts work smoothly. The lid fits, the drawers slide in and out without effort, and every surface is smooth and clean. If it is a country piece, like a Windsor chair, a pine table, or any piece that was normally painted, then we may leave a few traces of paint in the cracks, around the pins, in the crevices of deep turnings, in nicks and carvings and such. Finishing country pieces too well would make them look slick, which they were never meant to be.

No trace of paint should remain on formal pieces, veneered furniture, or anything made of mahogany but the piece should look its age. If a restored piece looks like a good reproduction, the restoration was a failure.

All new parts will, of course, look new. The removal of the old finish may have stained them a little, but probably not enough, and they certainly will stand out. The first step of our refinishing process will be to blend these new parts into the general tone of the whole piece.

BLENDING IN

Now get out the oil colors mentioned earlier. If the new parts are small, first wipe them with a little boiled linseed oil and then work in some color, probably burnt umber, perhaps with a little yellow ochre or burnt sienna mixed in, until the proper tone is reached. A little white will add a chalky character to the tone, if that seems desirable; if it looks as if we have the wrong color, a little turpentine will remove the whole mess and we can start anew. We can use a brush, a small rag, or even our fingers, depending on the nature of the surface. In my own work I usually apply the colors lightly from a small artist's palette with a square-ended half-inch brush, blending with my fingers wherever necessary.

On light woods with prominent grain, like birch, for instance, we may have trouble with this procedure. The difficulty arises from the unpleasant sharpness that the color imparts to the grain, so that patches now stand out more than ever, even if it looked as if

247

the grain were fairly well matched before we applied the color. One way out is first to coat the patch with dilute shellac to seal the pores and then sand the surface almost to the bare wood. When we now apply the color, it cannot sink in and we can obscure the grain just enough to blend in the patch.

It would not be wise to obscure the grain on large new surfaces, for the wood surface must have a certain depth in order to look natural. Instead of tube colors, use water or alcohol stains wherever possible, and oil stains in all other cases. We have discussed the preparation of these stains in chapter 9.

To prepare for water staining, first sand all surfaces with the usual grades of silicon carbide paper (see p. 243), with *water* as the cutting fluid. The purpose is to raise all the grain that is to be raised and sand it off. When the wood is as smooth as you want it, dry it off and wipe on the water stain. Once the stain is on, the surface cannot be sanded any more.

In my own work, I use water stain on maple, cherry, and walnut, but a friend tells me that I am just being a masochist. Alcohol stain, he says, is just as good and gives much less trouble with the grain. What is more, he says, the aroma is delicious.

Pine is difficult to stain without making it look artificially colored. One has to try it and see. In the end it is probably better to stain pine less rather than more and let time do the rest.

It is best to try out any mixed stain on a scrap of wood and rub it with boiled linseed oil to see what the finished job will be like before we try staining the carefully made new parts. This precaution has paid off handsomely more than once. The final color of stain is not easy to judge, and we may have to make several tests before we get the right tone

and intensity. Coarse woods should be filled before staining, using the filler described on page 185, and sanded clean. Now apply the stain with a small rag, wiping quickly but carefully to leave no streak, and let it dry for several hours. One coat should produce the desired color. If it does not, then we may go over the surface again, but the result may be streaky. As I said, we should experiment with scraps first.

A good uniform ground tone is necessary, and it must look right in any kind of light. For that reason I always do my blending by daylight. When the ground tone is just right, I let it dry, rub with boiled linseed oil, and then put on the finishing touches.

These touches will tend to imitate the nicks and irregularities that inevitably distinguish old surfaces from new ones. If traces of paint are still visible on the old surfaces, then we mix a little color of the same hue and put little flecks of it on the new parts here and there, wherever necessary to balance the new part with the old. If the old parts are stained in places, a few artificial stains are in order for the new parts. If a scratch comes right up to the new part and stops at the glue line, then we artfully extend it onto the new wood, not by scratching the new surface but by painting the scratch on. All these flecks and dabs of color must be oriented in such a way that they will distract the eye from the glue line without being obvious. We don't want the area to look like a study by Jackson Pollock, yet we do want to obscure the boundary between old and new.

Now all this discussion about coloring and imitation may have raised a few eyebrows. Let me allay any fears, if I can, on the subject of faking. Making a piece harmoniously uniform in color is not faking. A new foot is still a new foot, regardless of any paint job, however skillfully it may be done. Any expert will recognize the new parts without difficulty. The artistry merely serves to keep the new parts from standing out in a way that detracts from the esthetic appeal of the whole piece. It is my experience that all the staining and touching up that anybody could do would not make a new pine board look like an old pine board. Having sweated and cursed, with stain up to our elbows, if the new part still looks painfully new, we may decide that next time we will take the trouble of finding some old wood for such repairs.

Perhaps I need not say that we must never stain pine to look like walnut, maple to look like mahogany, and so on. If we must have mahogany for our decor, then let us find some mahogany; pending that, let us use the maple as it is. Henry Taylor wrote, *"Under no circumstances* stain any fine maple chests, high-post beds, Windsor chairs, early gate-leg or tavern tables to imitate mahogany. Persons have been summarily executed for lesser crimes."

CHOICE OF THE PROPER FINISH

The color of our piece is now pleasing and balanced, the piece is sound, and we can proceed with the final finishing. This is the step usually approached with the greatest fear, although, in reality, it is the easiest part of the job.

Somehow the myth has been spread that magic ingredients and mystic powers are needed for anything but the most amateurish kind of finish. The truth is that any beginner can produce an excellent finish *with patience.* And I might as well add that even a Swiss watchmaker will make a botch of things if he tries to rush the job.

There are, I think, only four finishes

that need concern us: wax, shellac, lacquer, and polyurethane. One of the four will do nicely for any piece I can imagine. The choice among them is governed by the kind of wood and by the use the piece is to be put to.

Hard, dense wood can be highly smoothed by the procedures we have discussed and has excellent wear resistance by itself. So if we desire an informal, soft effect, we can simply wax it. Oak, maple, and cherry are best waxed, birch and walnut less so, and mahogany better not, for it was seldom used for pieces that could be considered informal. The wax finish is quite unsuitable for pine, needless to say, for softwoods require a stronger-surfaced finish, if only to avoid splinters. For that matter, I would hesitate recommending a wax finish for any chair seats or table tops, no matter what kind of wood they may be. Wax gives a delightful semi-mat surface, easy to clean and simple to repair if damaged. However, it is not a strong finish and will not withstand much wear.

A shellac finish can be made mat or glossy and can be used on any wood, hard or soft, dense or porous. Fine mahogany furniture, elegant veneered pieces—in short, "parlor" furniture—is the type of stuff I would use shellac on. It is hard and permanent, but it is fairly brittle and can be scratched without half trying. Perhaps I should explain that shellac is brittle only by comparison with lacquer. Shellac is mighty durable compared to such things as spar varnish or some of the cheap factory finishes. However, shellac is attacked quite severely by the sort of beverages that some of us occasionally enjoy, and even a glass of cold milk, left standing on a shellacked mahogany table, can produce a ring that may be hard to remove.

A lacquer finish is very durable, and I recommend it highly for table tops and all other surfaces that receive heavy wear. Neither hot dishes nor strong drink will harm it, and water has no effect on it, hot or cold. It is an easy finish to clean; a wet sponge will remove anything from spilled ink to children's crayons. The finish itself is tough so that it adds strength to the surface of soft wood and makes it more resistant to impact. Lacquer fills up the pores in wood so that no other filler is required. It takes a lot of work to produce a good lacquer finish, and the raw material itself is rather expensive, but the product is worth the trouble.

A polyurethane finish is even stronger than lacquer although not quite as clear. For pine cocktail tables and splintery plank-bottom chair seats there is nothing like it.

In spite of the many sterling properties of lacquer and polyurethane, I would hesitate to use them on very fine antique furniture. These new, hard, permanent materials are alien to the homemade character of early cabinetwork. Again, it is a matter of taste. If you like your Hamlet in modern dress, so be it. I don't.

THE WAX FINISH

I have already discussed the preparation of the wax on page 185, and I have mentioned that the wood must be as smooth as we know how to make it—almost polished. If the wood is maple, first rub it hard with a small piece of soft cloth soaked in boiled linseed oil to bring out the grain and give depth to the surface. The oil must be worked well into the surface, all excess wiped off, and the piece allowed to dry for a week.

We may have doubts about putting oil on cherry. It brings out what grain the wood has, but it also makes the wood considerably darker. This is a matter of personal preference—if you like a dark tone in furniture, oil your cherry pieces. I always do. The color of oak is not greatly affected by oil, but the grain is much enhanced, so we might as well oil oak before we wax it. Birch is a little too coarse for the wax finish, but it certainly should be oiled. Mahogany and walnut are even coarser and may become very dark when oiled. However, if we wax them without oiling, they may look drab and lifeless. Furthermore, any fat will badly stain most dark woods that are waxed but not oiled.

When the oil has dried, we seal the surface with a quick and uniformly brushed coat of very thin shellac (as little as one part shellac to five parts alcohol for the densest woods). The perfectionist will now sand again with no. 400 or 500 silicon carbide paper and turpentine, just enough to remove any irregularities in the sealing coat. A fairly heavy coat of wax follows, applied with a soft cloth and allowed to dry for an hour or so. A quick rub with a medium-firm shoe brush, a piece of lamb's wool, or simply a square of soft flannel will produce a semblance of a finish. A second, thinner coat of wax and another rubdown will greatly improve things, and additional coats will ultimately create a fine mellow surface—smooth but not shiny, calm, and elegant. Time will dull the sheen, but another waxing or sometimes just a cursory buffing will quickly restore its beauty.

THE SHELLAC FINISH

With the surface nicely smoothed (but not necessarily polished), we first give a rub with linseed oil, as we have just mentioned, and allow it to dry for a week. We have selected a dark tone of "white" shellac, as already discussed on page 184; we now dilute it with denatured alcohol, about one part alcohol to two parts shellac of the "three-pound cut" density, or one to one with "four-pound cut" shellac. We brush on this mixture with a good, fairly dry brush, working quickly and making sure that the shellac does not run anywhere. We let it dry several hours and apply a second coat. When that coat is hard (preferably the next day, for soft shellac will not sand well), we rub it down lightly but thoroughly with no. 0 steel wool. For pine and other softwoods, that may be all that is needed. A coat of wax may follow, to add smoothness, but nothing else is really necessary.

A much more elaborate shellac finish, however, is in order for the higher-grade woods and elegant pieces in general. We apply the first two coats and rub down with steel wool as before. Now the piece must be thoroughly wiped to remove every last particle of steel wool, and another coat of shellac follows. We let it dry overnight and rub it down again, this time with no. 360 wet silicon carbide paper, using turpentine as the cutting fluid. This sanding is a little tricky: we must rub hard enough to smooth the surface but lightly enough not to remove all the shellac. That takes a bit of care, especially on edges and corners. Two or three more coats follow, each rubbed lightly with no. 360 paper. Now the final coat is applied and uniformly brushed on with great care, left to dry, and rubbed with no. 500 or even 600 paper, with turpentine.

That may do on most pieces, but some coarse, unfilled woods, like walnut, may require more intermediate coats to produce a finish free from tiny pockmarks caused by the pores of the wood. And if the soft luster produced by the no. 500 paper does not suit our fancy, we may feel inclined to polish the piece. Prolonged hand rubbing with a cloth saturated with a paste made of a little sweet (olive) oil, a little turpentine, and some very fine (no. 4F) cabinetmaker's powdered pumice (plus a lot of patience) will produce a lustrous satin finish. For a high gloss, use rottenstone in the paste instead of pumice. A thorough wiping with a turpentine-saturated rag is absolutely necessary to remove the last traces of the sweet oil; this oil never dries but just sits there and collects dust. If the piece we are finishing has many intricate moldings, corners, and other nooks and crannies that are likely to hold the oil, then perhaps we should use raw linseed oil to make up the pumice paste. Linseed oil is not as effective for rubbing as sweet oil, but it does dry eventually, and we need not worry quite so much about leaving a little of it behind.

The reader may think, at this point, that there surely must be an easier way. Well, naturally there is. And it always looks it.

FRENCH POLISH

There is still another way of applying a shellac finish. It is done with a little ball of cotton wrapped in a small piece of soft cloth and goes by the name of French polish. There are many varieties of this somewhat delicate procedure, but I shall describe only the one I have found most satisfactory. There may be better ways, for all I know.

To begin with, French polish is best suited for dense woods with rich grain, such as crotch mahogany, curly maple, or figured cherry. It is ideal for finely veneered surfaces.

The wood must be well prepared and highly polished, as we have already described. We may oil it or not, according to taste, although I usually do. Then brush on a quick sealer coat of dilute shellac and let dry. Now make a small ball of cotton, fairly stiff and about 1½ inches in diameter, wrapped in a soft cotton cloth to make a tampon. Saturate the tampon with shellac diluted about one to one with ether so that the tampon is thoroughly moistened but not dripping. Put two drops of sweet oil on the pad and rub the wood hard, a small area at a time, with quick, circular strokes, never stopping on the surface until the pad is dry. Saturate the pad again, add two more drops of oil, and go at it again until the whole surface is well covered. The grain now stands out deep and lustrous, and the surface appears highly polished except for a few smears of oil here and there.

Now leave the surface alone for a few hours until it has hardened. If the finish appears too thin, make a new ball and repeat the process to build up a sufficient layer of shellac. Let it harden again, remove the oil with a turpentine-soaked rag, and you have a high yet light and rich finish—perfect for a finely inlaid Hepplewhite sideboard, for example. Some cabinetmakers use alcohol to remove the oil, but that is a tricky business. A final light waxing and a polish with lamb's wool will remove the last traces of oil and add the ultimate luster.

THE LACQUER FINISH

Having selected a good grade of nitrocellulose (acetate) lacquer or polyurethane finish (I shall use the word lacquer to describe them both, albeit loosely), and having oiled (or not oiled) the wood as discussed on page 250, we proceed much as we did with shellac, except that the lacquer is best used full strength. No matter how coarse the wood, the lacquer will produce a smooth finish, but it may take quite a few coats, each rubbed down with no. 360 paper and turpentine. After the first two coats, we might even use water as the cutting fluid, but the piece must be bone dry before the next coat of lacquer goes on. Lacquer gives a tough coat and sands off less easily than shellac, particularly on the corners. Some professional finishers like to spray their lacquer, for it goes on much faster that way, and a skillful operator with a good spray gun can produce a coat so smooth that it requires a minimum of rubbing. Spraying makes quite a mess, though, and can be downright dangerous if we don't have a properly ventilated spray booth with good forced draft. The fumes are both toxic and explosive (when mixed with air in the right proportions). The spray gun is not an easy tool to use and is a nuisance to clean. For those reasons I stick to brushing on lacquer. On small jobs it is less work in the long run.

The finish coat may be polished with pumice or rottenstone, which will give a gloss almost as good as on shellac, but I usually skip the polish and merely wax lightly after the last rubbing. Lacquer is my choice for strength. Where gloss is required, I use shellac.

In all these processes the secret of success lies in the rubbing. Elbow grease is the most essential ingredient in any first-rate wood finish, and it is really too bad that one cannot buy it in jars.

MAINTENANCE MANUAL (AND SECRET RECIPES)

What do you have to do to preserve your antique furniture? What mysterious rites and secret ingredients are required for conservation? Come with me, and I shall initiate you.

TEMPERATURE AND HUMIDITY

Ideally, wood objects should be kept at a constant temperature and humidity to minimize expansion and contraction. In practice, that can be achieved in closed areas of low traffic with a fair degree of success, but only at great expense in both apparatus and the power to run it. Elegant museums can afford that, but in the average family's home the special air-conditioning machinery and its controls would cost at least as much as the house itself. The power bill would be prodigious. The benefit would be dwarfed by the expense.

Very high humidity may cause mildew and rot, and for that reason antique furniture should not be stored in warm, damp basements. Other than that, if *you* can survive the temperature and the humidity, your furniture will survive as well. Just keep the place ventilated when the air conditioner is out for some reason in very humid weather. On the opposite extreme, cold makes no difference. Freezing will not harm furniture, unless the pipes burst.

DAMAGE BY INSECTS

Wormholes, as we have said, are not a proof of great age but could be a sign of real danger if the infestation should still be active. Fortunately, the problem is rare in the United States, and a treatment with strong insecticide in dust form usually takes care of it.

Furniture left standing on dirt floors in cellars or in barns for a long time may be attacked by termites. They can do very serious damage, particularly to the feet. Termites range from Maine to Florida and can attack any wood that is in contact with the ground. If you have to store furniture on a dirt floor, first spread some plastic sheet.

Silverfish (*Lepisma saccharina*) do not damage wood, but they like starch and will eat sized or pasted paper and starched cloth. They can do serious damage to books, textiles, wallpaper, paper linings in trunks and boxes, framed prints, and labels on furniture. The label on the back of the mirror in figure 14 shows the kind of damage silverfish do. Moth crystals are effective against them.

MAINTENANCE

Antique furniture requires a lot of maintenance, doesn't it? Actually, honestly, no. The more you leave it alone the better. Over the long run, diligent dusting and persistent polishing will do more harm than good. Yes, I know— furniture gets dusty and dingy and finger marked, and the guests might get the wrong impression of your household. And then there are those miraculous compounds insistently advertised to help you spend your time cleaning. Forget it. You have my permission to wipe your furniture with a proper polish three times a year—no more. And what is a proper polish? Read on.

YOUR OWN SECRET FURNITURE POLISH

Pay no attention to all those advertised concoctions but go to a good art supply store and buy a pint can of turpentine and a half-pint can of boiled linseed oil. Any kind of turpentine will do. The steam-distilled variety costs more, smells better, but some people say they are allergic to it. The synthetic kind is harmless, unless you drink it. Both kinds are highly flammable, so be careful.

Empty the contents of the two cans into a clean quart (or liter) bottle, shake it all up until the solution clears, then pour it back into the two cans and dispose of the bottle, properly, of course. Now label the cans MY OWN SECRET OIL POLISH. Use the little one to work with and the big one to refill the little one when it gets empty. How is that for arcane directions?

As we all know by now, oil darkens some woods, and there have been times when dark wood was fashionable and other times when it was not. If you like your cherry pink, your walnut tan, and your mahogany strawberry blond, then the oil polish is not for you. Instead, pour a pint of turpentine into a wide-mouth jar and add either 4 tablespoons of grated dry carnauba wax or unbleached genuine beeswax, or about twice that quantity (½ cup) of a high-grade paste wax. The measures are not critical. Sometimes I put in more and other times less, and it does not make much difference. Suit yourself. Now warm the jar in a bowl of hot water (NOT ON THE STOVE!) until the wax dissolves, then pour the cleared solution back into the can and label it MY OWN SECRET WAX POLISH. Shake before using.

A soft, absorbent rag, saturated (but not dripping) with either of the secret solutions, will clean and polish in one operation, but the wax polish has to be buffed with a soft woolen rag or with a lamb's-wool shoe polisher when it is dry. That makes it more work, but it looks better on smooth polished hardwood like maple and on hard-finished surfaces generally. It certainly does not darken the wood. The oil polish I prefer for pine, oak, teak, and old finishes, be they painted, varnished, or japanned. It even helps some of the chalky old buttermilk paints.

BRASSES

Brasses become brownish green over the years, almost black, and I like to leave them that way. Why? Because there is no harmless way of polishing them. Brass polish stains the wood around the brasses, and the stains are difficult to remove. All polishes are abrasive and wear the brass in time; what's more, polishing brass is hard on your hands. But if you insist on shiny brass, gleaming in the candlelight, polish it carefully, wash off every trace of polish with warm water, let it dry, and then coat the brasses with clear lacquer from a spray can. That will preserve the shine for a while but not forever. Next time you want to polish, you will first have to remove the old lacquer with acetone. If that seems like too much work, and if gleaming brass is one of those necessities to you, consider having it gold plated. It is not as expensive as it sounds and makes for good conversation.

———

And that is about all there is to it. How does it feel to be an expert?

APPENDIXES
BIBLIOGRAPHY
INDEX

APPENDIX A:
INSURANCE

Should your antiques be insured? That is a very personal decision that only you can make. Some people can't sleep unless they know that everything they own is fully and properly insured against all foreseeable risks. Other people think it is enough to maintain some financial reserves as a cushion against possible catastrophic losses, but in smaller problems they are willing to take life's chances. Myself, I belong to the latter group, but many of my friends feel otherwise and this Appendix is intended to serve their interest by briefly outlining the insurance problems of the collector of antiques.

Insurance always costs more than the statistical value of the protection it gives. The premium you pay has to cover not only your share of the losses but also the agent's commission, the insurance company's record keeping and operating expenses, all that imaginative advertising, and taxes, as well as a little profit for the stockholders. Without the profit, the company would soon disappear, as many insurance companies have over the years. The total premiums collected must add up to much more than the total losses paid, but peace of mind is worth something, too, and that is why people insure.

HOMEOWNER / TENANT POLICY

The collector of antiques may want insurance in two basic categories: fire and theft. Fire insurance is likely to be straightforward, but the theft angle may be a problem, as we shall see. The usual fire insurance is called "fire and extended coverage." It protects you against loss from fire, smoke damage, water damage as a result of fire, explosion, and various other, usually minor, risks related to fire, regardless of its origin. For antique furniture, that is the primary coverage to consider.

Theft insurance covers "losses from burglary and larceny incident thereto, and robbery, including observed theft" but may exclude or limit "mysterious disappearance." It normally covers breakage from "forcible entry" but may require specific locking devices on doors and windows. If the clumsy thief smashes the lid of your secretary while

257

searching for the gold coins he thinks you have in there, the insurance company will pay for the repairs. If the damage is extensive and if you can show that the value of the piece has been reduced no matter how skillfully it may be repaired, you may expect to be reimbursed for that difference also. This breakage aspect is an important reason for having theft coverage on antique furniture.

Theft insurance is not usually sold separately but is included, along with the extended fire risks, in the popular homeowner / tenant policies, which also cover liability, water damage, additional living expense related to a loss, losses away from home, and lots of other things that insurance companies think people worry about. Everything we have mentioned so far is just ordinary household insurance for the contents of a home, be it owned or rented by the insured.

For the purpose of insurance, regular antiques are just high-grade furniture, unless you want to claim some special values—historic, artistic, or whatever. The average good, genuine antique piece costs no more than a well-made, equivalent new item in a fine furniture store. The difference is that new furniture depreciates but antiques do not. Experienced underwriters know that and will not be upset when you tell them that your home is furnished with antiques. They will probably ask you to prepare a "schedule" (as they say in the business), which is merely a list of all the valuable pieces in your collection, each individually identified (preferably with a photograph) and appraised by a competent expert, usually from a reputable local auction house. Preparing such a schedule may seem like a lot of trouble, but knowledgeable adjusters tell me that it is absolutely essential even if the agent does not ask for it. A proper schedule filed with the insurer at the time the policy is written will save a lot of trouble in adjusting the claim in case of a loss. The schedule, like the policy, should be kept up to date and in a place separate from the articles it covers.

FINE ARTS COVERAGE

If the value of your stuff is greater than what you would expect to pay for good furniture, or if you have some special pieces—signed, perhaps, or historically important—or if your collection is larger than what you would normally need to furnish a home, then you should consider a "fine arts policy," also known in the trade (perversely, perhaps) as a "personal property floater." Such insurance covers all risks of loss or damage, on or off your premises, from any cause short of war. The only exclusions are normal wear, damage by insects, and what underwriters call "inherent vice," meaning any form of trouble that was inherent in the object before it was insured. A complete schedule is required for the fine arts policy, and the total of the schedule is the amount of the insurance. The fine arts insurer may also demand that large collections be protected by fire and burglar alarms. Besides furniture, almost anything can be insured under the fine arts policy: paintings, sculpture, silverware, porcelain, glass, rugs, books, manuscripts, stamps, coins, jewelry—even furs, cameras, firearms, golf clubs, and things like that—but the cost of insuring furniture is very much less than the premium for jewelry or coins, for example.

HOW TO FIND THAT FRIENDLY AGENT

Finding an agent willing to write insurance on your antiques may be fairly easy, rather difficult, or almost impossible, depending mostly on where you live. Insurance agents have lists of areas where they would rather not write insurance because the losses there have been too high for their comfort. These lists are usually arranged by zip code, so that all the agent has to do is ask your exact address and right away he knows whether or not he wants to do business with you. It is a form of redlining, a practice frequently denied but obviously useful and, therefore, often encountered in high-crime areas.

Insuring your things will be easiest if you own your home. It is usually most advantageous to insure the real estate and the contents of the home with the same company. In some high-risk areas, the insurer may be reluctant to write homeowners' coverage and may want you to settle for "extended fire." The problem lies in the theft aspects of the homeowners' policies. The insurance industry is understandably disturbed about the thriving practice of burglary.

If you rent your home, your chance of finding an insurer depends very much on where you live. Out in the country you should have no problem unless your location is so remote that the fire department could not get to you in time. The place may be idyllic to you, but the underwriter thinks of that long drive on unpaved country roads and knows that any small fire is likely to become a total loss. In the suburbs it will be a matter of the local crime rate; in the city it's the same, only worse. You may be renting the most charming house on the most historic street, but if you have the wrong zip code, insurance agents will avoid you.

In such difficult situations it helps a lot to be introduced. A reliable dealer (one of those antiquarians I mentioned in chapter 2), an auctioneer, or a business friend may recommend a reputable insurance agency and be willing to introduce you. Insurance is to a very large extent a matter of confidence, and things have a way of going much easier once that confidence is established. Insurance agents tend to be very conventional, and they get rattled by customers who just walk in off the street, unannounced.

THE PRICE OF INSURANCE

The difficulty in shopping for homeowners' or fine arts insurance is that the cheapest is usually not the best. It's not just a matter of the premium; one also wants to know about the reputation of the insurer for satisfactory settlements in case of a loss, and that kind of information is not always easy to obtain. Consumers' organizations and state insurance departments or commissions may offer facts and figures, and the reputation of the various agencies in the community may be ascertainable. Most revealing, I think, is a good chat with the agent himself. Is he just selling insurance or does he know what you need? Does he understand what you mean by "antiques"? Does he agree that you should prepare a schedule or does he make light of the idea? Where was he and what did he do the last time one of his good clients suffered a large loss? Finally, does he know his arithmetic? Some agents make lots of mistakes, usually not in your favor.

The cost per $1,000 of homeowners' insurance will depend on a number of seemingly unrelated considerations. At the risk of boring you, here is a quick summary of what the premium depends on:

1. The total amount of insurance— large properties cost less to insure (per $1,000) than small ones.

2. Whether you own or rent—the contents of a home you own will cost less to insure than the same contents of a home you rent.

3. The number of families on the premises—contents of a single-family house cost less to insure than the same contents of an apartment in a multiple-family dwelling.

4. The distance from the nearest corner of your home to a fire hydrant—if it is less than 600 feet, your insurance will be a little cheaper; if it is more than 4 miles from your house to the nearest firehouse, your rate will be higher. (These numbers may not be exact. Different companies use slightly different standards.)

5. The type of construction—if the house is masonry (including veneered construction) and has an approved roof, the contents will cost less to insure than if they were in a frame house with a wood-shingle roof, for example.

6. Occupancy—if your house stands empty during working hours, or if you often leave it unoccupied for a few days or longer, your theft risk will be much higher than usual, and you can expect to pay for that in premiums.

The cost of fine arts insurance tapers off only slightly as the amount increases and is the same whether you own or rent, regardless of the size of the dwelling. There may be special charges for high-risk items and for problem locations. If you already have a homeowners' policy, additional fine arts coverage may cost less than increasing the homeowners' policy by the same amount.

THE DEDUCTIBLE

Small claims are a lot of trouble for insurance companies and greatly increase their cost of doing business. That accounts for the growing popularity of "deductibles" as a way to reduce the cost of insurance. The deductible is a specified amount to be deducted from each separate claim you may make for losses. The higher the deductible, the lower the cost of insurance. It means, in effect, that you are not insured for losses smaller than the deductible, but the resultant savings on premiums usually make that more attractive than it seems at first.

. . . AND IN CASE OF A LOSS

If (perish the thought!) you should suffer a loss covered by insurance, you would be required to notify law enforcement authorities and the insurer as soon as practicable after the loss is discovered. If your own agent does not answer the phone, you may call the company directly, but the responsibility is yours to notify them promptly. You would also be obligated to take all necessary steps to prevent further losses. If a burglar jimmied your back door so that it no longer can be locked, you are required to repair it enough to secure the property again. If a fire has damaged part of your house, you must make reasonable efforts to salvage what is left. The company will not be liable for additional losses that arise from your own negligence. Expenses of protecting the property after a loss will most likely be reimbursed to you as part of the final settlement of your claim.

One more aspect of insurance should be mentioned before we leave that dreary subject. When you have reported a loss, your friendly agent has a chance to be very helpful, but it is possible that he may not quite rise to the occasion. At times you may find yourself dealing with a sharp, brisk, hard-boiled adjuster, either a permanent employee of the company or one of the independent adjusters hired by the company on a free-lance basis. His interest will be to satisfy you at the lowest cost to the company, and that, of course, may not turn out to be in *your* best interest. If you have serious doubts in the matter and if your loss is large, you may find it advisable to retain a certified public adjuster (also called "public adjuster" or "adjuster to the people") to represent you against the company's adjusters. The public adjuster will charge a fee (rarely more than 15 percent and negotiable downward, depending on the size of the claim and the difficulty of the job), and in some cases that may be money well spent. All these people are listed under "Adjusters" in classified directories.

APPENDIX B:
SUPPLIERS

BOOKS ON ANTIQUES (in print)

Adams Brown Co.
(specialty: clocks and watches)
P.O. Box 399
Exeter, NH 03833

The Collectors' Shelf of Books
23 Crandall Street
Westfield, NY 14787

Book Shop
Colonial Williamsburg
Williamsburg, VA 01566

Book Shop
The Edison Institute
Greenfield Village and
   Henry Ford Museum
Dearborn, MI 48121

Museum Gift Shop
Old Sturbridge Village
Sturbridge, MA 01566

Ox Bow Shop
North Progress at Doehne Road
Harrisburg, PA 17110

The Reference Rack
Box 445C
Orefield, PA 18069

Sleepy Hollow Book Co.
45 Main Street
Tarrytown, NY 10591

Smithsonian Bookstore
National Museum of History and
   Technology
14th and Constitution Avenue, N.W.
Washington, DC 20560

Winterthur Museum Bookstore
Winterthur, DE 19735

WOOD IDENTIFICATION LABORATORIES
   (Write for instructions before sending a
   sample)

Center for Wood Anatomy Research
U.S. Forest Products Laboratory
P.O. Box 5130
Madison WI 53705

Gordon K. Saltar
2208 Lorelei Road
Ardentown
Wilmington, DE 19810

WOODWORKING TOOLS AND SUPPLIES

Brookstone Co. (tools)
124 Vose Farm Road
Peterborough, NH 03458
(branches in Boston, MA, Braintree, MA,
and Philadelphia, PA)

263

Albert Constantine and Son, Inc.
(tools, supplies, veneer, fine lumber)
2050 Eastchester Road
Bronx, NY 10461

Minnesota Woodworkers Supply Co.
(tools, supplies, veneer)
Industrial Boulevard
Rogers, MN 55374

Garrett Wade Co. (fine tools)
302 Fifth Avenue
New York, NY 10001

Woodcraft Supply Corp.
(fine tools, supplies, books)
313 Montvale Avenue
Woburn, MA 01801

GOOD REPRODUCTION HARDWARE

Ball and Ball
463 West Lincoln Highway
Exton, PA 19341

Faneuil Furniture Hardware
94 Peterborough Street
Boston, MA 02215

Horton Brasses
P.O. Box 95
Nooks Hill Road
Cromwell, CT 06416

Period Furniture Hardware Co.
123 Charles Street
Boston, MA 02114

MILK PAINT

The Old-Fashioned Milk Paint Co.
Box 222
Groton, MA 01450

SEATING MATERIALS

John K. Burch Co.
(cane and imitation rush, upholstering supplies)
40 Cherry Street S.W.
Grand Rapids, MI 49502
(branches in Berwyn, IL; Cincinnati, OH; Dallas, TX; Hayward, CA; Mission, KA; Oak Park, MI; Philadelphia, PA)

Newell Workshop
(cane, imitation rush, sea grass, rattan splint)
19 Blaine Avenue
Hinsdale, IL 60521

Peerless Rattan & Reed Mfg. Co.
(cane, rattan splint)
P.O. Box 67
Towaco, NJ 07082

H. H. Perkins Co.
(ash splints, genuine rush, sea grass, cane, fiber, rattan)
10 South Bradley Road
Woodbridge, CT 06525

Savin Crafts
(cane, imitation rush, sea grass, rattan splint)
P.O. Box 4251
Hamden, CT 06514

BIBLIOGRAPHY

The following selected books for further reading are all illustrated. Many are now out of print and can be found only in libraries and occasionally in secondhand book shops, particularly those that specialize in books on collecting.

HANDBOOKS FOR BEGINNERS

BECK, DOREEN. *Book of American Furniture.* London: Hamlyn, 1973, 96 pp.

Lively primer of American antique furniture styles with 101 excellent pictures, many in color.

BISHOP, ROBERT. *How to Know American Antique Furniture.* New York: Dutton, 1973, 224 pp.

Once over lightly (with lots of pictures) from Pilgrim to Art Deco.

CORNELIUS, CHARLES OVER. *Early American Furniture.* New York: Century, 1926.

Analysis of style development in the light of the social forces that brought it about. Profusely illustrated.

KIRK, JOHN T. *The Impecunious Collector's Guide to American Antiques.* New York: Knopf, 1975, xvi + 178 pp.

Well-written and nicely illustrated analysis of simple furniture with many new ideas and emphasis on the esthetic.

————. *Early American Furniture.* New York: Knopf, 1970, xii + 210 pp.

Superbly illustrated scholarly discussion of style and quality. The index, however, is garbled.

NAGEL, CHARLES. *American Furniture 1650–1850.* London: Parrish, 1949, 110 pp.

Sensitive, concise, and well-illustrated summary of the development of American furniture styles (by the director of the St. Louis Art Museum).

ORMSBEE, THOMAS H. *Field Guide to Early American Furniture.* Boston: Little, Brown, 1951 (and later editions), xxxix + 464 pp.

Well-organized and highly useful pocket-sized book that lists the principal types with more than 300 small but clear sketches and gives dates and comparative value for each.

PETERSON, HAROLD L. *How Do You Know It's Old?.* New York: Scribner's, 1975, 166 pp.

Cool and perceptive primer for detecting fake artifacts in wood, metal, porcelain, bone, horn, tooth, and stone by the chief curator of the National Park Service.

SACK, ALBERT. *Fine Points of Furniture—Early American.* New York: Crown, 1950, xvi + 303 pp.

Broadly critical analysis of what is really fine in antique American furniture, with 800 carefully selected photographs.

SMITH, NANCY A. *Old Furniture: Understanding the Craftsman's Art.* Indianapolis: Bobbs-Merrill, 1975, 191 pp.

Good technical discussion of American antique furniture detail, with excellent close-up photographs and some crude drawings.

VOSS, THOMAS M. *Antique American Country Furniture: A Field Guide.* Philadelphia: Lippincott, 1978, 383 pp.

Compact primer of type, age, style, and value, intended for the serious beginner, illustrated by many small, accurate drawings.

YARMON, MORTON. *Early American Antique Furniture.* New York: Sterling, 1952.

Nicely illustrated booklet for the serious beginner.

THE GREAT STYLE ENCYCLOPEDIAS

LOCKWOOD, LUKE VINCENT. *Colonial Furniture in America* (2 vols.). New York: Scribner's, 3d ed. 1929 (reprinted several times), xxiv + 398 pp., xx + 354 pp.

Over 1,000 photographs of well-selected pieces, Pilgrim to Empire (not just Colonial) and a matter-of-fact descriptive text.

MILLER, EDGAR G. *American Antique Furniture* (2 vols.) Baltimore: 1937; reprinted by Barrows (New York: n.d.) and, slightly abridged, by Greystone (New York: 1950) as *The Standard Book of American Antique Furniture,* 1,114 pp.

Over 2,000 good photographs of fine pieces (mostly in private hands) with emphasis on Maryland and nearby states. The lengthy text is lightly sprinkled with inaccuracies.

NUTTING, WALLACE. *Furniture Treasury* (3 vols.). Framingham, Mass.: 1928; New York: Macmillan, 1948 (and later reprints), vols. 1 and 2 unpaginated, vol. 3 550 pp.

By far the best of the style books—over 5,000 photographs (many good but some none too clear) of every conceivable type of American antique furniture, with brief but witty captions. The third volume combines good advice with cantankerous philosophy and many fine measured drawings.

THE EXPERT'S LIBRARY
OF SCHOLARLY WORKS, TOPICAL MONOGRAPHS,
AND ILLUSTRATED CATALOGS
OF IMPORTANT COLLECTIONS

ANDREWS, EDWARD DEMING and FAITH. *Shaker Furniture.* New Haven: Yale University Press, 1937; reprinted by Dover (New York: 1950), 133 pp.

Furniture made by the Shakers, viewed against the religious, social, and economic background of that communal sect. Forty-eight large photographs.

BAILLIE, G. H., CLUTTON, C., and C. A. ILBERT. *Britten's Old Clocks and Watches and Their Makers,* 7th ed. New York: Bonanza, 1956, 518 pp.

The bible of watch and clock collectors, with a comprehensive list of makers in both America and Britain.

BALTIMORE MUSEUM OF ART. *Baltimore Furniture: The Work of Baltimore and Annapolis Cabinetmakers from 1766 to 1810.* Baltimore: Baltimore Museum of Art, 1947, 195 pp.

One hundred twenty-five large photographs of Maryland pieces, mostly of the Federal period, including the famous griffin table now known to be a monkey.

————. *Maryland Queen Anne and Chippendale Furniture of the Eighteenth Century.* Baltimore: Baltimore Museum of Art, 1968, 128 pp.

Nicely printed catalog of 76 good pieces, giving brands, labels, and biographies of Maryland cabinetmakers and clockmakers.

BATTISON, EDWIN A., and PATRICIA E. KANE. *The American Clock, 1725–1865.* Greenwich, Conn.: New York Graphic Society, n.d., 207 pp.

Splendid catalog of 48 fine clocks in the fabulous collection at Yale University.

BELL, J. MUNRO, ed. *The Furniture Designs of Chippendale, Hepplewhite and Sheraton.* New York: McBride, 1938.

Representative selection of drawings from the original works of the three great masters.

BISHOP, ROBERT. *American Furniture 1620–1720.* Dearborn, Mich.: Edison Institute, 1975, 32 pp.

Good catalog of Pilgrim furniture in the Greenfield Village and Henry Ford Museum. Would you believe that the "Brewster" armchair on the cover is a splendid fake?

BISSELL, CHARLES S. *Antique Furniture in Suffield, Connecticut.* Hartford: Connecticut Historical Society, 1956, ix + 128 pp.

Finely illustrated and well-documented local study.

BJERKOE, ETHEL HALL. *The Cabinetmakers of America.* Garden City, N.Y.: Doubleday, 1957, xvii + 252 pp.

A biographical dictionary of unusual quality.

BRAZER, ESTHER STEVENS. *Early American Decoration.* Springfield, Mass.: Pond-Ekberg, 1940 (and later reprints).

The definitive work on painting and stenciling furniture, walls, floors, and accessories, with hundreds of superb illustrations (many in color) and detailed technical instructions, including advice on restoration of painted antiques.

BURROUGHS, PAUL H. *Southern Antiques.* Richmond, Va.: Garrett & Massie, 1931.

Over 200 good illustrations, mostly of authenticated southern pieces, Pilgrim through Federal.

CARPENTER, RALPH E., JR. *The Arts and Crafts of Newport, Rhode Island, 1640–1820.* Newport, R.I.: Preservation Society, 1954, 218 pp.

Finely illustrated presentation of Newport furniture, portraits, and silver. One hundred sixty-six clear photographs, 103 of them showing furniture.

CESCINSKY, HERBERT, and GEORGE LELAND HUNTER. *English and American Furniture.* Garden City, N.Y.: Doubleday, 1929, 311 pp.

Scholarly discussion of the great English styles (Gothic through Sheraton) and their adaptations in America. Many good photographs.

CHIPPENDALE, THOMAS. *The Gentleman & Cabinet-Maker's Director,* 3d ed. London: 1762; reprinted 1938 by Towse (New York —variant with "plate XIV") and 1966 by Dover (New York—variant with "plate XIIII"), 20 pp. + 200 plates.

The book that shaped American tastes in elegant furniture during one of its greatest periods.

CHRISTENSEN, ERWIN O. *The Index of American Design.* New York: Macmillan, 1950, xviii + 229 pp.

Handsome review with 378 renderings of handmade articles of American origin (many in color).

CONNECTICUT HISTORICAL SOCIETY. *Connecticut Chairs (Catalogue No. 1),* and *The George Dudley Seymour Collection (Catalogue No. 2).* Hartford: Connecticut Historical Society, 1956 and 1958, 67 and 141 pp.

Large photographs and brief, thoughtful descriptions of the furniture in these most interesting collections.

CORNELIUS, CHARLES OVER. *Furniture Masterpieces of Duncan Phyfe.* Garden City, N.Y.: Doubleday, 1922, reprinted by Dover (New York: 1970), xii + 86 pp.

Literate, well-illustrated discussion of Phyfe, his work, and the New York where he lived and worked, with measured drawings of his furniture.

DISTIN, WILLIAM H., and ROBERT BISHOP. *The American Clock.* New York: Dutton, 1976, 359 pp.

Comprehensive survey listing 6,153 clockmakers, covering clocks from 1723 to 1900 (but mostly in the latter part of that period), with 785 photographs (some good, some fuzzy, but many in color).

DOWNS, JOSEPH. *American Furniture: Queen Anne and Chippendale Periods.* New York: Macmillan, 1952, xl + 452 pp.

A magnificently printed book with about 390 photographs of selected pieces from the fabulous Winterthur collection—no primitives here.

ECKHARDT, GEORGE H. *Pennsylvania Clocks and Clockmakers.* New York: Devin-Adair, 1955, 229 pp.; reprinted by Bonanza (n.d.).

Friendly but rambling discussion, including theory and repair, with many good pictures and a 54-page list of makers.

FALES, DEAN A., JR. *American Painted Furniture 1660–1880.* New York: Dutton, 1972, 299 pp.

Lavishly illustrated survey (511 photographs, many in color) of all the best painted pieces around.

GREENLAW, BARRY A. *New England Furniture at Williamsburg.* Charlottesville, Va.: University of Virginia Press, 1974, viii + 196 pp.

Nicely illustrated catalog of plain and fancy furniture and clocks made in New England.

GUSLER, WALLACE. *Furniture of Williamsburg and Eastern Virginia, 1710–1780.* Richmond, Va.: Virginia Museum, 1978.

Finely illustrated monograph demonstrating the strong English influence on the local style.

HAGLER, KATHARINE BRYANT. *American Queen Anne Furniture 1720–1755.* Dearborn, Mich.: Edison Institute, 1976, 52 pp.

Concise but richly illustrated guide based on the collections of the Greenfield Village and Henry Ford Museum.

HEPPLEWHITE, GEORGE. *The Cabinet-Maker and Upholsterer's Guide,* 3d ed. London: 1794, 24 pp., 124 engraved plates; reprinted by Dover (New York: 1969).

The style guide that greatly influenced the taste in American furniture of the Federal period.

HIPKISS, EDWIN J. *Eighteenth-Century American Arts: The M. and M. Karolik Collection.* Boston: Museum of Fine Arts, 1941, xx + 407 pp.

Superlatively illustrated and handsomely printed catalog of this outstanding collection of late Colonial and Federal art, furniture, and accessories.

HORNOR, WILLIAM MACPHERSON, JR. *Blue Book of Philadelphia Furniture, William Penn to George Washington.* Philadelphia: Philadel- phia Museum of Art, 1935, xv + 340 pp.; reprinted 1977 by Highland House (Washington, D.C.).

Extensive, rambling treatise with much historical material and profuse but undistinguished illustrations.

HUMMEL, CHARLES F. *With Hammer in Hand: The Dominy Craftsmen of East Hampton, New York.* Charlottesville, Va.: Winterthur Museum and University of Virginia Press, 1968, 424 pp.

In-depth study of a miraculously preserved collection of tools and documents of a family of woodworkers, clockmakers, toolmakers, and wheelwrights active about 1760–1840, meticulously researched and documented.

———. *A Winterthur Guide to American Chippendale Furniture.* New York: Crown, 1976, 144 pp.

Brief but elegant guide to a choice collection, richly illustrated.

KANE, PATRICIA E. *300 Years of American Seating Furniture: Chairs and Beds from the Mabel Brady Garvan and Other Collections at Yale University.* Boston: Little, Brown, 1976, 319 pp.

A thoughtful survey from Pilgrim to present day, meticulously documented and beautifully illustrated.

KAUFFMAN, HENRY J. *Pennsylvania Dutch American Folk Art.* New York: Dover, 1964, 146 pp.

A good summary, including a fair amount of furniture.

KENNEY, JOHN TARRANT. *The Hitchcock Chair.* New York: C. N. Potter (Crown), 1971, xii + 339 pp.

Comprehensive, well-illustrated treatment of the subject in all its ramifications, including much autobiographical detail about the reestablishment of the manufactory.

KETTELL, RUSSELL HAWES. *The Pine Furniture of Early New England.* Garden City, N.Y.: Doubleday, 1929; reprinted by Dover (New York: n.d.), 475 pp.

Superbly illustrated (229 photos, 55 drawings) discussion of the humbler varieties of furniture, mostly Pilgrim and Colonial. Working drawings of selected pieces.

LICHTEN, FRANCES. *Folk Art of Rural Pennsylvania.* New York: Scribners, 1946, xiv + 276 pp.

A treasury of Pennsylvania Dutch art forms and handicrafts including furniture (mostly Federal), with emphasis on design. Magnificent illustrations.

LIPMAN, JEAN. *American Folk Decoration.* New York: Oxford, 1951, xii + 163 pp.

Well-selected designs and good technical instructions for painting and stenciling.

LUTHER, CLAIR FRANKLIN. *The Hadley Chest.* Hartford, Conn.: Case, Lockwood & Brainard (Connecticut Historical Society), 1935, xxii + 144 pp.

Scholarly discussion of this rare type of late Pilgrim furniture. Catalog of 114 known pieces with 67 fine photographs.

LYON, IRVING WHITALL. *The Colonial Furniture of New England.* Boston: Houghton, Mifflin, 1891 (and later reprints).

A pioneer collector's story, with quotations from old documents, bills, inventories, price lists, and such and 113 fine full-page illustrations, mostly of Pilgrim furniture.

McCLELLAND, NANCY. *Duncan Phyfe and the English Regency.* New York: Scott, 1939.

Exhaustive study of Phyfe and his competitors. Three hundred illustrations, including many facsimiles of contemporary cabinetmakers' labels. Good detail drawings of carving, etc.

MEADER, ROBERT F. W. *Illustrated Guide to Shaker Furniture.* New York: Dover, 1972, xii + 128 + 18 pp.

Detailed guide for dealers and collectors, with 235 very clear photographs and a facsimile catalog of Shaker chairs made in the Mount Lebanon factory.

MONTGOMERY, CHARLES F. *American Furniture: The Federal Period in the Henry Francis du Pont Winterthur Museum.* New York: Viking, 1966, 498 pp.

Magnificent catalog of a superlative collection, including a wealth of documented detail essential for attribution, labels and biographies of cabinetmakers, and a rich bibliography—a masterpiece of scholarship.

PALMER, BROOKS. *The Book of American Clocks.* New York: Macmillan, 1956, viii + 318 pp.

Concise text, 307 photographs (many by Wallace Nutting), and a 180-page list of American clockmakers.

PARSONS, CHARLES S. *The Dunlaps and Their Furniture.* Manchester, N.H.: Currier Gallery, 1970, 310 pp.

Thoughtful study of a famous cabinetmaking family and their products, conspicuous by the elaborate treatment of skirts and cornices.

———. *New Hampshire Clocks and Clockmakers.* Exeter, N.H.: Adams Brown, 1970, 356 pp.

Detailed summary of movements, dials, and cases, with many labels and biographies of makers and 550 illustrations.

(POESCH, JESSIE J.). *Early Furniture of Louisiana, 1750–1830.* New Orleans: Louisiana State Museum, 1972, 86 pp.

Good catalog of 61 pieces of mostly simple furniture; all but the armoires are extremely rare.

RANDALL, RICHARD H. *American Furniture in the Museum of Fine Arts, Boston.* Boston: Museum of Fine Arts, 1965, xviii + 276 pp.

Accurately researched catalog of a magnificent collection, offering much technical information, illustrated with crisp photographs, and beautifully printed.

(SACK, ISRAEL, INC.). *American Antiques from the Israel Sack Collection.* Washington, D.C.: Highland House, 1975–, 1,112 pp. in 4 vols. published thus far.

Collected reprint of the advertising brochures issued by Israel Sack since 1957. The photographs (many in color) are the best that can be had and illustrate some of the finest pieces in the trade. They are arranged roughly in the order of appearance in the showrooms and are accompanied by usually accurate captions. The introductions can be skipped.

SCHIFFER, MARGARET BERWIND. *Furniture and Its Makers of Chester County, Pennsylvania.*

Philadelphia: University of Pennsylvania Press, 1966, 280 pp.

Long list (261 pages) of recorded craftsmen who worked in Chester County from 1682 to 1850 and 164 good photographs of documented pieces, all carefully cross indexed.

SCHWARTZ, MARVIN D. *American Furniture of the Colonial Period.* New York: Metropolitan Museum of Art, 1976, xvi + 93 pp.

Excellent catalog of a very important collection, with much technical detail and fine illustrations.

SNYDER, JOHN J., JR. *Philadelphia Furniture and Its Makers.* New York: Main Street-/Universe Books, 1975, 158 pp.

Collection of 26 articles reprinted from *Antiques,* 1924–75, covering all aspects of the subject, repaginated and indexed.

J. B. SPEED ART MUSEUM. *Kentucky Furniture.* Louisville: J. B. Speed Art Museum, 1974, 93 pp.

Remarkable catalog of 86 authenticated pieces of great rarity, mostly Federal.

STONEMAN, VERNON C. *John and Thomas Seymour, Cabinetmakers in Boston.* Boston: Special Publications, 1959, 393 pp.; *Supplement,* 1965.

Elaborate and thorough presentation of their work, superbly illustrated with 292 photographs.

U.S. DEPARTMENT OF STATE. *Guidebook to Diplomatic Reception Rooms.* Washington, D.C.: U.S. Department of State, 1975, vi + 154 pp.

Nicely illustrated guide to a fine collection, rich in protocol.

WADSWORTH ATHENEUM. *Connecticut Furniture: Seventeenth and Eighteenth Centuries.* Hartford, Conn.: 1967, 156 pp.

Elegant catalog of a superb exhibition of 275 pieces of Connecticut provenance.

WARING, JANET. *Early American Stencils on Walls and Furniture.* New York: 1937. Reprinted in part by Scott (New York, n.d.), 85 pp.

Thoughtful study of the art of stenciling and excellent illustrations of selected examples.

WARREN, DAVID B. *Bayou Bend: American Furniture, Paintings, and Silver from the Bayou Bend Collection.* Houston: Museum of Fine Arts, 1975, xvi + 192 pp.

Neatly illustrated catalog of the rich collection of Ima Hogg. The furniture ranges from Pilgrim to Civil War.

WILLIAMS, H. LIONEL. *Country Furniture of Early America.* New York: Barnes, 1963, 138 pp.

Review of simple types, particularly valuable for the clear and precise drawings showing technical detail.

YALE UNIVERSITY ART GALLERY. *The Eye of the Beholder: Fakes, Replicas and Alterations in American Art.* New Haven: Yale University Press, 1977, 95 pp.

Instructive and occasionally hilarious exhibition ranging from honest repairs to malicious mischief with furniture, ceramics, glass, silver, pewter, paintings, and prints. The pedantic text adds to the humor of the catalog.

ACCESSORIES, TOOLS, AND UTENSILS

BULAU, ALWIN E. *Footprints of Assurance.* New York: Macmillan, 1953, xii + 319 pp.

Exhaustive summary with 1,796 illustrations of fire marks from all over the world, covering their forms since 1649 in England and since 1736 in America.

GOULD, MARY EARLE. *Early American Wooden Ware.* Springfield, Mass.: Pond-Ekberg, 1948, xiv + 230 pp.

———. *Antique Tin and Tole Ware.* Rutland, Vt.: Tuttle, 1958, xiv + 136 pp.

Profusely illustrated discussions of tin and wooden ware, and their use and manufacture in early America.

KAYE, MYRNA. *Yankee Weathervanes.* New York: Dutton, 1975, 236 pp.

Friendly and informative, but illustrated only with line drawings, albeit good ones.

KETCHUM, WILLIAM C., JR. *Early Potters and Potteries of New York State.* New York: Funk & Wagnalls, 1970, 278 pp.

Thorough town-by-town history of the manufacture of domestic pottery with a 48-page list of recorded potters.

McCosker, M. J. *The Historical Collection of Insurance Company of North America.* Philadelphia: INA, 1967, 213 pp.
Profusely illustrated catalog of ship models, fire insurance memorabilia, and miscellaneous Americana.

Mercer, Henry C. *Ancient Carpenters' Tools Together with Lumbermen's, Joiners' and Cabinet Makers' Tools in Use in the Eighteenth Century.* 5th ed. Doylestown, Pa.: Bucks County Historical Society, 1975, 339 pp.
Folksy but comprehensive survey based on the fantastic collection in the Mercer Museum in Doylestown, Pa.

Montgomery, Charles F. *A History of American Pewter.* New York: Praeger, 1973; reprinted by Weathervane (Crown), n.d., 246 pp.
Readable and scholarly, technical but clear, this is an excellent introduction to the subject, with fine illustrations of marks and detailed instructions on identification, cleaning, and even photography of pewter and a table of chemical analyses.

Orlofsky, Patsy and Myron. *Quilts in America.* New York: McGraw-Hill, 1974, xiv + 368 pp.
Comprehensive, thorough, and readable reference on quilts, including brief instructions for repairs.

Pennington, David A., and Michael B. Taylor. *A Pictorial Guide to American Spinning Wheels.* Sabbathday Lake, Me.: Shaker Press, 1975, 100 pp.
Clear pictures and brief descriptions of every kind of spinning wheel, including a few from Europe.

Sloane, Eric. *A Museum of Early American Tools.* New York: Funk & Wagnalls, 1964; paperback, Ballantine, 1973 (and reprints), 108 pp.
Lively, accurate sketches of preindustrial tools and implements, with clear explanations of their functions.

Webster, Donald Blake. *Decorated Stoneware Pottery of North America.* Rutland, Vt.: Tuttle, 1971, 232 pp.
A thorough guide, arranged by decorative design, illustrated by 300 clear photographs, and including a rather complete checklist of makers with dates. The chapter on the potter's technology is weak.

MATERIALS AND METHODS OF RESTORATION

Comstock, Ruth B. *Cane Seats for Chairs,* Bull. 681; *Splint Seats for Chairs,* Bull. 682; *Rush Seats for Chairs,* Bull. 683. Ithaca, N.Y.: Cornell University College of Human Ecology (Ithaca, N.Y. 14853), revised 1976, each 16 pp., 30 cents.
Elaborate instructions with many detailed photographs.

Constantine, Albert, Jr., and Harry J. Hobbs. *Know Your Woods.* New York: Scribner's, 1975, xvi + 360 pp.
Useful manual of modern woods available to amateur woodworkers.

Gibbia, S. W. *Wood Finishing and Refinishing.* New York: Van Nostrand, 1971, 192 pp.
Detailed technical discussion of the advantages and disadvantages of materials and procedures.

Hough, Romeyn B. *The American Woods.* Lowville, N.Y.: n.p., 1893–1923, 14 vols.
A labor of love without peer and still the classic of macroscopic wood identification, this is the largest collection of actual wood slices ever assembled. It is now a rare book and valuable but available in major libraries.

Lorini, M. Campbell, and H. L. Williams. *How to Restore Antique Furniture.* New York: Pelegrini & Cudahy, 1949.
Good discussion of materials, techniques, and procedures.

Panshin, A. J., and Carl de Zeeuw. *Textbook of Wood Technology,* vol. 1. New York: McGraw-Hill, 1970.
Standard text on the identification of American woods, highly technical but clearly presented.

Plenderleith, H. J. *The Conservation of Antiquities and Works of Art: Treatment, Repair, and Restoration.* London: Oxford, 1956 (and many later editions; 1966 ed. has xvi + 376 pp.).

The conservators' gospel according to the British Museum. Comprehensive discussion of methods and techniques with startling before-and-after illustrations.

RODD, JOHN. *The Repair and Restoration of Furniture.* London: Batsford, 1954, 180 pp.
————. *Restoration and Repair of Antique Furniture.* New York: Van Nostrand, 1976, 240 pp.
A fine craftsman tells how he does it, with excellent drawings.

SCHIFFER, NANCY and HERBERT. *Woods We Live With.* Exton, Pa.: Schiffer, 1977, 202 pp.
Good color photographs of woods used in antique furniture, including actual samples of 26 woods on a folding chart. The text is unreliable.

SOBER, MARION BURR. *Chair Seat Weaving for Antique Chairs.* Plymouth, Mich.: r.p., 1964 (and later reprints), 64 pp.
Exceptionally clear and accurate instructions for all kinds of seats, available from the author (Box 294, Plymouth, Michigan 48170).

U.S. FOREST SERVICE. *Wood: Colors and Kinds.* U.S. Department of Agriculture, Agricultural Handbook 101, 1956.
Superb color plates of transverse, radial, and plain-sawed cuts through 32 native American woods with brief description of each kind.

INDEX

273